Towards a Common European Immigration Policy

Rechtspolitisches Symposium
Legal Policy Symposium

Herausgegeben im Institut für Rechtspolitik an der Universität Trier
von Bernd von Hoffmann und Gerhard Robbers

Band 1

PETER LANG
Frankfurt am Main · Berlin · Bern · Bruxelles · New York · Oxford · Wien

Bernd von Hoffmann (ed.)

Towards a Common European Immigration Policy

Reports and Discussions of a Symposium held in Trier on October 24th and 25th, 2002

PETER LANG
Europäischer Verlag der Wissenschaften

Bibliographic Information published by Die Deutsche Bibliothek
Die Deutsche Bibliothek lists this publication in the Deutsche Nationalbibliografie; detailed bibliographic data is available in the internet at <http://dnb.ddb.de>.

ISSN 1610-8906
ISBN 3-631-51296-1
US-ISBN 0-8204-6468-6

www.peterlang.de

TABLE OF CONTENTS

PREFACE

Recently, immigration policy has become a very controversial subject for legal policy discussion in the European Union. The conventional wisdom has been that Europe is not – and should not be – a region open to immigration for third-country nationals. Dramatic demographic changes make it evident that immigration is one of the means for replacing an ageing labour force and maintaining the social system. On the other hand, previous experience shows that immigration must be accompanied by integration of the immigrants into the host country; ghettoization creates social tensions within the host country. A comprehensive immigration policy has to take into account the needs of the labour market, efficient selection procedures and the cost of integration. Human rights standards have to be observed without inviting illegal immigrants. Different member countries have attempted to develop comprehensive immigration policies. Exchange of experience between them allows mutual learning. Since 1999 the European Community has competence to enact Community legislation on immigration. The Commission has drafted several directives, which have however, not yet been enacted by the Council. As a result, a comprehensive EC immigration policy is some years away.

In 2002 the Institute for Legal Policy at the University of Trier invited eminent specialists from different European countries to present papers on different aspects of immigration and integration in an interdisciplinary way. Those papers were discussed at a workshop on October 24/25 in Trier. These papers and the discussion reports are contained in this volume. The editor gratefully acknowledges the cooperation of all contributors in editing their papers.

A special word of thanks goes to two collaborators of the Institute. Cordelia Faulenbach did the organisation for the workshop and Julia Stunz edited the book. Invaluable assistance was also given by the Trier Law Students André Eichhofer, Sören Havenith, Hauke Kuder and Anna Radjuk. They prepared protocols of the discussions: under the coordination of Wim Kreytenberg. Stephanie Lühl was the secretary during the workshop and Claudia Lehnen prepared the manuscripts for the printer.

Trier, February 2003

Bernd von Hoffmann

I. GENERAL ISSUES

RAINER MÜNZ

MIGRATION AND DEMOGRAPHIC CHANGE IN EUROPE

I. European Migration in the Second Half of the 20th Century

During the 1950s a majority of countries in Western Europe still registered a negative migration balance.[1] Some countries – in relative terms most notably Portugal and Ireland, in absolute terms also Italy, Spain and Greece – lost a substantial number of their citizens emigrating for economic reasons overseas as well as to other European countries: in particular to Belgium, France, (West) Germany, Switzerland and Sweden. There the recruitment of foreign labour had already started on a larger scale or, as in the case of France and Switzerland, had resumed after an interruption during World War II. In West Germany ethnic German immigration from East Central Europe and the inflow of GDR-citizens also played a significant role.

Since the 1960s, immigration started to outweigh emigration in other Western European countries as well; namely in Austria, Denmark, the Netherlands and Norway. For economic and demographic reasons, the inflow of labour to these countries had started five to ten years later. All aforementioned countries stopped recruiting foreign labour in 1973-74. Although many labour migrants returned to their countries of origin, others remained and were joined by their dependent family members (i.e. spouses and minor children).

In the 1980s and 1990s migration balances also turned positive in Finland, Great Britain, Ireland and later also in Greece, Italy, Portugal and Spain for the first time. With the exception of Great Britain all these countries had been traditional sending countries of economic migrants. Initially, their migration patterns changed as labour migrants returned home from the Benelux, France, Germany, Sweden, Switzerland and the UK. But during the 1990s, they all experienced an inflow of foreign labour and other foreign immigrants (see Table 1).

For four decades, between 1960 and 2000, Western Europe's population increased by 4.3 per cent through a net inflow of some 16.7 million people. In absolute terms the main receiving countries were Germany (net migration balance 1960-2000: +8.5 million), France (+3.9 million), the Netherlands (+1.0 million), the UK (+0.9 million) and Switzerland (+0.8 million). Relative to population size the largest net gain through international migration was registered in Lux-

1 I.e. the difference between the number of emigrants and the number of immigrants.

embourg (1960-2000: +22.8 per cent of total population), Switzerland (+11.2 per cent), Germany (+10.4 per cent), Sweden (+7.6 per cent) and Austria (+7.5 per cent).

Slightly more than half of Western Europe's demographic net gain through legal migration took place during the last decade. Between 1990 and 2000 this net gain amounted to an additional 8.7 million people. In absolute terms during this period Germany (net migration balance 1990-2000: +3.6 million), Italy (+1.2 million) and the UK (+0.8 million) had the largest net inflow. Relative to population size the net migration balance was again the largest in Luxembourg (1990-2000: +9.7 per cent), followed by Germany (+4.4 per cent), Greece (+4.2 per cent) and Austria (+3.6 per cent of total population).

In 1950, Western Europe (the current 15 EU countries, Liechtenstein, Norway, and Switzerland) was home to only 3.8 million foreign citizens. By 1970-71, this number had risen to almost 11 million and, by the beginning of the 21st century, their number had risen to approximately 20 million. Another 8 million people are foreign-born but not foreign nationals, as they either came as citizens of a European country or had in the meantime obtained citizenship in the country of residence.[2]

II. East Central Europe and the Balkans: Flight, Emigration, Transit

In Central and Eastern Europe and the Balkans, the "iron curtain" and various administrative measures kept the number and proportion of emigrants low as they prevented people from travelling to Western countries. Emigration was high only in years of political crisis (e.g., 1956 from Hungary, 1968 from Czechoslovakia, 1980-81 from Poland and 1989 from the GDR). In "normal" years only members of ethnic or ethno-religious minorities with strong support from a Western nation were able to leave, namely ethnic Germans (*Aussiedler*), Jews, ethnic Turks, slavophone Muslims and ethnic Greeks. The main exception was former Yugoslavia, where already during the 1960s, citizens were allowed to work as foreign labourers in various Western countries. Later, Poland followed this example. The situation changed in 1989-90 with the fall of the "iron curtain" and the end of bureaucratic travel restrictions. Immediately following those momentous events, there was a short intensive wave of emigration from Central and Eastern Europe. More importantly, civil wars and ethnic cleansing in Croatia, Bosnia and later in Serbia/Kosovo led to massive emigration and expulsion to neighbouring countries and Western Europe.

---

2 Council of Europe, 2001; *Münz*, 2002.

As a result of economically, politically and ethnically motivated emigration, most countries of Central and Eastern Europe and the Balkans posted a negative migration balance. Between 1960 and 2000 the whole region lost at least 4.7 million people (almost 3 per cent of its total population) through migration. In absolute terms, the main sending countries were former Yugoslavia (net migration balance 1960-2000: -1.2 million), Poland (-1.1 million), Romania (-1.0 million) and Albania (-0.7 million). Relative to population size the net loss through international migration was by far the largest in Albania (-21.3 per cent) and Bulgaria (-10.6 per cent), followed by former Yugoslavia (-5.5 per cent) and Romania (-4.6 per cent). More than half of the net outflow from this region occurred during the last decade (1990-2000).

1. Demographic Impact

From a demographic point of view, one major change is obvious. During the1950s and 1960s, in most European countries changes in the size and the structure of the population could largely be explained by changes in fertility and mortality determining natural increase. In the 1950s, Ireland and the GDR were the only exceptions. There the negative migration balance was higher than the natural increase.

During the early 1970s, at the first peak of labour migration within and to Europe, only West Germany's and Austria's positive migration balance exceeded natural increase. In the late 1980s and early 1990s, this was already the case in eight of 17 Western European countries. Among them were Austria, West Germany, Greece, Italy, Sweden, and Switzerland – all countries with a positive migration balance – but also Ireland and Portugal, where the negative migration balance was higher than the natural increase.

Since the early 1990s, demographic development in the majority of Western European countries as well as in a growing number of Central and Eastern European countries is characterised by a situation where changes in the size of the total population are influenced to a larger extent by net migration rather than by natural increase or decrease[3].

Thus, immigration has played an important part in boosting population growth in Western Europe over the last decade in some countries, while balancing the excess of deaths over births in others. In contrast, emigration from Central and Eastern Europe has been high, with only relatively little immigration or return migration balancing the net loss.

---

3 Council of Europe, 2001.

2. *Origin and Growth of Europe's Foreign Resident Populations*

A person's citizenship does not necessarily distinguish migrants from non-migrants. A significantly larger number of people have immigrated to Europe since 1945 than those listed as foreigners. Apart from naturalised expellees, refugees and migrant workers, the available data usually does not include ex-settlers, soldiers and other return migrants from former colonies who were born as British, French or Dutch subjects. Nevertheless the size of foreign resident populations in Western Europe gives an idea of the changing course of international migration.

National statistics[4] (see Table 2) show sharp increases in the foreign resident populations of almost all Western European countries between the 1950s and the early 1970s, but only minor or no increases during the 1980s when immigration control had become a major political issue. Finally in the early 1990s, the size of foreign resident populations began to rise again.

Between 1950 and the early 1970s, the number of foreigners in the present-day European Union (EU-15), and in Liechtenstein, Norway and Switzerland tripled. In 1950, more than 4 million foreigners lived in 18 Western European countries; in 1970/71, their number reached almost 11 million. Ten years later, in 1982,[5] some 15 million foreigners were living in the Western half of Europe. In 1997, this number reached almost 20 million. This trend clearly shows the ongoing internationalisation of Western European labour markets and societies, but it does not constitute a situation in which Western Europe could be seen as overrun by foreigners. Only 5 per cent of the 383 million people living in this region are not citizens of their country of residence. One third of the immigrants were citizens of a Western European country.

By 1970, West Germany was already the country with the largest number of foreigners living on its territory (3 million = 4.9 per cent of its total population). It was followed by France (2.6 million foreigners = 5.3 per cent of its total popula-

---

4 Tables 1 and 2 are based on an evaluation of the OECD/SOPEMI statistics, on data published by the Council of Europe (2001), the UN, Eurostat population statistics, and on official population statistics published by the countries themselves. The quality of SOPEMI data and the data published by Eurostat and the Council of Europe is dependent on the quality of the national data collection procedures. In general we can assume that in countries like Germany or Switzerland, having a population register for foreigners, the quality of the data is higher than in countries like Britain, where estimates are based on special surveys (see OECD/SOPEMI 2001; Council of Europe, 2001; EUROSTAT 2000, 2001).

5 1982 was chosen (instead of 1980/81) as year of reference because of the higher quality of data for this year (see *Fassmann/Münz*, 1994).

tion), Switzerland (1.1 million = 17.4 per cent), Belgium (700,000 = 7.2 per cent), Sweden (410,000 = 5.1 per cent), the Netherlands (260,000 = 1.9 per cent) and Austria (210,000 = 2.8 per cent).[6] Large proportions of these foreigners, often the majority, were migrant workers.

In 2000-01, the largest share of foreign population was still to be found in European mini-states like Liechtenstein (35.6 per cent), and Luxembourg (37.6 per cent). Germany still had the largest number of foreigners living on its territory (7.3 million = 8.9 per cent). Following Germany were France (3.3 million = 5.6 per cent), the UK (2.5 million = 3.3 per cent), and Switzerland (1.4 million = 20 per cent; see Table 2, Figure 2 and 3).

At the beginning of the 21st century Western Europe[7] had some 388 million inhabitants. Of them, some 20.5 million were foreign nationals: 6 million nationals of other Western European countries and 14.5 million third-country nationals. Another 7-8 million people were foreign born but later naturalised, or they already came as citizens of the country to which they immigrated (Figure 4).

Therefore, the number of foreigners in a country is not only determined by net immigration but also by nationality laws, birthright citizenship, family formations, and fertility patterns. In most EU countries the children of legal foreign residents born in the country become foreign nationals according to the citizenship of their parents (*ius sanguinis*). But in the United Kingdom and in Ireland most children born on British or Irish soil automatically become British or Irish citizens regardless of the citizenship of their parents (*ius soli*).

In 2000 Germany also has introduced ius soli citizenship for children with foreign parents born in the country.[8] In France ius soli citizenship is accorded to grand-children of foreign immigrants if the parents of the children are born on French soil. However, as a rule, legally established foreign adolescents are naturalised in France at the age of 18. Naturalisation also plays a major role in several other countries, particularly in the Netherlands and in Sweden.

---

6 Austria was the only country where the number of foreigners decreased between 1950 and 1970. In contrast to the situation in 1950, by 1970 all displaced persons and refugees as well as Hungarian refugees of 1956/57 who were still living in Austria had been naturalized.

7 Western Europe: EU-15, Iceland, Liechtenstein, Norway, Switzerland.

8 At least one part has to be a legal foreign resident with eight or more years of residence in Germany.

III. Demographic Trends in the 21st Century

Most Europeans share the same demographic destiny, characterized by the ageing of their societies. One reason for this is a pervasive low fertility rate. The other reason – unrelated to the first one – is a high, and in most parts of Europe still rising, life expectancy. As a result, in most countries the number of people above 65 years of age will increase until the year 2025 by 10 to 100 per cent and, until the year 2050 by 30 to 150 percent. The increase will be particularly marked in countries with higher fertility, which today still have a relatively young population. The increase will be less significant in countries with very low fertility rates, as smaller birth cohorts will be reaching retirement over the next decades (see Figure 5).

In Western Europe the number of people aged 65 or more will increase from 63.4 million (2002) to 92 million by 2025 (+37.2 per cent) and then gradually decline to 84.3 million (2050). In Central and Eastern Europe and the Balkans the respective numbers are 16.6 million (2002), rising to 23.6 million in 2025 (+41 per cent) and to 29.2 million in 2050.

An obvious consequence of low fertility rates in Europe are the declining numbers of natives and young legal foreign residents entering European labour markets, which can be expected to lead to an overall contraction of the working population (aged 15-64). In the absence of significant immigration this group would decline in most European countries up to the year 2025 by 2 to 22 per cent, and by a further 10 to 55 per cent by the year 2050. The sole exceptions are countries that today still have a relatively young population and high fertility rates (e.g., Albania, Ireland; see Figure 4). Moreover, over the next decades in countries such as the United Kingdom, France and the Netherlands the population aged between 15 and 65 will register only a moderate decline. Thus, in France the projected decline is only -0.2 million (-0.5 per cent) up to 2025, but is expected to reach -4.3 million (-8.4 per cent) by 2050. Similarly, the United Kingdom will register almost no decline up to 2025 (-0.2 million or -0.6 per cent), but this will rise to -4.8 million (-12.3 per cent) by 2050. On the other hand (and in the absence of mass immigration) countries with very low fertility rates would experience the largest contraction of their active populations. Thus, Germany's active population is projected to decline sharply by -6 million or -10.7 per cent up to 2025, and by a further -15.7 million or -28.2 per cent until 2050. In neighbouring Poland the decline is projected to reach -2.3 million (-8.6 per cent) and -7.7 million (-29.1 per cent) by 2025 and 2050, respectively. Italy will also experience a significant decline in its active population by -5.7 million (-14.8 per cent) and -16.3 million (-41.9 per cent) up to 2025 and 2050, respectively, while Spain's active population is projected to contract by -3.9 million

(-14.8 per cent) up to 2025 and by a further -16.3 million (-41.5 per cent) by 2050. The situation is similar for most other Central and Eastern European countries.

Thus, in Western Europe in the absence of mass immigration the population between the ages of 15 and 65 is projected to decrease from 259.4 million (2000) to 237.3 million (-8.5 per cent) by 2025 and to 162.8 million (-37.2 per cent) by 2050. The population in Central and Eastern Europe is expected to decline from 88 million (2000) to 80 million (-9.2 per cent) by 2025 and to 61 million (-30.9 per cent) by 2050.[9] However, the relative decline in the economically active population would be smaller as only 60 to 80 per cent of this age group (15 to 65) are currently either employed or self-employed.

The recourse to several possible strategies may offset or at least mitigate the foreseeable absolute decline in the population aged between 15 and 65.[10] The first and most obvious strategy is to create disincentives to early retirement.

Already today, in a majority of EU countries, over half of those between the ages of 55 and 65 are already retired or economically inactive. The main exceptions are Sweden and Denmark. Higher participation rates among those aged 55+ would keep more people in the work force. The main prerequisite to ensure their continued active involvement is the creation and/or maintenance of employment opportunities (most importantly a functioning labour market) for members of this age group.

Another strategy is to increase the participation rate of women. This would be particularly promising in Southern Europe, Belgium and Ireland, where participation rates are still very low. However, to be successful such an approach would require changes in the attitude of women and, in particular, of housewives and mothers towards working outside the home, as well as at the institutional level, where it would be especially important to foresee better childcare facilities as well as the extension of school attendance to cover the major part of the day (all-day schools).

A third strategy would aim at compensating future gaps in the labour market through recourse to immigrants. To be successful, such an approach presupposes

---

9 All these projections published by UN Population Division (2002) are based on the optimistic assumptions of stable or slightly increasing fertility rates and further increases in life expectancy. The UN projections analyse population dynamics in the absence of mass immigration or emigration.

10 These measures include: raising fertility rates, increasing labour supply, improving the training and education levels of the existing workforce, reducing unemployment and reforming the financing of health care and pension systems (*Coleman*, 1995; *Feld*, 2000).

the capacity to determine the nature and extent of such likely gaps and the possibility to recruit expatriate workers and professionals with the requisite skills to meet the unmet demands in European labour markets. This of course also requires that the target immigrant population is, in fact, mobile and willing to move to a particular European country or region. In the short term, the recruitment of foreign labour does indeed appear to be the simplest way to fill vacancies.

In the medium term (i.e. until 2020-25), countries which either experience no or only a modest decline in the number of people of working age (less than -5 per cent), for example Ireland, France, the UK and the Netherlands, are not likely to face demographically-induced labour shortages. However, future potential mismatches between the demand for particular qualifications and the skills provided by the national education systems, still render the recruitment of foreign workers necessary. Countries which in the absence of significant immigration register only a relatively modest decline in their active population (-5 to -10 per cent) together with low or medium labour-force participation rates (less than 75 per cent: e.g., Belgium, Portugal, Greece) have the possibility of either encouraging labour immigration or expanding the participation rate of the domestic labour force. Countries with a significant decline of the population of working age (more than -10 per cent) and low or moderate labour-force participation rates may find it necessary to combine the recruitment of foreign labour with an expansion of the domestic work force. Germany, Italy and Spain fall into this category. Countries experiencing in the absence of immigration a significant decline in their populations of working age, together with high employment rates (e.g., Denmark, Switzerland, Sweden) will increasingly have to rely on recruitment of foreign workers (see Table 3).

In the long run (up to 2050) and in the absence of mass immigration, nearly all European countries will experience a decline in the size of their active population aged 15 to 65 of between 10 and 50 per cent. This will almost inevitably lead to the systematic recruitment of both skilled and semi-skilled or unqualified foreign labour on a larger scale than it is currently the case.

However, as demonstrated in several studies,[11] mass migration will not be able to reverse the process of population ageing in Europe. But, this strategy can be useful in mitigating its impact on the work force. In order to stabilize the size of the working population in the European Union (current EU-15), an annual net gain of some 550,000 foreign workers and professionals would be necessary up to 2010 and another 1.6 million p.a. between 2010 and 2050, resulting in a total

11 E.g., UN Population Division (2000).

net inflow of 68 million people between 2003 and 2050. This would equal 16.8 per cent of the total population of the EU-15, or an annual net immigration of +3.8 per 1000 inhabitants (as against an annual average of +2.2 per 1000 during the 1990's and of +0.7 per 1000 between 1960 and 1989). Given that only about two-thirds of the current population of working age are gainfully employed, the current EU Member States would need an additional 46 million labour migrants up to 2050 to keep the work force constant.[12]

The countries of Central and Eastern Europe and the Balkans are facing similar problems. Until 2025 they would need a net inflow of 8 million people to stabilize their working-age population. At the moment this seems to underestimate the size of the necessary inflow, as many studies predict that during the first 15 years following EU enlargement, some 3-5 million citizens of Central and Eastern Europe will move to Western Europe for economic reasons.[13] However, over time the Central and Eastern European countries will themselves become the target of labour migrants, while demographically-induced labour shortages will reduce their emigration potential (see Figure 5, 6).

Future demographic trends appear to be clear. Europe faces an ageing and declining population. Western Europe can look back on its experience of labour recruitment as a practical solution to labour shortages. However, two main questions remain unanswered: Are people in Europe in fact willing to accept large-scale immigration, not as a temporary phenomenon but as a deliberate and permanent process? And will the countries of Europe develop a common strategy to attract skilled immigrants or will they become competitors in this field?

---

12 As many of them will be followed by dependent family members, the likely size of total immigration is correspondingly higher.

13 *Fassmann/Münz*, 2002.

Table 1: Net Migration Flows in Western Europe, 1960-2000

	Average annual net migration balance			Cumulative net flow					
	1960-1990	1990-2000	1960-2000	1960-1990		1990-2000		1960-2000	
				in 1,000	as % of population	in 1,000	as % of population	in 1,000	as % of population
Austria	1.3	3.6	1.9	308	4.0	294	3.6	602	7.5
Belgium	0.9	1.5	1.0	247	2.5	153	1.5	400	3.9
Denmark	0.6	2.5	1.1	97	1.9	129	2.4	226	4.2
Finland	-1.0	1.3	-0.5	-140	-2.8	64	1.2	-76	-1.5
France	2.1	1.0	1.8	3,270	5.8	585	1.0	3,855	6.5
Germany	2.1	4.4	2.6	4,857	6.1	3,638	4.4	8,495	10.4
Greece	-0.1	4.2	1.0	27	0.3	442	4.2	469	4.4
Iceland	-1.4	-0.4	-1.1	-9	-3.5	-1	-0.4	-10	-3.5
Ireland	-3.0	2.4	-1.6	-285	-8.1	91	2.4	-194	-5.1
Italy	-0.6	2.0	0.0	-904	-1.6	1,177	2	273	0.5
Luxembourg	5.4	10.0	6.5	58	15.2	42	9.7	100	22.8
Netherlands	1.5	2.3	1.7	644	4.3	360	2.3	1,004	6.3
Norway	0.8	2.0	1.1	98	2.3	88	2	186	4.2
Portugal	-4.6	0.3	-3.4	-1,197	-12.1	35	0.4	-1,162	-11.6
Spain	-0.3	0.9	0.0	-286	-0.7	358	0.9	72	0.2
Sweden	1.9	2.2	2.0	476	5.6	194	2.2	670	7.6
Switzerland	3.0	3.3	3.1	569	8.3	235	3.3	804	11.2
United Kingdom	0.1	1.5	0.4	114	0.2	827	1.4	941	1.6

Source: UN Population Division (2001); Brücker, 2000 – Calculations: Boeri, 2001 and Humboldt-University Berlin.

Table 2: Foreign resident population (FRP) in 18 Western EuropeanCountries, 1950-1996, (FRP in 1,000 and as share of total population)

	1950		1970/71		1982		1990		2000/01 (4)	
	FRP	%	FRP	%	FRP	%	FRP	%	FRP	%
Luxembourg	29	9,8	63	18,5	96	26,3	113	29,3	165	37,3
Liechtenstein	3	21,4	7	33,3	9	34,1	11	38,1	11	35,6
Switzerland (2)	285	6,1	1.080	17,4	926	14,4	1.100	16,3	1.444	20,0
Austria	323	4,7	212	2,8	303	4,0	456	5,9	730	9,1
Germany (1)	568	1,1	2.976	4,9	4.667	7,6	5.338	8,4	7.320	8,9
Belgium	368	4,3	696	7,2	886	9,0	905	9,1	862	8,4
France	1.765	4,2	2.621	5,1	3.660	6,7	3.597	6,3	3.263	5,6
Sweden	124	1,8	411	5,1	406	4,9	484	5,6	477	5,4
Denmark	*	*	*	*	102	2,0	161	3,1	257	4,8
Netherlands	104	1,0	255	1,9	547	3,8	692	4,6	652	4,1
Great Britain	*	*	2.000	3,6	2.137	3,8	1.723	3,0	2.450	4,1
Norway	16	0,5	76	2,0	91	2,2	143	3,4	184	4,1
Ireland	*	*	137	4,6	232	6,6	80	2,3	127	3,3
Italy	47	0,1	122	0,2	312	0,6	781	1,4	1.271	2,2
Spain	93	0,3	148	0,4	183	0,5	279	0,7	896	2,2
Portugal	21	0,2	32	0,4	64	0,6	108	1,1	191	1,9
Finland	11	0,3	6	0,1	13	0,3	27	0,5	91	1,8
Greece	31	0,4	15	0,2	60	0,6	173	1,7	165	1,6
Western Europe Total (3)	3.788	1,7	10.857	3,3	14.694	4,2	16.170	4,5	20556	5,3

* *Data not available.*

(1) 1950-1990: West Germany, since 1991: united Germany. Allied troops stationed in Germany, their civilian staff and family members are not included.

(2) Without seasonal workers and employees of international agencies.

(3) Without allied troops stationed in Western Europe.

(4) France 1999, Greece 1998.

Source: Council of Europe, 2001; OECD/Sopemi, 2001; Münz, 2002.

Table 3: Labour Force Participation and Prospected Population Decline 2000-2050 in selected European Countries, Age Group 15-64 years

	Labour Force Participation Rate 2000, Age Group 15-64 years (Persons aged 15-64 years employed or searching employment as percent of total Population aged 15-64 years)			
Prospected Population Decline 2000 to 2025, Age Group 15-64 years		>75%	66-75%	<66%
	>10%	Switzerland (81.8; 15.7)	Austria (70.3; 11.1) Finland (74.2; 10.8) Germany (72.2; 10.7) Czech Republic (71.6; 12.1)	Italy (60.3; 14.8) Spain (65.3; 10.4) Hungary (60.2; 15.6)
	5-10%	Denmark (80.0; 5.2) Sweden (78.9; 8.7)	Portugal (71.1; 5.1)	Belgium (65.2; 5.6) Greece (63.0; 9.7) Poland (65.8; 8.6)
	<5%	United Kingdom (76.6; 0.6)	France (68.0; 0.5) Netherlands (74.6; 2.1) Ireland (67.4; -19.2) Slovak Republic (70.1; 3.6)	

Source: United Nation, 2001; OECD Online-Database, www.oecd.org, update 4-2002 – Calculation: Humboldt-University Berlin.

Figure 1: Foreign Population in Western Europe by Citizenship, 2000

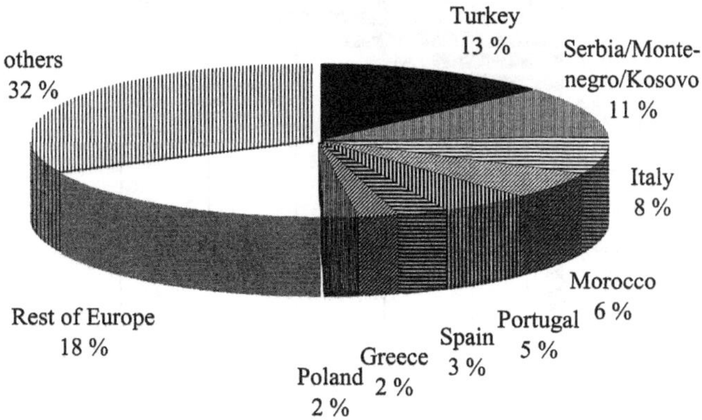

Source: See Table 2

Figure 2: Share of Foreigners in Europe by Countries, 2000/01

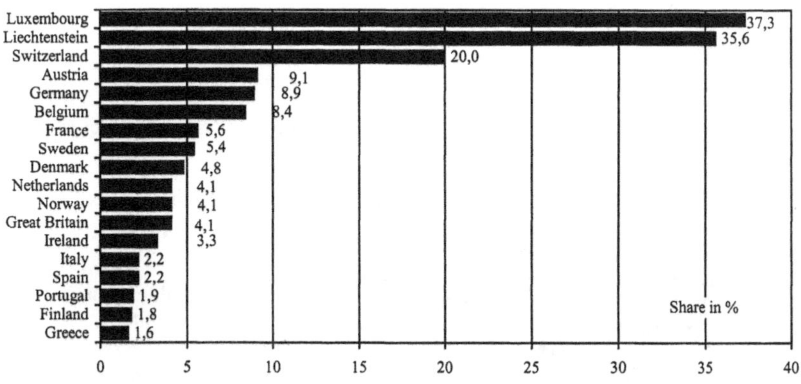

Source: Council of Europe, 2001; OECD/SOPEMI 2001; Fassmann/Münz, 1994.

Figure 3: Foreign Population in Europe by Countries, 2000

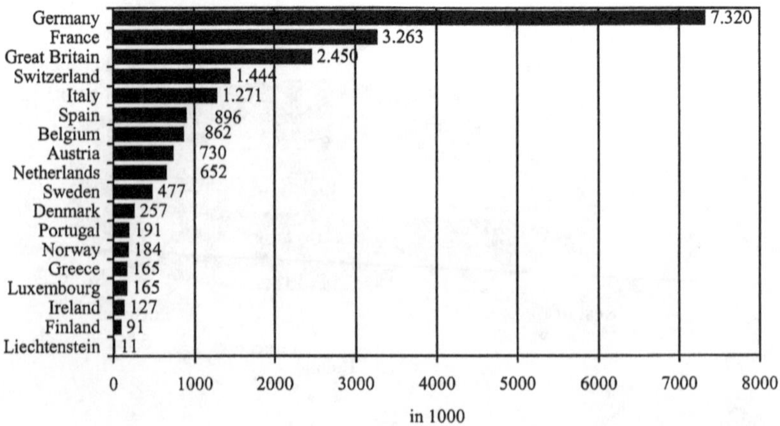

Source: Council of Europe, 2001; OECD/SOPEMI, 2001; Fassmann/Münz, 1994.

Figure 4: Population of Western Europe by Place of Birth/Citizenship

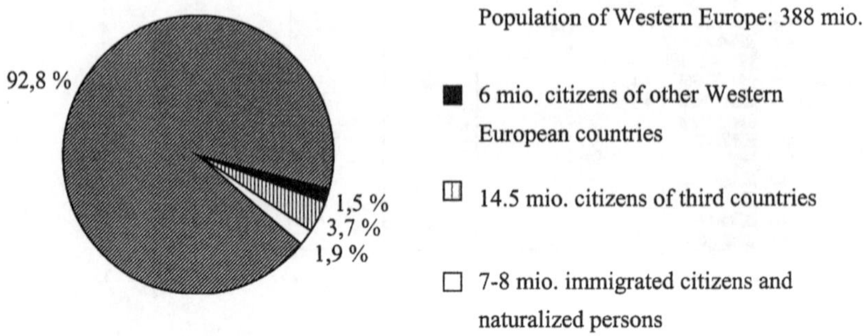

Western Europe: EU-15, Liechtenstein, Norway, Switzerland

Source: Council of Europe, 2001; Münz, 2002.

Figure 5: Relative Population Decline in selected European Countries, 2000-2050, Age Group 65+ years, as %

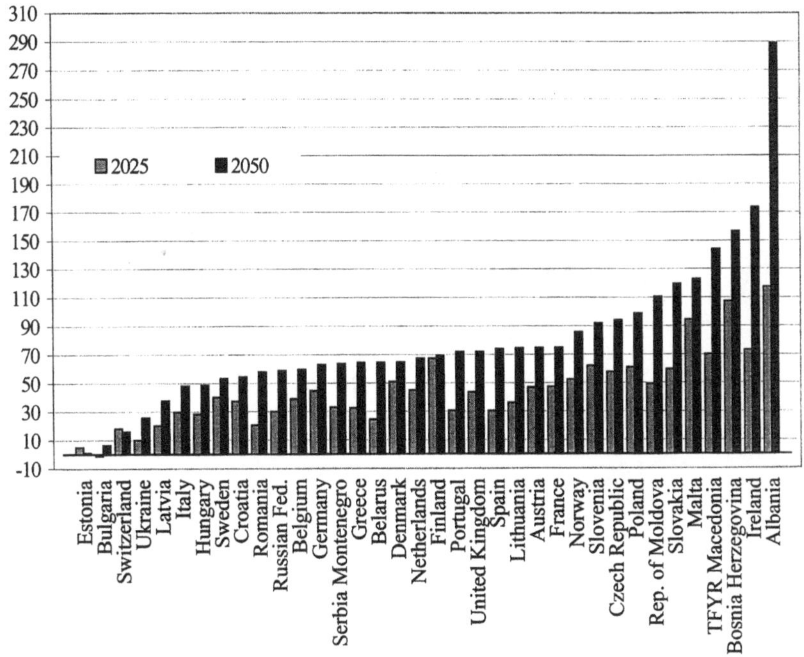

Source: United Nations, 2001; OECD Online-Database, www.oecd.org, 5-2001 – Calculation: Humboldt-University Berlin.

Figure 6: Relative Population Decline in selected European Countries, 2000-2050, Age Group 15-64 years, as %

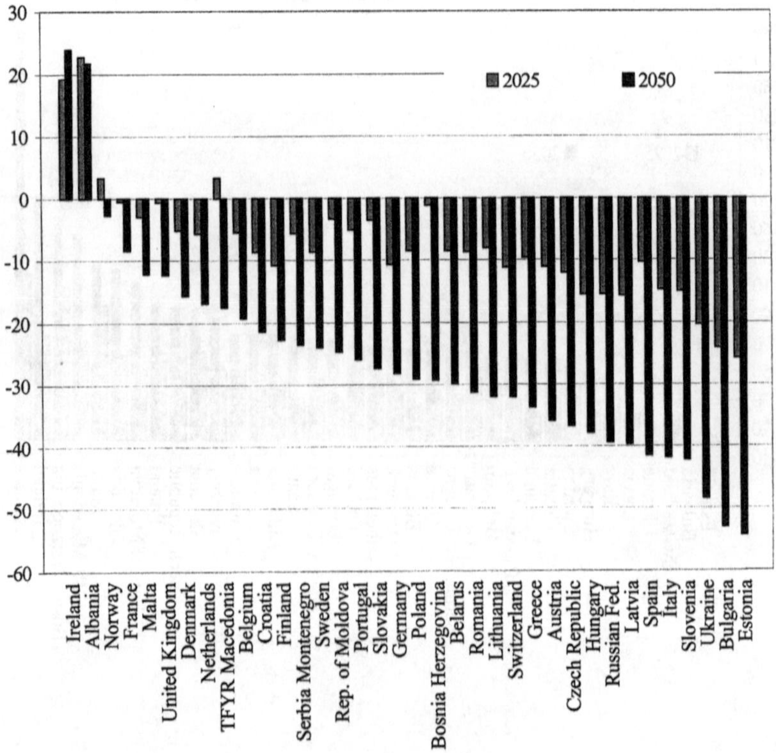

Source: United Nations, 2001; OECD Online-Database, www.oecd.org, 5-2001 – Calculation: Humboldt-University Berlin.

Figure 7: Population Dynamic in Europe by Age Groups, 2000-2050

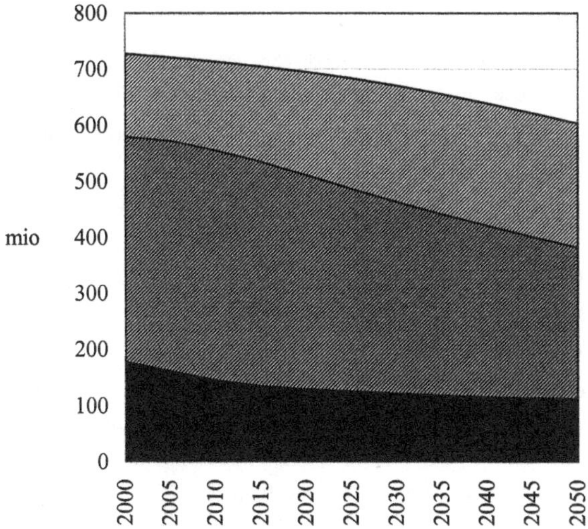

Source: UN Population Division 2000 (medium scenario) – Calculation: Humboldt-University Berlin.

References

Boeri, T./Brücker, H. et al. (2001), The Impact of Eastern Enlargement on Employment and Labour Markets in the EU Member States, European Commission, DG Employment and Social Affairs, Brussels (http://www.diw.de/english/abteilungen/wlt/ publikationen).

Brücker, H. (2002): Can International Migration Solve the Problems of European Labour Markets?, http://www.unece.org/ead/sem/sem2002/papers/Brucker.pdf.

Coleman, D. (1995): International Migration: Demographic and Socio-Economic Consequences in the UK and Europe, in: International Migration Review 29,1, pp. 155-206.

Council of Europe (2001): Recent Demographic Developments in Europe. Strasbourg: Council of Europe Publishing.

Eurostat/Europäische Kommission (2000): Europäische Sozialstatistik – Wanderung.

Luxemburg: Amt für amtliche Veröffentlichungen der Europäischen Gemeinschaften.

Eurostat/Europäische Kommission (2001): Europäische Sozialstatistik – Bevölkerung. Luxemburg: Amt für amtliche Veröffentlichungen der Europäischen Gemeinschaften.

Fassmann, H./Münz, R., eds. (1994): European Migration in the Late 20th Century. Cheltenham: E. Elgar.

Fassmann, H./Münz, R. (2002): EU Enlargement and Future East-West Migration, in: IOM International Organization for Migration (ed.): New Challenges for Migration Policy in Central and Eastern Europe. Geneva: IOM.

Feld, S. (2000): Active Population Growth and Immigration Hypotheses in Western Europe, in: European Journal of Population 16, pp. 3-40.

Münz, R. (2002): Europe and its Immigrants, in: Cavanna, H. (ed.): Governance, Globalization and the European Union. Which Europe for Tomorrow? Dublin: Four Courts Press, pp.183-210.

OECD (1991): Migration – The Demographic Aspects. Paris.

UN Population Division (2000): Replacement Migration: Is it a Solution to Declining and Aging Populations? New York: United Nations.

UN Population Division (2001): World Population Prospects: the 2000 Revision. New York: United Nations.

United Nations Population Division (2002): World Population Prospects – Population Database, http://esa.un.org/unpp/.

DISCUSSION

The chairman, Mr. von Hoffmann, opened the discussion. Ms. Apap made the first remarks: She mentioned the issue of replacement migration as a possible solution to demographic problems caused by a low fertility rate in many European countries. She then reported that according to some experts, the present demographic decline was due to a cyclic movement of birth rates. Therefore, births might only be delayed and occur five or six years later. Mr. Münz agreed that there were cycles of birth. He added, however, that these cycles were unrelated to postponed births. As a result, the working generation of today would become a burden to the society of tomorrow, since there would only be a small generation of young people left to support them. In the short run, the cycle theory could therefore not provide a solution because about 30 per cent of the younger generation would die childless.

He also stressed the importance of investing in human capital, especially in the human capital of women. Herein, the focus should be put on the labour force participation of women. As a consequence there would be a need for general provisions for day care of children and for all-day schools that take care of school children.

According to his view, due to the improvement of the economic situation of women, the vital point was no longer the cost of children, but the career opportunities for women. He stated that today the correlation between fertility and employment rates of women in Europe was positive: High fertility could mostly be found in the countries with a high labour force participation of women, e.g. in Scandinavia and France.

Mr. Münz admitted, however, that the argument of "birth-postponement" might nevertheless be true for East Central and Eastern Europe. Until recently, fertility patterns in these countries had been similar to those in Western Europe and Germany in the 1960s, including child bearing at the age of 20-22. In countries like Slovenia and Estonia, births might indeed just be "postponed"; due to the fact that women who now took part in the labour force would become mothers at an older age. But in his view, those small countries could not provide for the demographic relief of Western Europe. That would be the task of countries such as Germany, Italy, Spain, France and Great Britain.

In this context, Ms. Apap stressed that it would be necessary to coordinate policies for women in the labour market alongside policies for migration and against unemployment.

Mr. Werner, however, was doubtful as to whether high fertility rates could be explained by positive family policies alone. He submitted that fertility rates were high in France, the Scandinavian countries and the United States, while only the first two had adopted policies to encourage women to join the labour force, including childcare facilities.

Mr. Münz replied that in order to increase the employment rate of women, it was necessary to decrease the risks involved in being a mother. Women would have to be able to sustain themselves and to care for their children at the same time, without being totally dependent on a husband or father who might leave the family after a divorce.

He then pointed out the differences between the approach in France and Scandinavia and the US model. In France and Scandinavia, there was an education system taking care of the children from a very early stage on: kindergartens, childcare facilities and all-day schools. These facilities allowed women to pursue their career and be mothers at the same time, leading to an increase in fertility.

The US situation, on the other hand, was different because of two reasons: one was immigration. Even if it was proven that immigrants adapt their fertility patterns to the native society, it had to be considered that the U.S. had mostly immigrants from high fertility areas such as Latin America, and parts of Asia. Secondly, he added that the average white American had 1.8 children, which is close to the French level. In his opinion, the lack of social welfare provisions compared to Europe, e.g. 43 million Americans without a health insurance, gave rise to the idea that children are still seen as a last security in the case of emergency (illness etc.). He therefore concluded that the high fertility rate in the U.S. was due to the fact that children played a more important role in the security thinking of Americans than that of Europeans.

At this point Mr. von Hoffmann raised the question whether states pursuing positive family policies were in fact more successful in producing higher birth rates.

Mr. Münz stressed that the distinction of terms was crucial in this respect. In general, birth rate meant the births of a particular year divided by the population. States could do very little about it, because the birth rate did not only depend on the total number of births, but also on the age composition of the population, which determines the number of potential parents. The number of potential parents was defined by the absolute number of births 30 years ago and by the migration intake of the particular age group. The average number of children per woman/man, on the other hand, could be influenced by the states.

In her contribution, Ms. Langenfeld first referred to the statistics given by Mr. Münz, and asked whether it took account of people with dual citizenship. Her second question was whether Mr. Münz had heard about any attempts to have foreigners or foreign-born people counted in the statistics more effectively. As an example, she mentioned the issue of statistics relating to schoolchildren, where German born children with foreign parents were treated similarly to foreign children. In her opinion there was a need to change the statistical system. She concluded by stressing the influence of society on a mother's choice to leave her job. In her opinion many German women are not prepared to join the labour force because here, especially in rural areas, the attitude still prevails that the responsibility for the education of and care for children lies primarily with the mother. Mr. Münz replied that her perception seemed to him not fully correct. Even in rural areas, there were many women entering the labour force. This was the reason why many of them were not having children. They did not want to "waste" the time and the money that they and their parents had invested into their education. On the other hand, there were not enough adequate jobs for women available. Sometimes the mothers would resign if there were no schools with day care facilities available to take care of the children.

As far as the second question was concerned, he reported that there were no attempts to change the counting system. In Germany there was no system to count people by place of birth. Dual nationals were counted as German citizens. In France dual nationals would be counted at the same time as French. Ms. Langenfeld's suggestion would have the effect that Germany would change to the American system where people are counted by their place of birth. The drawbacks would be that (for example) a Turk would stay a Turk in this concept, even if he had a German passport. People would thus be "labelled" within an ethnic box (Hispanic, Turkish etc.) both for life and for generations if one did not accept naturalization statistically. However, he noted that it made sense to distinguish between foreign born and native born.

In the opinion of Mr. Bisopoulos, it made no sense to talk about fertility and birth rates. The real issue was to start initiatives and to pass laws that help women to take part in the labour market.

Using the example of former Yugoslavia and referring to Mr. Münz' statistics, Ms. Medved pointed out, that it was crucial to show the impact of internal migration that transfers into international migration. As an immigration country, Sweden has statistics distinguishing foreign nationals and foreign-born population, it does not have however an ethnic census. Ten years ago she was surprised over this fact. For example, a hundred years from now this may cause some trouble to a researcher when trying to statistically trace certain "ethnic" groups. On the other hand, she has changed her mind concerning ethnic identification questions in censuses, precisely because of the problems mentioned (labelling people).

Mr. Münz added that there were only a few European countries with statistics on foreign-born people, e.g. the Netherlands. There has so far been no attempt to harmonize on the European level. Britain (and the Netherlands) tried to identify the minority population in detail. In the Soviet Union or the Balkans this system made sense, because identity was constructed around ethnic origins, but in Scandinavia they try to avoid it, and in France it was forbidden to ask that kind of question, even in private surveys. In France the underlying reason was that it would be against the Republican idea that all citizens are equal. French law, for example, does not recognize ethnic groups. If we did not label people like that, every 10 years, this identity marker would be reduced.

Mr. Münz stated that considering just the last 30 years was much too short a period to make a reliable statement on the German perception. German society pushed people with a foreign background into categories, even without an ethnic census. As examples he mentioned successful "Turks" such as the businessman Vural Öger or the politician Cem Özdemir both holding German citizenship without being recognized as Germans by their fellow German countrymen. This was the result of an everyday labelling process.

KARIN OELLERS-FRAHM

NATIONAL IMMIGRATION POLICIES IN COMPARATIVE PERSPECTIVE

I. Introduction

During the last 30 years international migration has constantly increased. This development is certainly also due to the unlimited means of information which raise incentives to go to those countries where the standard of life is seen as attractive. This had the consequence that in addition to the influx of refugees, the influx of foreigners seeking admission for economic reasons required new policy orientations and legislative regulation. In particular the admission of foreigners to the labour market is not, in the first place, orientated to assist foreigners in economic deplorable situations, but to recruit workers for jobs, which cannot be filled by national workers. This means that the primary interest concerning "economic" immigration are issues of market policy, not the interests of the foreigners themselves as is the case for refugees. As the national interests in admitting foreigners are different, the immigration regulations are also rather different depending on the need to admit a foreign working force. The provisions concerning the admission of foreigners are, as a rule, threefold. They concern

a) the admission of asylum seekers, of refugees, which is largely regulated by the Geneva Convention on Refugees of 1951. This aspect will be treated only marginally in this paper because the regulation of this issue is only possible to a certain degree by the States themselves due to their international obligations and to the fact that their influence of who and how many refugees will arrive depends on such factors as the geographical situation which are beyond legislative rulings.
b) the admission of foreigners for humanitarian reasons, which can be approached by the asylum law because it concerns refugees from civil war countries granted admission in another State for the period of the civil war but who are not deemed to stay in the host country forever.
c) the admission of foreigners into the labour market, which is of particular relevance in the aspect of integration and of family reunification and is largely open to national legislation. In this context it is of special interest to see whether the aspect of integration is already given some consideration in the phase of admission and what the policies concerning integration of fam-

ily members, especially children, are. In this field the necessity of a common policy in the framework of the European Union is particularly important and therefore a comparative view on national legislation – which will include also Switzerland although not member of the EU – may help to find out those topics which are ready for a common policy and those where common endeavours are required. The data relied on in this paper are taken from T. Giegerich/R. Wolfrum (eds.), Einwanderungsrecht – national und international. Staatliches Recht, Europa- und Völkerrecht, 2001, an expert opinion elaborated at the Max-Planck-Institute for Comparative Public Law and International Law.

II. Immigration Policies in Comparative Analysis

1. Immigration-countries and non-immigration countries

First of all a distinction has to be drawn between formal or genuine immigration countries (United States, Australia, Canada and New Zealand) and those which declare that they are not but which, *de facto,* have in the meantime become immigration countries (i.e. Germany, France, Italy, Austria, Switzerland etc.). The difference between the policies of these two categories lies in the fact that genuine immigration countries utilise immigration law as an instrument in order to govern the admission of foreigners while the other countries, in denying that they are in fact immigration countries, consider the law of aliens as a special branch of public security law, reacting thus to the dangers which may result from the presence of foreigners – but without canalising the influx of foreigners in a consistent manner. This leads to the very important consequence that immigration countries provide for an effective system of selecting the foreigners to be admitted while the *de facto* immigration countries only react *ad hoc* to special situations without developing a consistent program concerning the admission of foreigners. A consistent approach right from the beginning could take into account rules or preconditions concerning the integration of the foreigners. Thus by simply ignoring the fact that they are immigration countries these States voluntarily omit to take adequate provisions in favour of the necessary integration of foreigners who, of course, are always to be granted respect and maintenance of their identity. The growing need for foreign workers in nearly all branches of economic activity finally favoured the conviction that further ignorance of the fact of being an immigration country only had negative consequences and that therefore it would be better to admit a *de facto* situation and to act in order to make the best of it.

2. *Limitation of Immigration*

When looking at the different systems of immigration policy, it firstly needs to be mentioned that no state is ready to admit all persons willing to immigrate. All states have erected obstacles to immigration at least in order to avoid a situation where foreigners fall to the financial charge of the state due to poverty. Therefore one of the main aims in regulating immigration concerns the limitation of the influx of foreigners – and these are in all Member States of the European Union exclusively foreigners from third states. As a rule it is for the legislator to provide the general rules on immigration. However, in nearly all states the executive has enough power to react to new developments. The limitation of immigration, which constitutes the central issue of immigration policy, is provided for rather in detail. The different models used by the legislator consist of requiring specified preconditions for the admission of foreigners, or in fixing each year quotas (Italy, Austria, Switzerland, Spain, Australia, Canada and the United States) or in combining both models. Those states that have not introduced quotas, namely Belgium, France, Netherlands, Sweden and Great Britain, provide for rather strictly defined preconditions for admission. Thus in Belgium the law clearly defines those foreigners who may be granted a residence permit, namely those who have a right under international obligations of Belgium, those who have the right to acquire or reacquire the Belgian nationality, women who have lost the Belgian nationality through marriage or the fact that their husbands have acquired another nationality than the Belgian one, members of family of a foreigner with a permanent resident permit if they have a right to family unification. There are some other possibilities for foreigners to be admitted; these are, however, also very limited, i.e. for a partner who has already lived together with a Belgian national for a long time, and in cases of humanitarian reasons, i.e. for Bosnian refugees, for foreigners, mostly women, being victims of slave trade etc. France has provided for comparable restrictive reasons by law, but has also, like Belgium, provided for rules concerning "economic" immigration. The limiting criteria are the preconditions for admission, which is granted in Belgium on the basis of a visa for only three months; a visa for a longer stay has to be requested from the home state and in case of "economic" immigration a working permit is required; the same is valid for France while, for example in the Netherlands the "economic" immigration presupposes also the existence of a working permit. Here, interestingly, it is the employer who has to apply for the working permit. The residence permit is then in general granted without further difficulty. In Sweden the admission of foreigners to the labour market is extremely restrictive, not more than 150 to 200 persons are granted a resident permission each year. The preconditions are the usual ones: a working permit, adequate housing etc. The United Kingdom provides for a series of different categories of immigrants, for each of which it has elaborated different preconditions for admission. Each of these countries, as is the case also for those countries having established a quota system, grant, in a first phase, only a timely restricted residence permit which can be prolonged and can, in the end, lead to a permanent residence permit.

The states which have introduced a quota system, namely Italy, Austria, Switzerland, United States and Australia, provide for a maximum quota of foreigners admissible to the state. This quota, which is fixed annually, is subdivided and attributed to the different territorial entities (*cantons, Länder*) and to different categories of foreigners, i.e. foreigners admissible to the labour market as employees or employers, foreigners admissible in the context of family reunification, foreigners admissible for seasonal work etc. Additionally they sometimes also provide for certain quotas of foreigners to be admitted coming from particular states. These cases are in general regulated by bilateral agreements. The admission within the specified quotas leaves some discretion to the administration but is, in any case, governed by economic reasons because it is based on the employment offers coming from the labour market.

In contrast to these systems, mention shall be made of the systems applied by genuine immigration countries (Australia, Canada and New Zealand), which sometimes also provide for quotas and other requirements, but which primarily base the admission of immigrants on a point system. According to the point system persons applying for immigration are admitted on the basis of an amount of points accorded for different qualifications. The maximum weight in terms of points is laid on the professional qualification of the immigrants and the needs of the labour market. In Canada a difference is made between employees – here the skilled workers scheme is applicable – and employers to which the Business Immigration Program is applicable. Other aspects, such as knowledge of the language, are also relevant and contribute to the amount of points available. An applicant who does not reach the minimum number of points is dismissed, while reaching even the maximum of points does not give a *right* to be admitted. In New Zealand the system is similar to that of Canada in that it also differentiates between several business categories. The selection of immigrants is adjusted very closely to actual needs; the number of points necessary for admission (the so-called pass mark) and which, in principle, leads to an immigration permit, is revisited *each week*, while the minimum number of points to be reached is fixed annually. The issues relevant for the point system are not only professional skill, but also professional experience, age, fortune, situation of accompanying persons, language knowledge etc.

In Australia the system is similar to that in Canada and New Zealand. Here, however, the point system works within a quota system, the quota being fixed annually.

The difference for admission of foreigners in immigration countries and non-immigration countries is striking in that the immigration countries consider not only the qualification of the applicant with regard to his economic capabilities but take account of factors favouring integration of the immigrant himself as well as of family members.

3. Requirements for admission to the labour market

As already mentioned, the requirements for admission to the labour market are, in all states, very strict, in particular for employees, who constitute by far the large majority of foreigners seeking admission for economic reasons. Relatively few foreigners seek admission in order to exercise an independent profession, which may in turn contribute to create new jobs; the provisions therefore, are less strict for this category of foreigners. Nearly all states, and here we are concerned with the Member States of the European Union and the traditional immigration countries United States, Canada, Australia and New Zealand, provide for application and admission to immigrate before entering the host country. This means that persons willing to immigrate in order to work, have to apply beforehand for a working place and have to demonstrate that they have a concrete working place and a working permission in order to be eligible for admission. Moreover, in order not to prejudice the national labour market, most states require that there are no national workers available to fill the working place. This precondition, which is provided for in all countries with the exception of Spain, is however not always implemented as seriously as for example in the United States, Austria and Switzerland. The proof of a lack of national employees lies with the employers who wish to employ foreign workers. In this context legally resident foreigners are also part of "national" employees in this sense, since the overall aim of immigration regulations is to avoid that foreigners – and possibly also their families – are at the charge of the public budget. In order to guarantee the priority of the national labour market, trade unions and employer associations are often involved in the process of admitting foreigners to the national labour market.

The permission to work is granted according to the national provisions established with a view to the national labour market laid down in laws and regulations. The easiest way to be granted a working permission is the situation where an employer requests a specific foreigner. This will, however, be mostly the case for highly qualified and specialised workers. For jobs requiring no or only little qualification most of the states establish lists showing open places. A special rule exists in Italy where citizens or legally resident foreigners may function as guarantors for foreign workers. That means that they take the obligation to pay for the foreigner who is admitted for one year, and who seeks an employment when already present in Italy. The number of persons for whom a guarantee may be adopted is limited to two persons a year. This provision is problematic under several aspects: firstly, the foreigner may "disappear" if he has not found an employment at the end of the year and secondly, if a large number of guarantors exist, there may be difficulties with a view to the quotas existing in Italy for specified jobs. On the other hand, a foreigner under "guarantorship" is part of the "national" workers which have priority in filling in vacant jobs.

While these requirements, in particular the existence of a working permit, are provided for in nearly all states and are to be considered as legitimate because economic immigration is aimed at serving primarily the interests of the receiving state, the means of selecting the individual foreigner differ widely between the states under examination and in particular between the genuine immigration states and those denying to be immigration states.

Those states which do not consider themselves to be immigration states – as is the case for the Member States of the European Union – leave the selection of foreigners to be admitted to the labour market. They only provide for the working permission and the visa and do not consider aspects of integration at all. In general, there are lists showing open working places; on the other hand there are foreigners looking for an employment who are placed on a waiting list. In the case that a working place is free, admission normally follows the waiting list. That means that no attention is given to aspects which would possibly favour integration, e.g. knowledge of the language of the receiving state, the most important precondition for integration. This disadvantage is due to the fact that these states do not proceed on the assumption that the immigration will be permanent. This is also the reason why, in a first step, they grant limited residence permissions only, in general for one or two years. But also when a prolongation of the residence permit or a permanent residence permit is requested, the granting of prolongation does not depend on any issues concerning integration, such as knowledge of the language, but generally depends upon the existence of employment and the social conduct of the foreigner.

In this respect, of course, the requirements are very different in the genuine immigration countries. As already mentioned, Australia, New Zealand and Canada have implemented a system of points according to which foreigners willing to immigrate are categorised. Although it must be admitted that the scale of points is also primarily oriented to economic factors and is in general combined with a quota system, there are, nevertheless, grades provided for, e.g. knowledge of the language of the receiving state which differ for different categories of foreigners. In Australia, for example, the knowledge of the language ranks higher, gives more points, for highly qualified independent workers than for example working experience; employees requested by the employer have to speak English. In Canada where the admission of foreigners is also regulated by a point system the number of points concerning knowledge of the language differs for different categories of workers.

Under the aspect of knowledge of the language, which is the precondition for integration, the provisions of the European States are insufficient. It must, however, be stressed that this deficiency has been recognised meanwhile so that the new German immigration law, for example, contains provisions concerning the knowledge of the language. It has to be borne in mind that requirements concerning knowledge of the language can be taken into consideration only for foreigners immigrating for economic reasons; for family reunification this is not possible and even less for refugees or immigration for humanitarian reasons. In these cases teaching of the language is one, perhaps the most important, part of integration programs for foreigners already in place; on the other hand, the interest to participate in integration programs may diminish when family reunification has taken place and the foreigner lives within a group of people of his nationality, which may lead to the unwelcome "ghetto-effect".

4. Family Reunification

a) International Obligations

A very important aspect of immigration policy is the admission of family members of foreigners already admitted in the framework of "economic" immigration. In fact, foreigners arriving under the label of family unification constitute the largest number of foreigners admitted. As a principle, all states allow the reunification of families rather generously. For the European States this results already from the obligations under Art. 8 of the European Convention of Human Rights (ECHR), but other international instruments, such as the European Convention on the Legal Status of Migrant Workers 1977 are also relevant. In particular, mention has to be made of the Convention on the Rights of the Child 1989. According to Art. 10 paragraph 1 of this Convention requests of children or their parents "to enter or to leave a state for the purpose of family reunification shall be dealt with by State Parties in a positive, humane and expeditious manner". Switzerland has made an explicit reservation to Art. 10, while Germany has made a "declaration" to the effect that the Convention may not be construed in a manner as to limit its competence to regulate the admission and the conditions of stay of foreigners or to differentiate between nationals and foreigners. Belgium has made a similar declaration, namely that it may not be prevented from making differences between nationals and foreigners and New Zealand has made a reservation according to which it is not prevented to differentiate in its legislation and practice between persons according to their residence status.

b) National regulations

In the framework of their international obligations states are free to regulate family reunification. In this context it is primarily of interest to compare who is considered part of the family, after what period of time the reuniting is possible and what the status of family members is. In general reunification of the family depends on whether enough means for subsistence and adequate housing exist. This is in line with the primary concern of states that foreigners should not be at the expense of social systems.

The period after which reunification is possible varies largely between the states: in Belgium, for example, the spouse and the dependent children are admitted if a foreigner has a residence permit for more than three months. The family must, however, follow within the year following the granting of the permission. Most of the other countries presuppose a longer stay of the person whose family shall be admitted; France and Italy require a stay of at least one year; the Netherlands allow reunification only if permanent residence has been granted. A special ruling exists in Austria where a special quota is fixed for family reunification; only the spouse and minor children of permanent resident foreigners have a right to family reunification. Therefore, in Austria the application for a residence permit has to state whether family members will follow or not. Sweden also requires a permanent residence permit before the family is admitted which is, however, granted only a timely limited permit of residence while in all other countries the period of the residence permit for family members follows that of the family member requiring reuniting.

Family reunification comprises in any case the spouse, increasingly also the unmarried partner, but in any case only one, even for persons from states where bi- or even polygamy is allowed (Belgium, France, Italy, Netherlands, where also couples of the same sex are admitted, Austria, Sweden, Switzerland, Spain and Great Britain) and minor children under the age of eighteen who are at the charge of the parents, independent of whether the children are children of one partner only or children of the couple, (Belgium, Italy, France, Netherlands,

Switzerland, Spain, Great Britain). In Belgium family reunification is limited to the family of the person who first immigrated; reunification of family members of the first immigrating person is not provided for. In Italy the family is defined as comprising also the parents and relatives to the third degree for whose maintenance the immigrant is obliged to pay. The person seeking admission for his family is, however, obliged to demonstrate that he has the means to house and to maintain the family for which special amounts are fixed according to the number of people following. Other states, as e.g. the Netherlands, require a declaration by which the person already admitted guarantees to maintain the following family members.

As already mentioned the aspect of integration cannot play a role in the context of family reunification and should be one of the central aspects of integration measures of each state, in particular with regard to children and their obligation to attend schools, but also for adults insofar as there should be an obligation at least to learn the language of the receiving state. This aspect will be treated in detail by another report and shall therefore be left open here. It has, however, to be stressed that this group of foreigners is the largest and that therefore integration incentives or also obligations have to be provided for in this context.

5. Relationship between immigration and refugees and asylum seekers

Since the number of refugees and asylum seekers is large in certain states of the European Union, it is of relevance to know, whether in the states that have a quota system for immigration, refugees and asylum seekers are comprised within the quota or whether their admission is independent of the quota. In all states with a quota system, Italy, Austria, Switzerland and Spain, the quota fixed for admission of foreigners does not comprise refugees or asylum seekers which seems to be consistent in that the number of refugees or asylum seekers cannot be foreseen and, moreover, the needs of the labour market cannot be made dependent on the admission of foreigners due to international obligations. However, in all states the asylum laws have been reviewed, or more precisely adapted to the community law, namely the Schengen and Dublin regulations, and tightened up in order to reduce the number of "asylum seekers" who in fact do not fall under this category as defined by law. Only for so called humanitarian refugees, that is refugees from civil war countries, as in particular people coming from former Yugoslavia, the admission follows special rules that fall neither under those concerning refugees or asylum nor those concerning immigration. The status of a "humanitarian" refugee can, however, be changed into that of an "immigrant" if the preconditions for immigration are fulfilled. Mention has to be made of the fact that recognised refugees or asylum seekers are part of the "national" work force and have to be respected before open jobs can be offered to foreigners.

6. *Illegal Immigration*

Until now the admission of foreigners has been regarded in the context of legal immigration. However, in order to appreciate immigration, illegal immigration also has to be taken into account for it is rather relevant in the context of comparative law to examine how illegal immigration is treated in different states. Illegal immigration is one of the main problems in the context of immigration and the number of "illegal immigrants" can, of course, only be estimated. Due to the fact that "illegal immigrants" pose a problem to the labour market and are, because of their illegal situation, more likely to become criminal than legal immigrants, nearly all states have sought to regulate the status of illegal immigrants by regularisation laws. It is understandable that from time to time the regularisation of illegal immigrants is helpful in order to counter the negative effects caused by illegal immigration, however, it must be borne in mind that regularly effectuated legalisation, as i.e. in Italy, is no remedy at long sight because the guarantee that regularisation will be enacted is even an attractive perspective for foreigners who are barred from legal immigration. These laws generally provide for a certain period within which "illegal foreigners" can apply for legalisation. In any case legalisation is not admissible for those foreigners who are a danger for the public security or who fall under the categories of foreigners who are excluded from admission by law which is the case for persons having committed certain criminal acts, slave or drug dealers etc. or who have been expelled, those who belong to legally defined "dangerous" persons (Italy).

Regularisation by law has taken place in Belgium, in France, in Italy (four times since 1987), the Netherlands and Spain (also four times since 1985). In several states regularisation is possible after a certain period of residence, in general 10 years (Netherlands) and on the basis of humanitarian considerations, such as family status. Regularisation is completely excluded in Sweden and in Switzerland, where the illegal stay is punished under criminal law and expulsion is mandatory.

In the context of free movement within the European Union, large scale regularisation poses a problem for those states which are the most favoured states for immigrants because of their social systems, such as e.g. Germany. This situation is in fact one of the reasons – not openly declared – for regularisation, as e.g. in Italy which is generally only used as transit country for illegal foreigners who intend to go to Germany or other countries. This seems to be one issue where a common policy of the European Union is needed for even the tentative to limit the freedom of establishment for those foreigners to a special European Unity Member State are not really promising.

Therefore the implementation of the national legislation concerning illegal foreigners plays a significant role. The amendment of immigration laws tightening up the provisions for illegal immigration by providing for sanctions such as prison and elevated fines can only avoid illegal immigration if consequently implemented; regularly repeated regulation laws are counter productive in this context. The expulsion of a foreigner residing illegally in a state should in fact be realized and in this context the Italian provision has to be criticised according to which an expelled foreigner has fourteen days free to leave the country. This seems to be quasi an invitation to disappear! What may, however, prove effective in the context of illegal immigration is the punishment of employers employing illegal foreigners which is provided for in nearly all states of the European Union which have rather recently enacted new immigration legislation.

7. Integration policies

The last aspect which shall be treated in this paper concerns the integration policies of the different states, for this aspect is the most significant in order to balance the admission of foreigners with their own cultural background against the interests of the receiving states to the necessary integration of foreigners in order to guarantee a peaceful social life. Only some states leave the integration of immigrants to the local political authorities or even to private organisations (Great Britain, Sweden, Austria, United States), while in general the integration of foreigners is regarded as a task of public interest thus requiring political control and financial support by the state.

In nearly all states integration programs have been drawn up and in some even special programs concerning in particular the integration of foreigners coming from Islamic countries, which constitute in all countries one of the biggest problems. The integration policies differ largely and shall be presented here shortly for the different countries because this topic is one of high priority for a common European immigration policy.

In Belgium the situation is interesting insofar as only the Flemish community realises an active integration policy which is based on three elements: in the first place the equality between foreigners and nationals as far as possible, but at least concerning working conditions; secondly, the integration of ethnic minority groups into social life and thirdly financial assistance in the health sector, the social sector and education, which also comprises language courses. This integration policy is developed and implemented with the participation of members of the minority groups.

The situation is similar in Switzerland where the integration of foreigners is described as a "task to be realised by the society and the central, cantonal, and local authorities together with the foreigners' organisations". The different authorities can propose special projects that have to be approved by the commission for foreigners in Switzerland. However, there exists no right to financial support by the Federation. The commission for foreigners itself plays an important role in the integration policy; it is composed of nationals and foreigners. The project concerning mandatory language courses is still on the way and has not yet been decided upon.

In Spain the integration policy comprises in particular the realisation of the full exercise of social rights concerning health services, education of foreign students, family reunification, free exercise of religion and means to facilitate nationalisation of foreigners. A special organ has been created for this purpose which shall also assist foreigners in finding employment and enhancing professional education.

As in Spain, France has also charged a special council with the question of integration policy which was created in 1989 and which has to be heard on all questions concerning foreigners. The nine members of the council are nominated by the President and proposed by the Prime Minister. The law of 1989 does not, however, explicitly provide for the participation of foreigners' organisations in the Council.

Italy provides for a large scale of integration provisions which comprise all levels and rely on the co-operation with foreigner associations, organisations and public and private authorities in the national states of the foreigners. Of special importance is the language education and cultural education which comprises not only Italian culture but also that of the states of origin of the foreigners. Also in Sweden, as is the case for Italy, special organs have been created in order to promote the integration policy in which foreigners are also represented. In Italy, the financial needs for the policy are covered by the so-called migration fund, which is composed of public means, as well as public, private or international support from organs and organisations.

The most interesting and ambitious integration policy can be found in the Netherlands. The Netherlands has provided for integration by a rather detailed law which follows the foreigner right from the entry into the country. The program is mandatory and is flexible in that it is adapted to the very special needs of the individual foreigner. To this end talks are held with the foreigner in order to check whether or to what degree he could become socially backward. In this context his general knowledge, professional experience and education, language knowledge as well as the aims pursued by the foreigner and the obligations incumbent upon him in the Netherlands are relevant. This enquiry may take up to four months. The educational organs and the employment exchange are involved in these talks. At the end of this enquiry, the local authority adopts an order fixing the integration program to be followed by the foreigner. The foreigner and the education organs then conclude a contract of education. The education comprises in any case the Dutch language as second language with approximately 600 hours language education for each participant; furthermore the education comprises social issues and professional orientation. At the latest one year after the inscription an examination concerning social and language knowledge has to be passed. In the case that the foreigner does not participate in the program the social welfare benefits can be reduced or even fines be imposed. Each foreigner is provided with a tutor, which is in fact decisive for the success of the integration courses, because this tutor assists the foreigner whenever necessary. The process of education is permanently controlled and the local authority permanently informed so that there is a continuous exchange concerning the integration of the foreigner. The integration program ends within six months from the date of the examinations. An important condition for the "dismissal" of the foreigner into the normal daily life is a conversation between the foreigner and a representative of the education organ and the employment exchange which leads to final proposals concerning the future of the foreigner. The local authorities then assist the foreigner in finding an employment and provide him with a certificate containing the program followed and the results reached.

The financial means for this program – which is rather expensive – are borne by the Government. The necessary financial means are fixed at the national level on the basis of the estimated number of foreigners to integrate. For the year 2000 e.g. 179,5 million Euro had been supplied for ca. 22.500 integration courses. The expenses for these programs are – rightly – regarded as investment in order to avoid even higher follow-up costs resulting from not or insufficiently integrated social groups.

Besides this very ambitious program for "newcomers" the Netherlands also has an integration program for minorities who have already lived in the Netherlands for some time. Out of this large group of foreigners the authorities concentrate on two groups: unemployed persons whose chances may increase after improving their language knowledge, and non-employed parents. The participation in these programs is, however, voluntary. Furthermore, mention should be made of the Dutch law for improvement of employment for minorities according to which employers with more than 35 employees are obliged to publish once a year how many of their employees belong to minority groups and what they intend to do in order to employ more members of these minority groups. This law is aimed at encouraging employers to employ more members of minority groups. Finally it should be mentioned that also private programs for integration are offered in the Netherlands. The enterprise TNT Post Group has instituted integration courses in order to recruit more foreign workers.

The rather extensive description of the integration policy in the Netherlands seems to be justified because it may be taken as a model in other states or even on the European level because according to the author's view it demonstrates in a convincing way that social peace can best be maintained by investing in the integration of foreigners who are indispensable for our Western economies. If we invite foreigners to come we have, on the one hand, to canalise the influx and on the other to take care of them and their integration.

III. Conclusion

Although the above remarks concern only some aspects of admission of foreigners in a comparative perspective, they show that Europe is far from a common policy of immigration. Diverging national interests govern national immigration laws. However, all states have in the meantime recognised that their economy needs foreign working force and that denying to be an immigration country does not solve the problems arising from immigration but increases them. The most recent immigration laws in various countries show that the states are ready to accept the situation and to remedy the deficiencies of former legislation by on the one hand canalising the immigration and providing for a stricter reaction against illegal immigration without affecting the rights granted to refugees and asylum seekers. On the other hand the recent legislation provides for active integration policy, however, sometimes fails to consider those large groups of minorities already present in the state, but generally not favoured by the new integration programs. Therefore, a common European immigration policy should put the emphasis on fighting illegal immigration and on integrating those who are admitted. In this context integration measures should, as is already practice in the Netherlands, not only aim at those foreigners who want to participate in the labour market, but also, and perhaps even more, the family members, in particular the parent responsible for the education of the children. The integration of the children is the precondition for future peaceful living together and reciprocal understanding. In this context, it would, however, also be welcomed to include at least basic information of foreign cultures and religion in the education of nationals because also those who invite and integrate foreigners have to make some efforts to understand and comprehend what may seem rather strange to them at first sight.

DISCUSSION

Ms. Apap began the discussion, bringing up several points of Ms. Oellers-Frahm's oral presentation: The first point referred to the idea that immigration had to be a two way-system, which benefits both immigrants and the hosting state's society. The benefits of immigration needed to be pointed out.

There would also need to be a discussion on the meaning of integration at a European level, as the different Member States of the EU had different perceptions and ideas of this. Until there was no clear definition and no framework, it would be difficult to make any process. Furthermore the ideas of immigration determined the need for integration. Insofar a common definition of integration would be important in order to elaborate concepts of integration policy.

Concerning family integration, Ms. Apap stated that there was neither in European Law nor in international law an explicit right to family reunification and that this fact was the reason why different countries were at different stages of the debate.

Some countries would still see family reunification as a kind flaw instead as a right to family, although all countries had been signatories of the ECHR. Family life did not only mean the family life of the EU nationals but was a universal concept; insofar as family integration means respect of the right to family life and should therefore be granted to all people living in the EU. That included also the need to allow family reunification not only after a period of several years, but quite rapidly.

Referring to the programme of family reunification, Ms. Apap contradicted the statement of Ms. Oellers-Frahm insofar as the French community in Belgium had such programmes but less funds than the Flemish community. Due to this fact, its results were less visible. Nevertheless they played an important role, as the percentage of foreigners and citizens with a foreign background was much higher than in the Flemish community as well as the unemployment and economical problems of foreigners. Most foreigners' parents had come to work in the mines. These had been closed down and a large number of immigrants moved to Brussels, where considerable economic problems already existed. The programmes in the French community were in fact less effective, which resulted from the economic and demographic background, whereas the Flemish community had higher funds and more financial resources to implement programmes. Moreover the different demographic situation in Flanders had a certain impact on this issue.

Concerning the legalization of illegal immigrants in Belgium, Ms. Apap explained, that this programme had not been set up purely to reduce criminal activities of illegal immigrants. It is true in fact, that illegal immigrants tended to commit more criminal activities than the average, and especially there was a problem of illegal employment, which was more typical for the countries of southern Europe.

There were certain conditions to be met (e.g. the candidate must have been present in Belgium for at least the last six years), in order to get an amnesty and be accepted, which prevented other immigrants from entering the country shortly before the start of the amnesty programme in order to abuse it.

Mr. Münz was of the opinion that the Dutch programme could be considered a good framework for benchmarking. Mr. Münz wondered, whether there was an argument, that European integration programmes need to be harmonized, or whether it would make more sense, to regulate immigration on a local basis in order to consider the local settings and needs.

Mr. von Hoffmann mentioned that comparative work too often would propose to adopt the at first sight best system by all other states, not regarding the local settings like legislation, demographic situation and economical conditions.

Mr. Werner stated that concerning the situation in the Netherlands, the unemployment rate of minorities was extremely high. The national programme theoretically seemed to be excellent, but in practice it did not work trouble-free.

Mr. Bisopoulos stressed that there was obviously in every country a link between integration and economic preconditions. Concerning the programme of regularisation, there should be a common way in the European Union. At the moment, Member States have different policies in regard to that point. Some tried to legalise illegal immigrants very quickly; others did it from time to time. Mr. Bisopoulos expressed his hope, that there would be a possibility to find a common way of regularisation in the European Union. He regarded the planned creation of a European Corps of Border Guards an important step that might help in this direction.

Mr. Weber considered comparative analysis to be essential for a potential harmonisation policy. Mr. Weber wondered, whether there was a competence of the European Union to regulate the integration within the European Union. Insofar the EC norms and papers are very reluctant. But the efforts made in asylum policy on the EU-level seemed to indicate that progress in integration Policy was also likely.

In the context of whether a harmonisation of the law on integration within the EU was desirable, Ms. Oellers-Frahm stressed the importance of comparing the legislation of the Member States and of lining out the differences and the common basics in order to determine, what kind of policy was likely to be accepted by the Member States.

Concerning the question of whether political or economical determines the quota system respectively by labour market or demographic interests, Ms. Oellers-Frahm explained that all aspects are important. Firstly the political decision has to be taken, but this decision is made with respect and in regard to the surrounding conditions, such as mentioned above. Insofar as the quota system serves the needs of an individual country it differs from country to country.

Responding to the remark of Mr. Werner, that immigration was not a recent problem within the EU, Ms. Oellers-Frahm stated that it had only recently been recognised that most EU Member States were immigration countries, which had been contested so far and ignored by the policy. Until then, just the symptoms of immigration had been treated, instead of accepting and canalising immigration.

With reference to the questions of Ms. Apap concerning the reasons for legalization, Ms. Oellers-Frahm stated that there were various reasons, depending also upon the juridical settings, such as whether or not a change from asylum seeker to the status of a "would-be-immigrant" is possible. The central aim was to take illegal immigrants out of their illegality in order to facilitate a normal life.

Concerning family, Ms. Oellers-Frahm explained, that all EU Member States recognised the right to family reunification despite the fact that Art. 8 ECHR does not provide for it. The state's practice was a mere outflow of Art. 8 ECHR and based on national law.

Ms. Apap emphasised that in order to manage integration of immigrants effectively, a common definition of that term was necessary. According to Ms. Oellers-Frahm only the basic aspects, which are generally accepted, could be taken into account by a common definition of "integration", such as for example the knowledge of the language, which Ms. Oellers-Frahm considered to be one of the most important elements.

FELICITA MEDVED

A COMMON EUROPEAN IMMIGRATION POLICY OR HOW COMMON IS COMMON ENOUGH?

I. Introduction

There is the increasingly apparent need for a "new approach" to immigration in Europe. The intensified debate and search for new immigration policies stem from a combination of deficiencies of policies evolving since the 1970s, the changing nature of migration and attitudes towards it. The "zero immigration" policy model, based on two major lines of action - the closing of borders to new influxes of immigrant labour and measures to promote the integration of the immigrant populations already in place - has proved inadequate in dealing with existing "stocks and flows". Likewise, there is hardly any evidence, that it would be flexible enough to deal with the current situation. Furthermore, the accompanying calls for a "common" European immigration policy are the result of the integration objectives of the European Union and the anticipated eastern enlargement. As a result of the Treaty of Amsterdam, immigration and asylum have become a "1st pillar" issue and the special meeting of the European Council held in Tampere, in October 1999, discussed the establishment of an "area of freedom, security and justice" and elaborated on the political guidelines for the coming years. It was agreed that "the separate but closely related issues of asylum and migration call for the development of a common EU policy". This would include the following elements: partnership with countries of origin, a common European asylum system, fair treatment of third-country nationals and management of the flows of migration.[1] But until recently, partly because of the developments of the 1990s which are closely connected with the phenomenon of "new migration", the political and practical agendas have been influenced predominantly by asylum, irregular immigration, smuggling and trafficking in human beings, with limited attention being paid to family reunion and even less to labour market requirements and to the integration of third-country nationals. There has been little debate about the role that immigrant labour might play in enhancing the competitiveness of European national and regional economies. There are signs, however, that this attitude may be changing. In the last couple

1 Tampere European Council, 15 and 16 October 1999, Presidency Conclusions, particularly points 10-27.

of years, issues as the shortages of skilled persons and the ageing and decline of populations, have been drawn to the public migration debate. Comprehensive immigration policies are being called for.

The problems now confronting governments are the result of a piecemeal approach to a specific problem-solving, which in turn led to a series of (im)migration-related policies, addressing a series of issues (such as asylum, labour, family reunion and formation, trafficking, illegal immigration and return) separately or in parallel rather than in an integrated fashion. An integrated management strategy is required to bring these together and to be applied over a long period of time. Failure to do so will only replicate the mistakes of the past where action in one direction has often resulted in creating new problems in another. The European Commission in its proposals on a Community immigration policy[2] supports such a management approach. Whether countries are able to develop their own integrated policies and are able to harmonise them with others, are questions that can no longer be avoided.

However, the feasibility of commonly agreed and consistent immigration policy objectives, that could underpin the elaboration of a legislative framework common to all Member States, may be questioned – not only on the sensitive issue of sovereignty, but on other issues as well. Among them is the highly diverse geography and experience of migration within Europe: three interlinked, but separate migration sub-systems have evolved within Europe in the last decade, which are characterised by different types and scales of movement. Although they are acting largely independently, at least in geographical terms, they are nevertheless largely influenced by economic globalisation. Consequently, the formulation of a common European immigration policy needs to include a common understanding of a multi-dimensional global matrix of movement involving capital, goods, services, ideas and people as well as taking into consideration the interests of the various actors involved in the process.

The EU immigration policy, as set out by the Commission, takes into account humanitarian, family reunion and economic types of migration. It is the purpose of this paper to look at this latter category and the ways in which the Community immigration policy attempts to tackle tensions between different actors involved in this process. Economic migration involves at least three main actors or three main interests. Firstly, there are the interests of the state. For the purposes of economic migration the state means a sovereign state, which has the capacity to confer nationality on individuals, and to recognise the nationality of non-

2 Communication from the Commission to the Council and the European Parliament on a Community Immigration Policy, Com (2000) 757 final, Brussels, 22.11.2000.

nationals; this to control their movement according to its purposes.[3] State can be subdivided into the state of destination, the state of origin as well as of transit. Here, however, I will focus on the interests of Member States of the European Union, who have declared strong interests in the regulation of labour migration regarding promoting, preventing and controlling its flow. Secondly, there are the interests of the economic sector, more specifically those of companies and business. These interests can be manifested in various ways. The employer may rely on the destination state to undertake recruitment of labour migrants, or the employer may recruit migrant labour directly, either in the destination state or abroad. Thirdly, there are interests of individuals, meaning the migrants themselves. An individual has an interest in economic migration both individually and as a part of a family and network structure and strategy.

In order to understand the dynamic relationship of these key interests and the evolution of the construction of a common EU immigration policy I will firstly discuss the interaction between "new migration" and "new" policy initiatives. This will be followed by a discussion on Community immigration policy in the demographic and economic context. Finally, it will be argued that the best model for a common European immigration policy would be the human rights approach.

II. The New Migration and Policy Responses

Over the last decade, there has been the highest level of migration in Europe since 1945.[4] Much of the academic literature on this issue has described the period as being characterised by "new" migrations.[5] These are identified in a number of ways, but at its heart are the dynamic relationship between geopolitical and geo-economic changes and the evolving patterns and processes of migration, normally traced back to 1989 and to the end of Europe's Cold War political division.[6]

---

3 *Guild, E.*: Member States' Labour Markets: Impact on Immigration. Paper presented at the conference "Extending the Area of Freedom, Justice and Security through Enlargement", Trier, 7-8 July, 2002.

4 This section is based on the author's paper Migration in Context of the European enlargement presented at the ERA Conference "State of Play on European Immigration and Asylum Policy: Patching up Tampere?", Trier, 25-26 April 2002.

5 *Koser, K./Lutz, H.*, (eds.), 1998: The New Migration in Europe: Social Constructions and Social Realities, Macmillan Press Ltd.

6 *Castles, S./Miller, M. J.*, 1993: The Age of Migration, London: Macmillan; *Gould, W. T. S./Findlay, A. M.* (eds.) 1994: Population Migration and the Changing World Or-

While any estimations of migration are clouded by the concerns of data deficiencies, a number of commentators have suggested that the extent of migration since 1989 in Europe alone allows for its qualifications as "new", as it outnumbers any other migration in Europe since the end of the Second World War.[7] However, in the 1990s it was political-military perturbations in Central and Eastern Europe, particularly the Balkans, that have affected the flow regimes, created human rights difficulties and injected major uncertainties into the policy-making process.

1. *New geography of migration*

Along with the extent of international migration a new geography of migration in Europe emerged.[8] The geographical patterning has altered greatly already since the early 1980s. In particular, the proportion of immigrants coming from other developed countries has declined significantly. Recent migration flows have emerged from new countries of origin; in the late 1980s and early 1990s there was a considerable escalation of flows into Western Europe from two sources: the East of the "South". Changes in the former Soviet Union and Eastern Europe have not resulted in the "mass" migration initially predicted, but these countries are nevertheless also significant new countries of origin for migration within Europe.[9] The wars in the Balkans dominated movements of the 1990s as they brought sudden and massive forced movements on a scale not seen since 1945. New countries of destination have also emerged. These include countries in Southern Europe as well as in Central and Eastern Europe. The larger southern European countries such as Italy and Spain became net immigration countries.[10] The new and newly democratic countries of Central and Eastern Europe increasingly find themselves playing the role of transit countries for migrants aiming to enter the EU as well as that of destination countries in their own right as the

---

der, London: Belhaven; *Richmond, A. H.*, 1995: Global Apartheid, Toronto: Oxford University Press.

7 *King, R.* (ed.), 1993: Mass Migration in Europe: The Legacy and the Future, London: Belhaven; *Fassmann, H./Münz, R.*, 1994: European Migration in the late Twentieth Century, Aldershot: Edward Elgar.

8 *King, R.* (ed.), 1993: The New Geography of European Migrations, London: Belhaven.

9 *Salt, J./Clarke, J.*, 1996: International Migration in Central and Eastern Europe, New Community, 22 (3), pp. 513-529; *Tränhardt, D.*, 1996: European Migration from East to West: Present Patterns and Future Directions, New Community, 22 (2), pp. 227-242.

10 *King, R./Rybaczuk, K.*, 1993: Southern Europe and the International Division of Labour: From Emigration to Immigration, in: *King, R.* (ed.), 1993: The New Geography of European Migrations, London: Belhaven, pp. 175-206.

process of economic transition advances and as the EU countries reinforce their controls.

With regard to immigration, European countries fall into several groups. The vast majority of immigrants in Central and Eastern European countries come from elsewhere in Europe, mainly from other countries of the same region, and with only small proportions from EU and EFTA states. Scandinavian countries also display a relatively high degree of "Euro self-containment", mainly from EU and EFTA states, and from "Other Europe" (largely Turkey and former Yugoslavia) with only small proportions of flows from Central and Eastern Europe. Germany's immigration field is strongly European, and along with Austria and Finland, receives a high proportion of its immigrants from Central and Eastern Europe. In contrast, almost a third of the UK's immigrants come from outside Europe. The Mediterranean countries also tend to look beyond Europe, as does the Netherlands. These differences in the migration fields of individual countries, reflect a range of historical (such as post-colonial links) and geographical (especially proximity) processes.[11] Finally, the patterns depicted reinforce the diversity of migration experience across Europe.

2. *New types of migration*

The new pattern of migration has often been associated with new types of migration and more generally, with the changing profiles of migrants. The emergence of a "post-industrial" pattern over the past two decades, represents the latest wave affecting post-war Europe, following the displaced persons resettlement after 1945, the "guest worker" phenomenon of the 1950s and 1960s and the subsequent phase of family reunification. This latest wave comprises three relatively distinct elements: high-skilled labour migration, refugees and asylum seekers and the irregular/ illegal or clandestine movement. The first of the three has, at least until recently, constituted an essentially "invisible" process in that it involves mainly professional, managerial and technically skilled workers who are relatively cosmopolitan in culture. They also play an important role in the economy and are likely to be on some form of temporary contract or posting from their home companies. However, there appears to have been a steady growth in the migration of the highly skilled across Europe as a whole. While the bulk of this movement is still westwards, the continent is now seeing an increasingly

11 *Salt, J.*, 2000: Current Trends in International Migration in Europe, Consultant's Report to the Council of Europe.

complex pattern of "brain exchange".[12] The second element consists of refugees and asylum seekers to whom most attention has been accorded in recent years, partly because they are closely monitored under international agreements and also because the numbers applying for asylum in the states of the EU exploded during the 1980s and early 1990s and, in the late 1990s also in some of the EU Candidate states. The third element consists of "illegal" migration. There is a commonly held view that an increasing proportion of immigrants are "illegal", either by entering a country in violation of that country's laws or by doing something to violate a condition for legal stay. This type of migration is largely labour-market related; the process is controversial, however. For example, even refugees and asylum seekers often appear to be little different from clandestine migrants, as many are believed to be basically "economic" refugees rather than people fleeing from fear of persecution. Furthermore, it is sometimes difficult to distinguish human trafficking from illegal immigration. Smuggling of migrants and particularly trafficking in human beings is currently one of the most urgent and complex human rights issues and a priority concern of the EU international cooperation in the fight against trans-national organised crime.[13]

A substantial amount of literature deals with each of these types. An important overall comment is that together they embody an increasing polarity in migration flows. In particular, this is manifested by a bipolar distribution according to skills, occupation and income. Another result of new migration is family fragmentation, bringing about a growing participation of women and children. A growing number of female migrants and minors are also reported as being the victims of trafficking in human beings, exploited through sexual and other industries in slavery-like situations.

3. New nature of migration

The term new migration may suggest that using the term "migration" has changed in some way. It is not immediately clear what is meant by "migration" and "immigration". Migration is a sub-category of a more general concept of "movement", embracing a wide variety of types and forms of human mobility, each capable of metamorphosing into something else through a set of processes which are becoming increasingly institutionally driven. What we then define as

---

12 *Rees, P/Stillwell, J./Convey, A./Kupiszewski, M.* (eds.), 1996: Population Migration in the European Union, Chichester: Wiley.

13 *Medved, F./Cullen, P.*, 2002: Counteracting Human Trafficking: An Analysis of European Policy, in: *Anderson, M./Apap, J.* (eds.) Police and Justice Co-operation and the New European Borders, The Hague: Kluwer International, pp. 183-218.

migration is an arbitrary choice, and may be time specific. In recent decades, "immigration" has been associated with some notion of permanent settlement, which for the most part occurred indirectly as a development of previous temporary labour migration, mainly through family reunion and family formation. Most voluntary migration in recent decades has featured temporary labour migrants. This is, however, an enormously diverse group, which can be blended with numerous other international movers. Today, "permanent" settlement may be associated with the return of former labour migrants or certain ethnic groups such as German *Aussiedler* or Romanian Magyars. It is important to see that diverse types of "mobility" (permanent migration, temporary labour migrants, asylum seekers, refugees, temporary protected persons, students, working holidaymakers, highly skilled) may easily be transposed into another. It does therefore not make sense to think of it in terms of rigid categories, nor to place "(im)migration" at some defined point on the mobility continuum.[14]

Eurostat reports that migration flows are now composed of a mix of people: asylum seekers, displaced persons and those seeking temporary protection, family members coming to join migrants already settled within the EU, labour migrants and growing numbers of business migrants. The flows have become more flexible – in particular there has been an increase in short-term and cross-border movements – with a complex pattern of people entering but also leaving the Union.[15] The European Commission's new approach to immigration sees new trends in migration through "the concept of migration as a *pattern of mobility*",[16] limited to the element of policy concerning partnership with countries of origin. In this sense flexibility of policy is concerned with encouragement of migrants to maintain and develop their links with their countries of origin rather than including the realisation that new migration as a "pattern of mobility", involving different "categories" of migrants, motivations, methods and roles of insertion into the societies into which they come is largely influenced and managed by different agencies and institutions. Categories are often rigid, and it is sometimes difficult for migrants to move from one category to the other. In my view, a new approach to immigration should also provide a framework for flexibility in this respect.

14 Cf. *Salt, J.*, 2000, op.cit.
15 COM (2000) 757 final, Annex 1.
16 COM (2000) 757 final, p. 8, emphasis original.

4. *Policy responses*

Immigration policies often emerge out of political, social and economic imperatives which have little direct relationship with migrants or migration itself. The extent to which the changes in policy-making have been a response to changes in migration, either stocks or flows, is hard to discern. It may be claimed, however, that simultaneously with the new migration, a "new" Europe and new policy responses have emerged. Political transformations have brought about a sharper focus to questions surrounding the definition of Europe and its boundaries. New migration is located at the centre of competition and conflict concerning the nature of organising principles, which can unify the "new" Europe. The first decade of the 21st century confronts Europe with challenges relating to five interrelated subjects in particular: the enlargement of the Union, the strive for a common foreign and security policy, the urge to provide a sustainable basis for employment and growth, the establishment of the Union as an "area of freedom, security and justice" and the decision to agree on a common asylum and migration policy. Hence, "new" migration cannot be understood in isolation from the economic, political and social orientation of the "new" Europe.

Despite this, it was before 1989 that the countries in Western Europe recognised that they had a "common interest" in the area of asylum and migration policy and began searching for a forum for strategy creation and coordinated action. When it became clear that guest workers "come to stay",[17] the initial reaction of most governments was to stop further recruitment of foreign workers, to try to induce those residing in the country to return, and to prevent family reunification. When this proved to be impossible, the problem of regulating international migration shifted in the 1980s to one of intensifying border control, increasing internal regulation of labour markets and integrating large, established foreign populations.[18] Controlling borders required a renewed emphasis on international cooperation, especially among the Member States of the European Community, committed to building a border free area, relaxing and eventually eliminating all internal borders, in order to complete the internal market. This process of integration was given new impetus by the Single European Act of 1986, which called for the elimination of all barriers to the movement of capital, goods, services and people within the territory of the European Community by January 1992. Given the desire of Member States to stop further immigration, creating a

---

17 *Rogers, R.* (ed.), 1985: Guests Come to Stay: The Effects of European Labor Migration on Sending and Receiving Countries, Boulder, Colorado: Westview.

18 *Brochmann, G./Hammar, T.* (eds.), 1999: Mechanisms of Immigration Control: A Comparative Analysis of European Regulation Policies, Oxford: Berg.

border free Europe meant reinforcing external borders. A series of intergovernmental agreements dealing with asylum, migration and security issues were drafted to help construct a kind of European migration regime. These include the Schengen Agreement of 1985, whereby EU governments, in exchange for common visa requirements to control the movement of third-country nationals, committed themselves to eliminating border checks, and the Dublin Convention of 1990, which requires asylum seekers to apply for asylum in the first "safe country" where they arrive. These agreements, with further "transgression" of the "European borders" in view of the eastern EU enlargement helped to establish buffer states in the Central and Eastern Europe.[19]

Project 1992 together with the Maastricht Treaty, ratified in 1993, launched the most ambitious program of regional integration and economic liberalisation in world history.[20] But just as this process was taking off, the strategic situation in Europe was turned upside down, with a crisis surrounding refugee migration and asylum seeking. A large percentage of those whose asylum claims were refused would remain in the host countries either legally – pending appeal of their case – or illegally. With continuing attempts to slow down or stop all forms of legal immigration, the number of illegal immigrants has increased steadily. New migrants, particularly asylum seekers and undocumented migrants, have become the focus for a brand of moral panic in many European societies, in which they represent a broader social symbol of immigrants who abuse the welfare state, commit crimes and threaten the employment of established citizens. In this context, the new migration has been associated with the current resurgence of extreme nationalist and racist movements in a number of European societies.[21] The construction of "frontiers of identity" against the "others" has intensified.[22] With the perception among Western publics that immigration is raging out of control and with the rise of right wing and xenophobic movements and political parties, governments have been reluctant to create new programmes for legal

19 *Hollifield, J. F.*, 1992: Migration and International Relations: Cooperation and Control in the European Community, International Migration Review 26/2, pp. 568-595; *Medved, F.*, 2000: Politika migracij in azila v transgresiji Evropske Unije (Migration and Asylum Policy in the Transgression of the European Union), Razprave in gradivo (Treatises and Documents) 36/37, Ljubljana: Institute for Ethnic Studies, pp. 207-226.

20 *Hollifield, J. F.*: Migration and International Relations: The Liberal Paradox, Paper presented at the ERA Conference "State of Play on European Immigration and Asylum Policy: Patching up Tampere?", Trier, 25-26 April 2002.

21 *Miles, R.*, 1993: Racism and Race Relations, London: Routledge; *Solomos, J./Wrench, J.* (eds.), 1993: Racism and Migration in Western Europe, Oxford: Berg.

22 *Cohen, R.*, 1994: Frontiers of Identity: The British and the Others, London: Longman.

immigration, or to expand existing quotas. Instead, the thrust of policy change has been in the direction of further restriction.[23] Policy changes that have taken place increased vulnerability of many migrants from asylum seekers deprived of welfare, to undocumented migrants indebted to smugglers and traffickers.

It is becoming clear that the new migration in Europe has a significance, which outweighs the changing patterns and processes alone.[24] Migration has assumed a growing importance on political agendas and opened new dilemmas. In addition, the meaning of the "new" migration has become the focus of competition and sometimes conflict between policy makers, new migrants and the resident populations – indigenous and immigrant – in Europe.

Most European governments recognise that they now preside over multicultural/immigrant societies, and attempts to ostracise settled foreign populations only feed the flames of xenophobia and racism. In the late 1990s, several European states passed laws to liberalise naturalisation and citizenship policy.[25] Furthermore, irregular immigration and trafficking in human beings have occupied much attention from both the media and the authorities. New national and international efforts have been launched to combat these phenomena.[26] In the meantime, acute shortages of skilled workers in the labour market and issues regarding the "demographic deficit" anticipated within the EU over the next 10 to 30 years have driven the debate on the question of relaxing immigration controls both in Member States and across the EU and added a wider dimension to the

23 For example, Germany in 1993 amended its constitution in order to eliminate the blanket right of asylum that was enshrined in Article 16 of the old Basic Law, France in 1995-96 enacted a series of laws that were designed to roll back the rights of foreign residents and make it more difficult for immigrants to naturalise. See e.g. *Brochmann, G./Hammar T.*, 1999, op.cit.

24 Of course, describing a phenomenon as 'new' corresponds with the modern desire to order and arrange societies according to certain characteristics of which the expression of time and sequential structure is a major principle. It is, however, an example of an a posteriori description and these have in other contexts been challenged at a later date on the basis of differing ordering principles. It follows that the description of recent migration in Europe as new is still preliminary and the validity of the notion new stands to be tested and proved in the long term.

25 *Medved, F.*, 2001: Interaction between Nationality and Integration/Interaction entre nationalité et integration, 2nd European Conference on Nationality: Challenges to National and International Law on Nationality at the Beginning of the New Millennium, Council of Europe, Strasbourg, 8 and 9 October 2001, Proceedings, pp. 23-39.

26 *Medved, F./Cullen, P.*, 2002, op.cit; *Medved, F.*: Is illegal migration the 'missing link' of a comprehensive immigration and asylum policy? Paper presented at the Conference "Extending the Area of Freedom, Security and Justice through Enlargement: Challenges for the European Union", Trier, 4-6 July, 2002.

arguments as to whether immigration can benefit the EU economically. European governments are now turning to new recruitment programmes, seeking to emulate some aspects of the U.S., Canadian and Australian dynamic and selective immigration policies, and make their own economies more competitive in a rapidly globalising world.

Regarding the competence of the European Commission over the field of immigration, the document on a Community immigration policy, with such keywords as "common legal framework", "new integrated approach" and "proactive immigration policy", appeared relatively late, stating that "in view of the strongly divergent views in the Member States on the admission and integration of third-country nationals, the Commission feels that it is essential to discuss these issues openly and to try to reach a consensus on the objectives of the policy to be followed" and that the purpose of the communication is to "stimulate this debate".[27]

III. A Community Policy on Immigration

A Community immigration policy as communicated by the Commission represents an attempt to synthesise the economic and demographic aspects of the arguments for a proactive immigration policy. It implicitly recognises the numerous tensions between Member States, business and individual migrants and it is my intention to look at how the balance between these competing, but also overlapping interests has been tackled by current proposals on the admission of economic migrants.

1. The demographic context

The role of migration in European population change has come under increasing scrutiny in recent years. This is a result of growing concerns about a cocktail of prospective changes to labour supply and demand. Issues raised include demographic ageing, shortages of working age populations, dependency ratios and payment of pensions, and possible shortages of both skilled and less-skilled labour. But while for demographers, migration is one of the three key variables affecting the size of population, for migration policy makers, the effects of migration on populations have mostly not appeared that interesting, perhaps because the slow demographic changes have been viewed as long-term concerns, which often appear to be beyond the politicians' horizon. The need for interac-

27 COM (2000) 757 final, Executive Summary, p. 3.

tion between demographic and migration policy goals has also been overshadowed by concrete concerns regarding, for example, illegal immigration, smuggling of migrants and human trafficking or difficulties in the integration. However, the United Nations Population Division report *Replacement Migration – Is it a Solution to Declining and Ageing Populations*? published in March 2000 attracted large publicity and brought the demographic facts and projections into the public debate on migration policy.[28]

During the 1990s the world's population increased more rapidly than ever before and looks set to continue its rapid growth, (rising to around 9.4 billion by 2050), with Europe's share becoming increasingly modest, halving between 1995 and 2050. Whether or not one subscribes to the notion of a "post-industrial society" coming into being in Europe, both in economic and social terms, it cannot be denied that contemporary demographic behaviour in Europe is very different from that which prevailed during the main period of demographic transition. Indeed, it can be claimed that demography is one of the main driving forces for change in Europe. Over the last three decades the continent appears to have embarked on "a second demographic transition", with the overall level of fertility moving below the replacement rate and alterations taking place in sexual and household-forming behaviour.

Main demographic features recently recorded by Eurostat included the generally low rates of fertility and mortality and the widespread occurrence of natural decrease. Net migration to the EU has declined rapidly over the last decade since peaking in the early 1990s at over 1 million per year before starting to climb again and reaching just over 700 000 in 1999. The general trend among all the Central and Eastern European countries is one of even slower population growth than that of the EU-15 for the first quarter of this century. The various European countries fare differently in the process, mainly according to their current levels of fertility but in spite of these disparities, across the EU as a whole it is net migration that has become the principal component of population growth.[29]

Irrespective of any future trends in the three basic demographic components these developments have put in train a variety of consequences, which will have repercussions lasting well into this century, and raise a whole series of important policy issues. The direct impacts of the likely changes in the number of people are modest compared with those arising from changes in the structure and composition of the population. The three aspects of population change have brought

28 UN, 2000: Replacement Migration: Is it a Solution to Declining and Ageing Populations?, New York: UN Population Division.

29 COM (2000) 757 final, Annex 1.

about the fundamental restructuring of the population over the past three decades and have set in motion a pattern of demographic development, which appears to contain a high degree of inevitability.

2. *The "greying" of population*

The "greying" of population is considered to be one of the most important changes to be affecting European populations. Certainly, the statistics on the growth of the aged population are impressive. All European countries have larger proportions of the elderly than ever before, a development, which will be strongly reinforced in many countries as their baby-boom generations reach retirement age. As shown in Table 1 the proportion of Europeans aged 65 years and older has been rising steadily over the past four decades being half as much again in 1990 as its 8.7 per cent level in 1950. Moreover, this growth is projected to accelerate as the baby boomers of the 1950s and early 1960s move into retirement age. It can also be seen that this phenomenon is widespread across Europe, though not entirely uniform, the biggest increases being for western and Southern Europe (reflecting the very low birth rates there) and the smallest for Northern Europe.

Table 1: Proportion of the population aged 65 years or more, and elderly dependency ratio, 1950-2025

Year / Area	1950	1970	1990	2010	2025
% aged 65+ Europe total	8.7	11.4	13.4	16.1	20.1
Northern	10.3	12.7	15.5	16.1	19.8
Western	10.1	11.4	13.4	16.1	22.3
Central	7.4	9.9	12.7	16.3	20.0
Eastern	7.0	10.4	11.3	13.5	17.6

Year / Area	1950	1970	1990	2010	2025
Dependency ratio Europe	13.2	17.9	20.0	24.3	31.7

Notes: Areas of Europe are arranged in order of percentage of persons 65+ in 1990. Dependency ratio refers to the number aged 65+ per 100 persons aged 15-64.

Sources: Warnes, A. M., 1993: Demographic ageing: trends and policy responses, in Noin, D./ Woods, R. (eds.), op.cit.; Champion, T., 1998: Demography, in: Unwin, T.(ed.): A European Geography, London: Longman.

This ageing has at least three major consequences. Firstly, it increases the costs of health treatment and personal care. Secondly, there is the problem of raising money to fund pensions, given that an increased population entitled to an pension will have to be supported by a shrinking number of people of working age. The dependency ratio has already risen from 13.2 to 20 in the 40 years preceding 1990, but it is projected to reach 31.7 by 2025. This represents a massive redistribution of economic, social and political power, which governments are currently grappling with. Thirdly, and particularly important for employment, is the ageing of the labour force. Much of Western Europe has already experienced a large downturn in the number of labour market entrants, but the next two decades will see a reversal in the balance of younger and older workers from around 1.2 20-39-years-old for every 40-59-year-old in the early 1990s to 1.2 40-59-years old for every 20-39 year old around 2015.[30] The accession states will experience a similar ageing of the population and challenges expected from the decline in their working-age population to those faced by EU-15.

Particular issues are also raised by the arrival of less skilled immigrants and of those of "non-European" culture.[31] These problems are often exacerbated by the uneven spatial patterns of immigrant's destinations, traditionally in areas needing low-wage labour for declining industries and more recently in the largest cities, where cheaper housing is more plentiful and job openings are expected to be more numerous.

Thus, the geographical patterning of population growth and decline across Europe has undergone some substantial changes during the post war period but

30 *Green, A./Owen, D.*, 1995: The labour market aspects of population change in the 1990s, in *Hall, R./White P.* (eds.): Europe's Population: Towards the Next Century, London, UCL Press, pp. 51-68.

31 *White, P.*, 1993: Ethnic minority communities in Europe, in: *Noin, D./Woods, R.* (eds.): The Changing Population of Europe, Oxford: Blackwell, pp. 206-225.

these lack consistency and provide a rather weak basis for anticipating future trends. One important development has been the convergence of birth and death trends across most of Europe, not only at national level but also intra-regionally within countries. The inter-regional range of natural change rates is much smaller now than in the past, and migration has become relatively more important in accounting for regional differences in overall population change.

3. Replacement migration

The United Nations Population Division has suggested that Europe might need replacement migration – in order to cope with the potential problems caused by the declining and ageing populations – ranging from around a million to 13 million new migrants per year between 2000 and 2050. For example, immigration required to keep the support ratios unchanged during the next five decades would mean a growth of the European Union's population from 375 million in 2000 to 1.2 billion, out of which 918 million, or 75 per cent would be immigrants or their descendants. Others have contested such a scale of immigration as being unnecessary or impractical.[32]

An OECD report, *Maintaining Prosperity in an Ageing Society*, emphasised that policy choices have to be made for the medium-long term in order to support pension and health systems.[33] Most frequently mentioned are those aimed to raise fertility rates or encourage greater immigration. There is also a need to understand better the capacity of labour markets to adapt to ageing work forces, and how it can be enhanced. It is suggested that most workers have the potential to remain productive up to and beyond the current standard are of retirement, provided they receive adequate training. However, these adjustments may not go as far, or proceed as rapidly, as desirable and it still remains true that older workers face elevated risks of skills obsolescence and poor health.[34]

Tapinos presented a useful framework for the future dilemmas. The issues related to migration, population ageing and population decline can be analysed with help of three time horizons. During the next ten years, the labour market will be the main focus of concern, and the relevant action parameters would be thus linked with labour market demand and supply. Impact on fertility and mor-

---

32 *Coleman, D. A.*, 1995: International migration: demographic and socio-economic consequences in the United Kingdom and Europe. International Migration Review, Vol. 29, No 1; Economist, September 9th, 2000.

33 OECD, 1998: Maintaining Prosperity in an Ageing Society.

34 See e.g. OECD, 2000: Reforms for an Ageing Society.

tality will be limited. In this time horizon international migration can play a decisive role. This seems to be the case in many industrial countries where labour shortages and mismatches in domestic labour markets have motivated special arrangements and measures facilitating immigration of the skilled labour especially. In the next 20-40 years, "structural imbalances of age distribution", and the threatening imbalance in the social security system will be the main concern. The impact of demographic trends, and the obviously weakening support ratios on the social security balance would be crucial but "a number of social economic and institutional variables may strengthen or dampen the demographic impact". In the "very long run" the concern is the total population decline, for which no meaningful option would exist other than an increase in fertility in order to sustain a stationary population, which is, for Tapinos, an unquestionable end for any society.[35] It is obvious that the key problems pointed out neither appear nor fade away in a subsequent period. It is rather that they have already started to emerge, and policies to counteract them would be better found as soon as possible.

Thus population projections and labour market shortages have been the main triggers for a new wave of debate and active search for the policy making, particularly in the search of a possible combination of the many issues, interests and concerns that are represented in the policy making. These are different and often conflicting and are articulated both in national migration debates and at the European Union level.[36]

Some EU Member States have already developed concrete policy initiatives to address labour market shortages, and implicitly the increasing demographic issue.[37] The European Commission has also identified a number of trends in the demographic situation in the EU, notably the decrease in population growth and a marked rise in the average age of the population. The decline in the working age population, beginning in the next 10 years and the long term rise in the percentage of the population who are over 65 are identified as issues of concern to the EU, both in terms of the economic consequences and the impact on social security regimes. The Commission recognises that increased legal immigration cannot, in itself, be considered as an effective way to offset these demographic changes, but should be part of an overall structural strategy to tackle these problems. In the short term, it could be an important element in population growth

35 Tapinos (2000) as referred to in: *Mattila, H. S.*: Search for new immigration policy in Western Europe, "European Population Conference 2001", Helsinki, June 7-9, 2001.

36 Ibid.

37 As for example Germany in the Report of the Independent Commission on Migration: Structuring Immigration, Fostering Integration, Berlin, 4. July 2001.

when accompanied by other responses such as more friendly family policies. Equally, controlled immigration may help to alleviate shortages provided it takes place within the context of an overall structural strategy dealing with labour market imbalances, including skill shortages, which should be addressed by an overall strategy of structural policies in the field of employment and human resources development.

In this sense, the Commission's paper on immigration policy, emphasised policy co-ordination in the EU concerning the area of employment, a process, which was initiated by the European Council in Luxembourg in 1997. According to Article 126 of the Amsterdam Treaty, Member States implement their employment policies – outlined in their National Action Plans – in a way, which is consistent with the employment guidelines and the broad economic policy guidelines drawn up each year by the Council. A number of weaknesses in the EU economy are highlighted as well, notably the high number of people still unemployed, insufficient participation of women and older people in the work force and long-term structural unemployment, with marked regional differences. Attention is also drawn to the need to modernise social protection systems and in particular to secure their sustainability in the face of an ageing population.[38] The Commission believes that the strategies, which came from the Lisbon European Council in March 2000, will reduce the effects of the ageing population in the EU and the level of dependency between those in work and those who have retired. With respect to social security systems the presence of legal labour migrants and their families may, at least in the short term, be a positive factor in the face of an ageing and declining population. The Commission recognises that there may be initial settlement costs, but that the availability of effective integration measures for third-country nationals would reinforce their socio-economic contribution to their "host" society and may be a smaller long-term cost to society than the absence of such policies, which lead to discrimination and social exclusion.

Actors' interests

The migration interests of the Member States in this context can be evident through the wish to maintain or increase revenues from a successful economy in order to pay for the social costs of an ageing population without disrupting so-

38 Communication from the Commission to the Council, to the European Parliament and to the Economic and Social Committee -The future evolution of social protection from a long-term point of view: safe and sustainable pensions COM (2000) 622 final.

cial solidarity. The interest of business is to have a flexible labour market with sufficient workers, either highly skilled or low skilled, to meet demand and to keep wages as low as possible in order to remain competitive in the global economy. The interest of individual migrants are to improve their living and working conditions, to achieve their full potential and not least to be able to exercise their right to family unification and formation.

However, the extent and the consequences of demographic changes should be looked at carefully. Projections as to net immigration figures vary significantly and this can have an impact on the importance of migration policy when seeking to redress any deficit. It is arguable that the demographic deficit will increase migratory pressures, as labour shortages will push wages up and bring unemployment down. A tight labour market attracts migrants and without them, labour market shortages could lead to reduction in growth and inflationary pressures.[39] Therefore, these aspects need to be considered seriously.

4. The economic context

A strategic goal of the EU for the first decade of this century is to "become the most competitive and dynamic knowledge-based economy able to sustain economic growth and create more and better jobs with greater social cohesion."[40] An overall strategy to this end was adopted by the Lisbon European Council, which also pointed to the problems caused by the under-development of the services sector, especially in the areas of telecommunications and the Internet, and the widening skills gap, especially in information technology.[41] Charting the progress, the Joint employment report 2000 stressed that further efforts are necessary, due to a worrying growth in skills shortages and miss-matches in supply and demand for labour, and reported that shortages in the traditional low-skilled areas, such as agriculture and tourism, are continuing even where there are high

39 *Medved, F.*, 1998a: Izhodisca za oblikovanje politike priseljevanja Republike Slovenije (The Outline of the Immigration Policy of the Republic of Slovenia) Porocevalec Drzavnega zbora Republike Slovenije (Parliament of the Republic of Slovenia) XXXIV, 38, pp. 9-77. *Medved, F.*, 1998b: Predlog nacel in ciljev imigracijske politike Republike Slovenije (The Proposition of Principles and Aims of Immigration Policy of the Republic of Slovenia), Javna Uprava, 34, 3, Faculty of Law, University in Ljubljana, pp.433-456.

40 COM (2000) 757 final, p. 26.

41 The strategy outlined by the Council is to raise the employment rate from an average of 61% in 2000 to near 70% in 2010, for women from 51% to over 60%.

levels of unemployment.[42] These shortages, in the view of the report, could threaten the European Union's competitiveness in the global economy.

Overall, the Commission's Communication on a Community Immigration Policy points to good macro economic prospects for the European Union and cites a number of benefits to the economy such as the introduction of the Euro and the completion of the internal market, as leading to improved growth and job creation with a consequent drop in unemployment. The Commission states that these prospects provide an ideal environment within which to look at the benefits of increased immigration.

Issues such as the possible downturn in the EU economy were not addressed. This, particularly in view of the document's timing, when slowdown of the US economy was already projected, and when a similar process could have been expected in the EU economy, reinforces the view that Community institutions as well as the Member States may be too slow to react quickly enough to significant and rapid changes in the labour market. Any Community policy, however, should be able to react rapidly to fluctuations in economy and changes in the labour market. As an example, the significant downturn and investment in the high technology and e-commence sectors, where rapid growth and skills shortages have been used by the Commission as an example of the need for immigration throughout the paper, has taken place just as these shortages have finally been acknowledged by the Member States, as well as by the Commission in its Communication.

5. *Actors' interests*

The fluctuations in the economy and the often changing needs for migrant labour highlight the differences between the competing interest groups. The interests of the Member States have historically been driven by the wish to have migrant labour for the shortest possible time (for example the "Gastarbeiter" approach when no commitment is given to the security of residence of individuals). From the employer's perspective, there is clearly no benefit in having a continuing obligation to employ migrant labour in the event of an economic downswing. From the individual's perspective, migrants' priorities are clearly the security of employment and residence, which will effectively compensate for their commitment to a specific labour market. There is a risk that if no such security is provided, migrants will be reluctant to take up employment and resi-

42 Joint employment report 2000 – Part I: the European Union – Part II: the Member States COM (2000) 551 final.

dence in a particular Member State. Such a reaction was evident in the poor response to the May 2000 German government's launch of a "green card" program, designed to recruit up to 20,000 highly skilled workers from outside the European Union. After criticism from human rights groups and gentle reminders from experts about the difficulty of preventing "guest workers" from settling, the government quickly revised its policy to allow for the possibility of settlement and family reunification.[43]

The new economic migration?

The Commission recognises that "there is a growing recognition that the "zero" immigration policies of the past 30 years are no longer appropriate."[44] It should be understood however, that the concept of "zero" immigration, brought into force in the following the economic crisis from 1973 onward, has largely been a fiction, maintained for political ends by Member States throughout the 1980s and 1990s. In reality, even after the official suspension of recruitment programmes, substantial migration has taken place as a result of powerful supply-push forces and networks giving migration the form of family rather than worker immigration and as a result of both the liberalisation of trade and the globalisation of the economy. All Member States have, to some extent, admitted economic migrants for the purposes of employment, business and investment during this period. The development of international business across frontiers has continued hand in hand with the transfer of personnel within international companies. Strict labour market testing has sought to protect local labour markets but the reality has been that migrants always possessed skills and experience, often sectorally based, which could not be found in Member States. The hypocrisy of the "zero" immigration policies has been that they have effectively sanctioned the continued economic migration, often on an entirely discretionary basis, where the grant of work permits has been an exception (or derogation) from the general rule that there should be no economic migration.[45]

Highly skilled labour – An acceptable face of immigration

Currently, there is no doubt that the demand for specialised skills within the EU labour market cannot be met by the existing workforce. This is particularly so in the information technology sector where, in some Member States, numerous high profile schemes and changes in existing rules took effect in the second half

43 *Hollifield, J. F.*, 2002, op.cit.
44 COM (2000) 757 final, Brussels, p. 3.
45 See below, section IV.

of 2000. The Commission's Communication reflects the arguments for an increased economic immigration, which have been driven largely by the "acceptable" face of migration – that of highly skilled and highly educated migrants, required by the economies of the Member States in its most buoyant sectors and makes it clear that migration for the highly skilled is necessary for the continued economic growth of the EU.

6. "Low qualified" migrants and undocumented labour – social difficulties of immigration

The assessment of the need for low skilled labour is unsatisfactory. While a certain need for low skilled labour is recognised, concerns are focused on the possible social difficulties of encouraging such labour migration to the EU. The question of low skilled immigration is looked at in the context of a number of problem areas and weaknesses identified in the EU economy, notably the high unemployment figures. While dispelling myths that immigration contributes to unemployment, the Communication identifies the economic benefits of migration as being more positive in respect of highly qualified migrants, as the "low qualified" may be competing with national workers for jobs. The Commission sees direct competition between low skilled migrants and national workers, with migrants undercutting local wage rates, as being susceptible to lead to some social unrest.[46]

It is clear from the experiences over the last decades, that low skilled migrant workers have filled jobs, which national workers do not wish to do. This is true even at a time of economic prosperity, where the shortage in these areas becomes more acute with the national labour force becoming more prosperous and better educated. Failure to fill these posts with legally resident labour leads to the use of undocumented/irregular/illegal migrant labour outside the formal economy, often undercutting local workforces and in cases, national minimum wage requirements. It may be argued that the problems of lack of employment and social protection for these illegal migrants is far greater than any perceived social tensions which the Commission believes may exist. The demand for low skilled immigration clearly exists and should be managed in a way that will bring these migrants within the legal framework of migration and social protection. It is clearly accepted within the Commission paper that labour shortages, which exist in a number of fields such as agriculture, construction and domestic services are often met by irregular/ illegal labour and that the demand for that

46 COM (2000) 757 final, Annex 1.

labour may add to trafficking in human beings and to migrant workers being exploited and unprotected. The problems of undocumented migrants are also recognised. The Commission observes that these problems have led to several Member States resorting to regularisation and amnesty measures. What is not pointed out is that these measures often lead to the polarisation of public opinion for and against immigration. A more rational immigration policy which aims to channel potential illegal migration into legal channels in order to satisfy the clear labour market demands would go a long way in eliminating both misery of undocumented migrants and the politicisation of the immigration debate.

Therefore, both the EU and Member States ought to take a realistic view as to the need for low skilled labour and should seek to influence the public debate on the need for migration in this context. More should also be said about the positive aspects of immigration in general. The Communication indicates, although tentatively, that immigration may contribute to economic growth and to growth per capita and that the fiscal impact of migration is generally thought to be positive. However, it has not been pointed out that there is little evidence that indigenous workers are harmed by immigration. When markets are functioning well, migration usually improves economic welfare, both for the migrant and for the indigenous population.[47]

Atypical work and service provision

One of the principal challenges facing Member States is to provide a flexible immigration policy, which reflects the recent structural trends in the labour market. The increasing incidence of atypical working, part-time, flexible and occasional work, as well as a move from the individual as employee to business person, has become more and more evident, particularly over the last decade. Furthermore, the EU as a whole needs to ensure that it is able to attract not only skilled individuals, but also investment. This can only be achieved by recognising the way in which successful individuals and companies operate within a competitive environment. If immigration policies for economic purposes are to be successful, they must encompass all types of migrants who would be a benefit to the EU economy. The Community institutions should therefore look carefully at encouraging and developing flexibility within their own policies.

Another issue is the increased liberalisation of trade in cross-border services. These issues are mentioned in passing.[48] Nevertheless, in the proposed Directive on the conditions of entry and residence of third-country nationals, for the

47 *Medved, F.*, 1998a.
48 COM (2000) 757 final, Annex 1.

purpose of paid employment and self-employed economic activities,[49] the Commission recognises that a successful policy should provide a place for such short-term migration to take place and encourages the Member States to apply the provisions of the General Agreement on Trade and Services (GATS) in this respect.[50]

Actors' interests

Hence, from the Member States' point of view, the demands for labour at both the top and bottom end of the labour market scale must be addressed. The public debate about illegal immigration is the result of inadequate arrangements at the bottom of the labour market. For business, there is an interest to be able to take on workers who are able to work legally with maximum flexibility. There is also an acute problem of business within the ethnic immigrant communities, which are often perceived as employers of illegal migrants, because the nature of their business involves the employment of low skilled workers. For the individual, the right to security of residence remains paramount, whether at the top or bottom end of the labour market scale.

7. Who decides on appropriate immigration levels?

The intention of the Community immigration policy is not to set "detailed European targets".[51] The responsibility for deciding on the need for different categories of migrant labour is firmly placed on the Member States. While accepting that quotas may be impractical for a flexible approach to changing economic needs, the Commission instead turns to establishing "an appropriate system of indicative targets". This would also take in account factors such as public acceptance, resources available for reception and integration, possibilities for social and cultural adaptation.

A mechanism established at EU level, based on co-operative exchange of information and reporting, was set out in the Communication on the open method of

49 Proposal for a Council Directive on the conditions of entry and residence of third-country nationals for the purpose of paid employment and self-employed economic activities, COM (2001) 386 final, 2001/0154 (CNS), Brussels 11.7.2001.

50 See below, section IV.

51 COM (2000) 757 final, p. 16.

co-ordination for the field of Community immigration policy.[52] The key elements of this method are multi-annual guidelines, approved by the Council, and accompanied by specific timetables for achieving the goals which they set in the short, medium and long term. They are then to be translated into national policy by the setting out of specific targets, which take into account national and regional differences.[53] According to the Directive referring to the admission of economic migrants, coherent and transparent policy and procedures should be established for opening the labour market to third-country nationals within the framework of the European employment strategy. The admission of economic migrants for economic purposes should, as far as possible, be done also in partnership with the countries of origin and in a transparent and coherent way, based on the procedures set out in the proposed Community legislation on the admission of third-country nationals for the purpose of taking up employment.[54] Member States will need to ensure, *inter alia*, that the changes which might be required should be decided in consultation with the social partners, national, regional and local authorities, non-governmental organisations, migrants' associations and other relevant organisations.[55] Under such a scenario, Member States would prepare annual National Action Plans, consisting of two parts; the first would review the development and overall impact of their immigration policy over the previous period, including the numbers of third-country nationals admitted under the various categories and their situation in the labour market; the second part would set out the Member States' future intentions on immigration, including a projection of labour migrants that they wish to admit as set in their National Action Plans for employment.[56] On the basis of these reports the Commission would prepare a synthesis report of the implementation of the common policy, drawing attention to common problems and identifying areas where European solutions might be appropriate. The preparation of this report will be co-ordinated with the corresponding reports on employment and social inclusion.[57] This entails that the responsibility for dealing with the labour market aspects of immigration should lie with the bodies responsible for the imple-

---

52 Communication from the Commission to the Council and the European Parliament on an open method of coordination for the Community immigration policy, COM (2001) 387, Brussels, 11.7.2001.

53 The Commission proposed six guidelines in the following areas: management of migration flows; admission of economic migrants; partnership with third countries and the integration of third-country nationals.

54 COM (2001) 386 final.

55 COM (2000) 757 final, pp. 9-10.

56 COM (2000) 757 final, p. 16 and COM (2001) 387, p. 12.

57 COM (2001) 387, p. 13.

mentation of the European employment strategy at both Member State and Community levels.[58]

The assessment of appropriate immigration levels is clearly left in the hands of the Member States. As they continue to be responsible for the selection of economic migrants and for deciding how many are needed to meet national requirements, it is likely that the indicative targets established under the Community immigration policy would effectively be treated as quotas and that migration over and above those quotas would politically be extremely difficult. However, the nature of economic migration is no longer one where the state is the primary determiner of the need for labour. The EU economy has moved from one where the state was the main employer of labour (and thus having competence to recruit labour itself) to one where many of the fields within state control in the 1950s, 1960s and 1970s have moved into the private sector.[59] Although, particularly in the area of health, the state retains an important remit in assessing the need for migrant labour, it is the market that takes the lead. The deregulation of the EU economy, a process brought about in no small part by the exercise of the Community's powers, has defined the role of the government as framing an economic environment within which businesses flourish, not as one in which the state should be directly involved in the economic decisions of those businesses. It is to some extent inconsistent to approach future EU immigration from a perspective which involves not only a major involvement by the Member States but also by the Community in the decisions of those businesses requiring migrants for their own success.

While it is certainly important to ensure that migration policy is complementary and consistent with other internal and external policy areas so that they are mutually reinforcing within a context of sustainable development, it is – to some extent – difficult to see the benefit of the synthesising of information on the admission of migrants and in laying down principles of the "common approach" to be implemented within the EU. Will this genuinely assist economic needs of business in a fast moving and highly competitive market? As has been seen in the recent past, translating the need of grass roots business for migrant workers, particularly the highly skilled, into positive action by Member States to allow for the admission of those workers, is often a lengthy process. A further exten-

58 In addition the Commission believes that a more open admissions policy should be accompanied by additional measures to eliminate undeclared work which itself encourages illegal migration, smuggling and trafficking.

59 See below, section IV.

sion of this process by the Community's common approach may not assist EU businesses and the economic sectors concerned.

In addition to assessing the level of migration, it is also important to recognise that European industries, particularly small and medium sized ones, often need to recruit migrants quickly. The application of assessment procedures, involving cooperation of a range of institutions (governments, regional and local authorities, social partners, non-governmental organisations, migrants and international bodies) could make the process extremely cumbersome and damage the flexibility of recruitment of labour from outside the EU.

8. Economic needs test

Finally, the principle of "respect for the domestic labour market situation" which is currently applied in all Member State is intended to be untouched.[60] The Commission recognises that industry should be assisted and that employers need "a practical tool" in demonstrating that there is a concrete shortage on the EU labour market.[61] However, it does not encourage enough flexibility on this issue. The "*economic needs test*" and "*beneficial effects test*" as the proposed criteria in the common legal framework on admission of third-country nationals to employed and self-employed economic activities need to address the realities of how businesses operate.

A practical tool for employers as designed in the proposed Directive, provides for an *individual assessment* of compliance with the requirements of the Directive: if employers have published a job vacancy via the employment services of several Member States, e.g. by means of the European Employment Services Network (EURES), for at least four weeks and if they have not received an acceptable application from within the EU labour market, from the Candidate States or certain persons privileged under international agreements, they will be allowed to recruit a third-country national.[62] As regards to self-employed persons, third-country nationals must show that the activity will create a job for them and will have a beneficial effect on the economic development of the Member State concerned.

---

60 COM (2001) 386 final, Article 6.

61 COM (2001) 386 final, Explanatory Memorandum, p. 2.

62 It needs to be added here that the exact terms of possible restriction of access of citizens of the new EU Member States to the labour market of the EU-15 will be determined in the Accession Treaties. Currently, the EU Common Position on Chapter 2 – Free Movement of Workers states that current Member States will introduce a preference for new Member State nationals over non-EU labour.

It is not difficult to see that most high skilled posts are not advertised by the employment services of Member States but through other means such as newspapers, specialised publications, recruitment consultants or the Internet. In many cases, it would be better not to apply the economic needs test, especially when there are recognised labour shortages in specific sectors and in cases where employment of migrant workers involves extremely highly experienced or skilled individuals and/or accompanying investments into the EU economy.

Some options are given in this direction to the states rather than employers. Member States shall have a possibility for a *horizontal assessment* to react – within "transparency provisions" of the Directive – to worker shortage in a specific sector, by establishing, for instance, national "green-card programmes" for the recruitment of certain specialists and to fix – at national level – appropriate *income thresholds*, based on the idea that the high-income sector of the European labour market needs less protection and that it can afford to be more open to global competition.[63] Another option or idea of "competing for successful models" is an "employer's contribution", an extra premium for recruiting a third-country national paid by the future employer to the competent authorities.

9. Common legal framework

The common legal framework on admission of economic migrants as one part of the "two-tier approach" on Community immigration policy was proposed at the same time as coordination mechanism.[64] The proposed Directive determines common definitions, criteria and procedures regarding the conditions of entry and residence of third-country nationals for the purpose of paid employment and self-employed. It also seeks to provide a single, simplified national procedure for issuing a combined title – residence and work permit in one administrative act – and standards of the differentiating rights of third-county nationals according to length of stay. The proposal also allows for special residence permits to be issued to certain other categories of persons such as "seasonal workers", "trans-frontier workers", "intra-corporate transferees", "trainees", "youth exchange"/"au pairs".[65] The Directive will apply except where bilateral or multi-

63 See *Joanna Apap's* contribution in this volume.

64 Other categories of migrants such as asylum seekers, family members of citizens of the EU or third-country nationals, third-country nationals established within the Community who are posted worker for the purpose of providing cross-border services or who provide such services are, or will be, covered by other directives or regulations.

65 The proposal defines also a number of other key terms, such as 'third-country nationals' or 'activity as an employed or self-employed person'.

lateral agreements contain more favourable provisions. These may also be applied to university students, artists, journalists, professional sportsmen, members of religious orders and representatives of non-profit making organisations.

The proposed creation of a single national application procedure leading to one combined title, will contribute to simplifying and harmonising the diverging rules currently applicable in Member States. For Member States this may be an incentive to streamline their internal administration and to avoid duplication of work. The residence permit will initially be valid for a period of up to three years and initially restricted to certain fields of activity or to paid employment in a particular region. It will be renewable for a further three years only. After five years the "horizontal" provisions of the draft Directive concerning the status of third-country nationals who are long-term residents[66] – once adopted – would phase in and workers who have fulfilled the conditions for "long-term residence status" could apply for it.

The holder of a "residence/work-permit" will enjoy various rights, notably: the right to enter and reside in the territory of the Member State that issued the permit, even after a temporary absence; the right to pass through other Member States and to exercise the activities authorised by the permit; the right to enjoy the same conditions as EU citizens (working conditions, pay, vocational training, social security, medical care, freedom of association). The latter catalogue of rights is aligned with the catalogue of rights proposed in Article 12 of the proposed Directive on long-term resident third-country nationals but is less exhaustive, in line with the principle that rights of third-country nationals should be incremental with their length of stay.

The Directive on economic admission leaves a high level of discretion to Member States. They may apply horizontal measures (ceilings and "quotas"). Member States must adopt the necessary provisions to comply with the Directive by 1 January 2004. However, Title IV of the EC Treaty (ECT) does not apply to the United Kingdom and Ireland unless they decide otherwise. Likewise it does not apply to Denmark. Furthermore, although Art. 63 of the ECT as a "five year window" for the "communitarisation" of specified migration measures is formally set out and the process should be over by 1 May 2004, measures to be adopted pursuant to points 3 (a) and 4 shall not be subject to a five year period. It is with this in mind that it should be considered what Europe has already agreed upon in "common" immigration policy.

---

66 Proposal for a Council Directive concerning the status of third-country nationals who are long term residents, COM(2001) 127 final, Brussels, 13.3.2001.

IV. Concluding Remarks

1. What has been achieved?

Until 1992, migration and refugee matters fell flat within the sovereign realm of Member States.[67] Building on the impetus of the Amsterdam Treaty, Tampere recognised that the EU needed a common migration policy based on a comprehensive approach. Various factors are contributing to its construction. Firstly, there is the increasing recognition amongst origin, destination and transit countries alike of the link between migration and demographic, economic, social, political and human rights conditions. Secondly, while the concepts of asylum and migration are distinct and entail different responses, the area of asylum constitutes a part of the larger migration debate. Thirdly, the construction of a common border highlighted the deficiencies of border control and migration management particularly with respect to illegal migration and human trafficking. Fourthly, despite a desire to restrict immigration and to mitigate migration flows, the immigration debate reoriented itself from one of restriction to one of a guarded overture in order to meet labour shortages. Fifthly, the link between migration and integration has been recognised. Concrete steps towards an integration policy are set out in the Tampere conclusions and the Charter of Fundamental Rights is seen as reference for the development of the concept of "civic citizenship" for third-country nationals in a particular Member State.[68] However, the rights of migrants remain the most elusive component of a common migration policy. And finally, efforts on controlling migration and on the harmonisation of migration policies and practice of Candidate States with those of EU

---

67 Whereas regularised control of immigration and aliens control have been traditionally an essential part of the state's territorial sovereignty and recognition of its jurisdiction upon all persons within its territory, refugee policy has been characterised by a clearly separated dual structure of policy-making at the international and the national levels. At the international level, 'political' asylum has been codified in an international regime, based on the 1951 Geneva Convention on the Status of Refugees with its 1967 New York Protocol and the activities of the UNHCR, acting as the guardian of the treaty. The core elements of this regime are general principles of international solidarity and cooperation for the protection of refugees, the norm of non-refoulement which prohibits the forced return of persons in situations where either persecution or other dangers are imminent. While there are rules and decision-making procedures laid down by the international regime, the right to grant asylum is left to the discretion of the sovereign nation-state.

68 COM (2000) 757 final, p. 19.

States called for a clearer vision of a comprehensive policy and more concrete migration objectives within the EU. Enlargement of the EU, which was the same date as "communitarisation" of specified migration measures (1 May 1994), inevitably broaches the issue of migration both from the perspective of Candidate States and concerning what the blueprint of an expansive EU (im)migration policy might look like.

2. *What model should the Community develop for economic migration?*

When constructing a viable common immigration policy for economic purposes we should bear in mind successes and failures of known models. Two main models were dominant in the post World War Two period. The first model, prevailing in the period of massive effort to reconstruct the war-ravaged economies of Western Europe, was based on bilateral agreements with labour-rich countries in Southern Europe and Turkey, allowing the recruitment of millions of guest workers during the 1950s and 1960s. In spite of some distinctions between European states, guest worker migrations were primarily seen to be economic in nature.[69] The international stage for providing both state and non state collective recruitment of labour was set by the 1949 International Labour Organisation Convention 97 concerning migration for employment.[70] The ILO framework, complemented by other ILO and the Council of Europe activities regarding the treatment of migrant workers, gives legitimacy to the authority of the state's monopoly over the means of movement to work and assists companies based in the destination state to find suitable workers. The individual is clearly the object of the labour recruitment activity, but there is little space allowed for the individual's active role. The protection of the individual migrant worker was, in theory at least, within the responsibility of the state of nationality or protected in accordance with the interests of the host and home states. Security of work and

69 Foreign workers constituted a kind of economic shock absorber ("Konjunkturpuffer"); they were brought into the labour market during periods of high growth and low unemployment, and they should be sent home during periods of recession and rising unemployment and it seemed logical that in such circumstances guest workers should behave according to the laws of supply and demand. See e.g. *Miller, M. J./Martin, P. L.*, 1982: Administering Foreign Worker Programs; *Lexington, M./Heath, D. C./Castles, S.* and *Kosack, G.*, 1973: Immigrant Workers and Class Structure in Western Europe. London: Oxford University Press; *Cornelius, W. A./Martin, P. L./Hollifield, J. F.* (eds.) 1994: Controlling Immigration: A Global Perspective. Stanford, California: Stanford University Press; *Joppke, C.*, 1998: Immigration and the Nation-State, Oxford: Oxford University Press.

70 120 UNTS 71.

residence and family reunification were excluded and the state's monopoly over security for aliens was broken only by the decisions of the European Court of Human Rights specifically concerning Article 8 of the ECHR.

Rising unemployment rates in Northern Europe combined with the rise in oil prices led to a political "stop" on state labour recruitment and sanction. The use of work permits changed and they became a mechanism of the state's protection of the domestic market. The political commitment to guarantee a right to work for their nationals created a direct conflict with the interests of companies in the recruitment of foreign labour. The test which was applied became one of determining whether indeed there was a need for the admission of migrant workers to fill labour market gaps described by private enterprises. As long as the state's political priority was to ensure the availability of employment for the domestic labour force, the interest of companies to import workers would be in principle illegitimate and only approved of as a matter of exception. The migrant's interest to a secure residence right, independent of employment, became paramount. A right to secure residence, which provides free access to the labour market has developed in EU Member States from approximately 1965 onwards.

With the rise of a new service industry, the corporate regulation of labour migration was negotiated within the World Trade Organisation Agreement. GATS as one of the integral parts of the WTO, includes services, which involve movement of persons. The provisions of GATS are designed to ensure market access for service providers or, in other words, to restrict the power of states to impede access to their territory by foreign competitors in the services field through the use of restrictive labour migration laws. The individual is dependent on the economic activity, both security of residence and family reunification are not regulated, and she or he is increasingly dependent on the company for protection against the control capacities of the state.[71]

Quite a different legal framework for labour migration has been worked out within the European Community. Movement of persons is seen as an important part of European economic integration and for this vision the role of individuals, as the means of production, has been critical. Two of the four freedoms, i.e. freedom of movement of persons and services involve the right of movement of natural persons. This alternative approach, expressed in the ECT (and earlier EEC Treaty), was developed for migration of nationals of the Member States and has been driven principally with a view to completing the Single Market. The Community put into place a model for migration which put a strong empha-

71 For a detailed discussion of both models refer to *Guild, E.*, 2002: op.cit.

sis on the rights given to individual workers, the self-employed and service providers and recipients – rights guaranteed by the Community and subject only to derogations by Member States in very specific circumstances. The Community's model clearly sought to balance the interests of the Member States in protecting their population from threats to public policy, the need of business for labour and the need of individual migrants to exercise a choice to move for economic purposes and to have security of residence and benefit from equal treatment. This has been a successful example of managing migration for an economic end, with the emphasis firmly placed on the right of the individual. However, the Community's experience of extending free movement provision to third-country nationals has been less successful.

The extension of economic migration rights to nationals of European Economic Area countries was uncomplicated, but numerous agreements with other third countries, starting with the 1970 Protocol to the Turkey Agreement, the 1976 Maghreb Agreements (replaced by the 1995/96 Euro-Mediterranean Agreements), the Europe Agreements and the Cooperation and Partnership agreements with the CIS states (P&C Agreements) have proved more problematic. This has been due largely to the reluctance of EU Member States to accept the extent of the free movement provisions contained in those agreements and implementing decisions. For example, some provisions of the Europe Agreements are delayed for some Candidate States. There are also sectoral limitations, which are to be lifted in accordance with a timetable and the possibility of temporary suspension of the provisions under specified circumstances. Partly, this is a result of the period of "zero" immigration in which these agreements have been negotiated, and the strong emphasis on aspects of policing and security rather than thinking about the economic benefits or implications of migration policy.

In the Community's approach to economic migration within and from outside the EU we can find aspects of both the ILO and GATS model. The emphasis on equal treatment in working conditions, remuneration and social security is reminiscent of ILO 97. It is found in the ECT and is incorporated into all of the Community's third country agreements, which include provisions on labour. Similarly the GATS approach is to be found in the Community's interpretation of the right of an enterprise within the Community to send its third-country national personnel anywhere within the European Union as to carry out service provision. Furthermore, the approach has been formally introduced into all of the post-1994 third country agreements of the Community, which include provisions on services. A more sophisticated version of the GATS provision is included in the Europe and the P&C Agreements, permitting enterprises to move their key personnel in order to carry out their service provision and establishment rights.

In conclusion, any European immigration policy must take place within the framework which protects the rights of migrants, meaning that a Community immigration policy should adopt a rights-based model. This does not mean advocating that there is a human right to migrate for any purpose whatsoever. Instead, it means that migration law regarding any form of migration should be set out in legally binding rules that can be interpreted and enforced by courts and tribunals, who can consider the merits of the authorities' decisions when applying those rules. This is the approach applied by Community law regarding entry of third country goods and capital, and to a large extent services and establishment. The binding rules need not be as liberal as the rules governing movement of citizens of the European Union, just as the rules governing the entry of third country goods, services and capital into the Community are not as liberal as the rules governing movement within the Community. Thus, the Community has to be brought into the relationship between the state, business and individual so that the enforcement of rights granted to an individual under Community law is also governed by Community law. According to my reading this view is endorsed by the Commission in its Communication on a Community immigration policy and in the long term such a common European immigration policy would be common enough to benefit all actors involved.

DISCUSSION

Mr. Münz made the first contribution, suggesting that the question of European immigration policy can be illustrated by a picture of three concentric circles of different size, crossed by 15 lines from the centre to the edge, dividing thus the circles into 15 equal parts. The image should represent the European Union and its 15 Member States. The outer circle should symbolize the issue of the rules for crossing the border of a respective country within Europe. The middle circle would stay for the requirements for legal rights of residing, and the smallest one would represent the subject of how the citizenship of a particular European state can be accessed. Each circle was to be entered through a new door, symbolising the respective juridical requirements ("three door model").

According to Mr. Münz, the question of harmonisation arises as soon as the first stage has been reached once the third-country national fulfils the requirements of entry to a Member State. As to the second and third steps, Mr. Münz considered a harmonisation on these levels as being open to doubt. European countries may not have any objections against naturalization of other European states – as long as it does not go beyond any reasonable extent – since the naturalized persons would normally stay in the naturalizing state and not move to other European countries. As a paradigm, he mentioned the German "Aussiedler". That is why the speaker expressed his uncertainty about any advantage of harmonizing the legal rules for obtaining citizenship to a single European state, which automatically gives access to EU citizenship.

Mr. Bisopoulos admitted that the harmonisation on the internal steps of the "three door model" as presented by Mr. Münz, is a controversial issue. However, he recognised that legislation has to be common at least as far as the outside circle is concerned. He disagreed with Ms. Medved, who esteemed the European Community as being slow at harmonizing. Citizenship has been a national question, so the Community is not competent for deciding on these matters. However, piece by piece the Community is steadily moving towards a more coherent approach on matters of immigration. Ms. Medved stressed that it was not her purpose to be critical of the European Commission's role at slow harmonizing. Nevertheless she wanted to emphasise, that this issue is still more intergovernmental than a matter for the Community. She did not touch on the issue of citizenship in her speech. Referring to the "three door model", the speaker added that there were already some signs to harmonize the first step, as e.g. admission for the purposes of employment, self-employment and study. However, due to various reasons such as history, extremely large differences could be seen among the rules governing residence permission. On this point, Ms. Medved held that it would be essential for Europe to have a common definition of the terms “immigrant” and “long-term resident”. The latter was particularly important, since the rights of long-term residents should be – according to the Tampere conclusions and later documents – as close as possible to the rights of EU citizens. In some Member States, long-term residents gain citizenship only after a 10 year period, which leads to a high number of third-country nationals. This can raise numerous issues, among them question of political participation. As to the nationality itself, it is bound to the Member State, so that there cannot (as yet) be identical criteria for naturalisation.

Mr. Münz remarked that as long as Europe is not a state, an EU citizenship independent from the citizenship of one particular Member State could not imagined.

Ms. Medved declared that she did not see any development towards a new content of EU citizenship either as a social or a political good until there is an agreement on the common conception of the political union.

Christian Calliess*

THE CONSTITUTIONAL FRAMEWORK OF A COMMON EUROPEAN IMMIGRATION POLICY – PAVING THE WAY TO FORTRESS EUROPE?

I. Introduction

In the discussion about the development of European immigration policy, argument can often be heard that Europe is building a fortress against immigrants. This argument implies that the EU is not willing to establish an open policy towards so called third-country nationals, neither with regard to economically motivated immigration nor immigration for political reasons (asylum, refugees). The Fortress-Europe-Argument is not new, of course; the last time it was brought up was with regard to the 1992-Project, the completion of the Internal Market. My contribution intends to examine, whether the Constitution of Europe, EU Treaty (EUT) or ECT, as well as its implementation in term of policies justify the Fortress-Europe-Argument. At the same time, my speech intends to look for a transparent model, which might establish a guideline, a framework for the developing European Immigration Policy. Only on the basis of a transparent model can be answered, if and to what extent, the Fortress-Europe-Argument paints a true picture of European Immigration Policy.

II. The Model

If we look into the Treaties to find hints for a transparent model framing European Immigration Policy we discover them in the system of the freedom of goods, especially in Art. 23 (2) and 24 ECT. In order to avoid any misunderstanding: referring to the freedom of goods does not imply the intention, that human beings can be compared with goods. With regard to human beings it is quite clear that any model has to take into account the ethical background of any Immigration Policy, which is legally based on human rights, especially by the rights of refugees and asylum as well as family-rights and political rights. My only intention in referring to the freedom of goods is that here we can find an

* I would like to thank my assistant Mrs. Mag. *Thérèse Zankel,* LL.M. (Brügge) as well as my assistant Mr. MMag. *Winfried Pöcherstorfer,* LL.M. (LSI) for their helpful support with regard to writing this article.

established system, that is simple and transparent. Therefore it may serve as a model for European Immigration Policy. Not at least, the definition of the Internal Market in Art. 14 (2) ECT is based on the freedoms of goods as well as the freedom of persons and capital.

1. The Idea of the Internal Market

The notion "Internal Market" already suggests an area determined by an internal dimension which in a way contrasts with its external aspects. This first etymological remark might somehow meet the idea of the fortress Europe. When we imagine a fortress we immediately think about big walls which cut off the world outside of the fortress from the life inside of it, those who are behind its secure walls and those who remain outside. Although it is true that the rules in and outside of the Internal Market are different this does not reflect its primary intention. The Internal Market is basically a form of economic integration in which the degree of involvement of participating economies is very closed. The Member States have agreed to remove all customs and quotas on trade passing between them. Moreover they apply a common level of tariffs on all goods entering or leaving the common market (This corresponds to a customs union in which goods can circulate freely.) The Internal Market additionally also guarantees the free movement of the factors of production namely labour, capital and enterprise. One of the consequences of the free movement of goods is that the best products in the eyes of the consumers are the most successful no matter where they are produced. Since labour and capital are two essential economic factors in the production of goods, it is important that their free movement is also guaranteed. The idea is to ensure the best possible allocation of resources within the Internal Market by enabling factors of production to move to areas where they are most valued.[1]

Art. 14 (2) ECT sums up the idea of the Internal Market which "shall comprise an area without internal frontiers in which the free movement of goods, persons, services and capital is ensured in accordance with the provisions of this Treaty".

In many respects the Four Freedoms have similar characteristics and the case law has developed in a parallel way. Since the free movement of goods constitutes the basic principle of the Internal Market we will start by presenting the model of the freedom of goods and then discuss if this model can also be transposed on the other freedoms.

---

1 *Swann*, The Economics of the Common Market, 1992, 11 in: *Craig/de Burca*, EU Law, 1998, 548.

2. The Model of the Freedom of Goods

Arts. 23 ff. ECT deal with the freedom of goods. They prohibit customs duties and charges having equivalent effect, quantitative restrictions on imports and exports as well as measures having equivalent effect between Member States. All of these prohibitions concern goods which circulate within the Internal Market. It is important to notice that the scope of application of these prohibitions includes not only goods which were produced inside the EC but also goods originating in third countries. Art. 23 (2) ECT explicitly states that "the provisions of Art. 25 and of Chapter 2 of this Title shall apply to products originating in Member States and to products from third countries which are in free circulation in Member States". This means that once foreign products have legally (see Art. 24 ECT: customs are paid; all due import duties are fulfilled) passed the common external boarder and entered the Community they are treated exactly the same way as if they had been produced within the EC. By virtue of Art. 23 (2) ECT they become more or less an EU-product.

This is the major difference between the free movement of goods and the free movement of persons; with regard to this point the model of the free movement of goods can not be transposed on freedoms related to persons: Unlike goods, third-country nationals who are in the territory of a Member State are not allowed to move freely to another Member State. For them the frontiers inside the Union do still exist and represent a barrier not that easy to overcome. In a certain sense the Internal Market is – with regard to that point – not yet fully completed.

III. Constitutional Gates Into the European Union

1. The Four Freedoms and Rights of Third-country nationals

Our main question therefore is: which constitutional gates can help third-country nationals enter the EU. Since the Four Freedoms constitute the heart of the Community System we will start by discussing how they can by used by non-EU citizens.

When we speak about the status of third-country nationals in the context of the Four Freedoms we immediately think about those freedoms which are directly concerned with persons, namely the freedom of workers as laid down in Art. 39 ff. ECT and the freedom of establishment (Art. 43 ff. ECT).

If we have a look at the wording of these provisions we notice that they either refer to "workers of the Member States" (Art. 39 (2) ECT) or to the "nationals of a Member State" (Art. 43 (1) ECT). This already indicates us that these rights were not designed for everybody but aimed to favour EU citizens.

Third-country nationals actually benefit only from these freedoms if they are somehow related to a national of a Member State. They do not have a right on their own but derive their rights from the rights of one of their family member who is a EU citizen. Regulation 1612/68 on the freedom of movement for workers within the Community[2] grants parallel rights to third-country nationals. Art. 1 of Directive 73/148[3] grants rights of movement and residence with regard to the freedoms of establishment and of services.

This extension of rights in favour of the family of an EU citizen expresses the will to respect and to protect family life and follows from Art. 8 EHRC.[4] This fundamental right to family life was the main reason why the Community legislator introduced the above provisions. Besides, the European Court of Justice (ECJ) also refereed to this fundamental right when it had to decide on the compatibility with Community law of certain national measures concerning third-country nationals. The Court used a proportionality test and balanced the right of protection of the family with other interests like public security or burden on the public finances of the host Member State.[5] Moreover, one might mention several other purposes of the extension of the freedom of persons to the family members such as "the importance for the worker, from a human point of view, of having his entire family with him and the importance, from all points of view, of the integration of the worker and his family into the host Member State without any difference in treatment in relation to nationals of that state"[6]. And last but not least, it is obvious that the effective exercise of freedom of movement of an EU citizen would be hampered if e.g. his wife, not being a national of a Member State, would not be entitled to apply for a job in this other Member State, where he was offered a new job.

2 Regulation (EEC) No. 1612/68 of the Council of 15 October 1968 on the freedom of movement for workers within the Community, O.J. 1968, L 257/2.

3 Council Directive 73/148/EEC of 21 May 1973 on the abolition of restrictions on movement and residence within the Community for nationals of Member States with regard to establishment and the provision of services, O.J. 1973, L 172/14.

4 Case C-60/00, Carpenter, [2002] not yet published, para. 38.

5 Cases C-259/99, MRAX, [2002] not yet published, C-413/99, Baumbast [2002] not yet published.

6 Case 249/86, Commission/Germany, [1989] ECR 1263.

2. Who are the family members who benefit from these Community rights?

a) The spouse[7]

In most of the cases it is easy to determine who falls within this category, there are however some cases where it is not easy to draw the boarder line.

Separated couples who not longer live together and who intend to divorce[8] are officially still married and therefore benefit from the rights related to their marital status.

On the other hand, former spouses of divorced couples do normally not have these rights, although, under particular conditions, they might indirectly still benefit from them. The *Baumbast* judgment which was delivered on 17th September 2002[9] deals with such a situation. A United States citizen married a Frenchman. They had two children and all of them lived in the UK. Since the divorce the children have stayed with their mother but still have had regular contact with their father who works and lives in the UK. The ECJ basically stated that the British government had to grant their mother a residence permit although she was no longer the spouse of a Member State national because "to refuse to grant permission to remain to a parent who is the primary carer of the child exercising his right to pursue his studies in the host Member State infringes" the right "conferred by Art. 12 of Regulation No 1612/68 on the child of migrant worker to pursue, under the best possible conditions, his education in the host Member State"[10]. In other words: the third-country national derived her Community rights not from her former husband but from her children who themselves benefit from Community rights.

Another question which might arise in this context is the position of registered partnership since they have been introduced in several Member States. For example, does Art. 10 (1) of Regulation 1612/68 also cover a homosexual partner? In a judgement from 1986 the ECJ decided that "Art. 10 (1) of Regulation No. 1612/68 cannot be interpreted as meaning that the companion, in stable relationship, who is a national of a Member State and is employed in the territory of another Member State must in certain circumstances be treated as 'his spouse' for the purpose of that provision"[11]. However, since the Dutch law granted resi-

---

7 Art. 10 (1) Regulation 1612/68 and Art. 1 (1) Directive 73/148.

8 Case 267/83, Diatta, [1985] ECR 567, para. 20.

9 Case C-413/99, Baumbast *not yet pubsihed.*

10 Baumbast, para. 73.

11 Case 59/85, Reed [1986], ECR 1283, para. 16.

dence rights to the unmarried foreign companions of nationals it had to grant the same rights to the companion of a Member State migrant worker. This case answers only part of our question namely that if a Member States decided to treat marriage and other forms of partnership equally, the companion of migrant work living in such a partnership falls under the scope of Art. 10 (1).

What happens if such a couple moves to a Member State which does not recognise this form of registered partnership? There is no case law dealing with this specific problem but the ECJ would probably interpret the legal term "spouse" on the basis of social developments and take into account the situation in the whole EU and not in just one Member State.[12] In the context of a recent staff case concerning a household allowance the ECJ has already considered the question of these new forms of partnership and came to the conclusion that "the fact that in a limited number of Member States, a registered partnership is assimilated, although incompletely, to marriage cannot have the consequence that, by mere interpretation, persons whose legal status is distinct from that of marriage can be covered by the term "married official" as used in the Staff Regulation"[13]. According to the ECJ it would be up to the legislator to take appropriate measures and amend the Staff Regulation if it wishes to include also other forms of partnerships. Would the ECJ decide in a similar way if it would have to interpret the term "spouse" of a migrant worker in the context of Art. 10 (1)?

b) The descendants

Beside the spouse Art. 10 (1) of Regulation 1612/68 and Art. 1 (1) Directive 73/148 also cover their descendants who are under the age of 21 years or are dependent as well as dependent relatives in the ascending line of the worker and his spouse. "Their descendants" should be understood as including not only the children of the migrant worker and his spouse but also the descendant of the EU citizen and those of his spouse stemming from another relationship.[14] Children under 21 are automatically covered whereas older relatives in the descending line and all relatives in the ascending line need to be dependent on the migrant worker. The decisive fact is that the migrant worker actually grants them maintenance, the existence of a claim to alimony is not important.[15] After the death of the migrant worker his relatives may remain in the host Member State but if a

12 Reed, para. 13.

13 Case C-122/99P and C-125/99, P/Council [2001], para. 39.

14 Baumbast, para. 57.

15 *Brechmann* in: *Calliess/Ruffert*, Kommentar zu EUV und EGV, 2002, Art. 39, para. 23.

migrant worker dies before the accession of his state of origin to the EC, his family members then have no rights under Art 10 (1).[16]

In this context one should also mention the proposal for a family reunification Directive which deals with the same type of family members but is supposed to concern only family members of third-country nationals who have a valid residence permit or are refugees – I will come back to that proposal at a later point of this report.

3. *Which other conditions must be fulfilled in order to benefit from these Community rights?*

a) It is actually not enough for a third-country national to be a family member of EU citizen, this EU citizen has to exercise either the freedom of movement of workers or the freedom of establishment or the freedom to provide services. The family members of persons who never exercised one of these rights do not fall under the scope of Arts. 10ff. of Regulation 1612/68 and Art. 1 (1) Directive 73/148[17] and therefore do not benefit from these special Community rights. Although a Member State national has ceased to be a migrant worker his children still benefit from educational rights in this foreign Member State according to Art. 12 of Regulation 1612/68.[18]

b) Moreover, it is worth underlining the necessity of a Community link. EC law does not grant any rights to third-country nationals who are family members of an EU citizen being in a purely national situation. This Community link might in some cases be easier to find than in others. It is easier for self-employed persons to pretend that they have business partners abroad than for workers to invoke a relationship to an other Member State.

   Even so-called reversed discrimination cases where somebody tries to benefit from Community rights in his own Member State might present such a Community link. In the *Singh* case[19] an Indian national married to a British national wanted the British authorities to grant him indefinite leave to remain. Before coming back to the UK Mr. and Mrs. Singh were employed in Germany. The ECJ decided that "a national of a Member State might be deterred from leaving his country of origin in order to pursue an activity (...) in the territory of another Member State if, on returning to the Member State of

16 Case C-131/96, Romero [1997], ECR 3659, para.17.
17 MRAX, para. 39.
18 The ECJ expressly confirmed this view in Baumbast, para. 54.
19 Case C-370/90, Singh [1992], ECR 4265.

which he is a national in order to pursue an activity there (...), the conditions of his entry and residence were not at least equivalent to those which he would enjoy under the Treaty or secondary law in the territory of another Member State"[20]. In other words in some cases it might be enough that this Community link had existed in the past.

Beside the rights third-country nationals can derive from their relatives who are EU citizens, non-Member State nationals might in the future also benefit from Community rights on their own. A proposal for a Directive concerning the status of third-country nationals who are long-term residents[21] is currently under debate. It aims to fulfil point 21 of the Tampere conclusions by granting to all third-country nationals who are long term residents in a Member State a set of uniform rights which are as near as possible to those enjoyed by EU citizens.

4. *Freedom of Services*

Since the free movement of services is closely linked to the person of the provider and of the recipient of the service, it also constitutes a gate through which third-country nationals might benefit from Community rights. Art. 49 (1) ECT prohibits restrictions on the freedom only in respect of nationals of Member States, but Art. 49 (2) ECT opens the possibility for the Council to extend the provisions of the Chapter on services to third-country nationals who provide services and who are established in the EC. Such an extension of the personal scope of Arts. 49 ff. ECT has not yet been achieved, but in 1999 the Commission made a first proposal for a Directive[22] which was amended in 2000[23] and which is currently under discussion.

Until the adoption of such a text by the Council, third-country nationals have already – under the current state of the law – some possibilities to benefit from the free movement of services.

In a similar way to the free movement of persons, the relatives of EU citizens who exercise the freedom of services benefit from the rights of movement and of residence granted by Directive 73/148. We therefore have to deal firstly with the question: when does a national of a Member State exercise the freedom of services, what is the personal scope of this freedom? Basically there are two possibilities: being a provider or a recipient of a service. In the first case the EU

20 Singh, para. 19.
21 Commission proposal COM (2001) 127 final, O.J. 2001 C 240 E.
22 Commission proposal COM (99) 3 final, O.J. 1997 C 67.
23 Amended proposal of the Commission COM (2000) 271 final, O.J. 2000 C 311 E.

citizen can go to an other Member State in order to provide a service there. A recent case, *Carpenter*,[24] illustrates such a situation: a national of the Philippines, married to a British national, applied for leave to remain in the UK. The couple lived in the UK but Mr. Carpenter travelled on a regular basis to other Member States for the purpose of his business, he sold advertising space in scientific journals and offered various administrative and publishing services to the editors of those journals. Since the services provided abroad made up a significant proportion of his business Mr. Carpenter was a provider of services within the meaning of Art. 49 ECT and his spouse had – according to Community law – the right to reside in the territory of the UK.

The other theoretical possibility of exercising the free movement of services is to travel to another Member State in order to receive a service there; a tourist would e.g. be included in that category.[25] Would, therefore, a third-country national have rights under Community law just because her husband, a EU citizen, goes on a regular basis to the hairdresser in the neighbouring Member State? The Member State national is only very temporary a recipient of services, during this short period of time her spouse benefits from the right of movement laid down in Directive 73/148 and is allowed to accompany her abroad. The ECJ would probably however not deduce a permanent right of residence for him like in the *Carpenter* case just because his spouse is occasionally a recipient of services in another Member State!

Arts. 49 ff. ECT does not only apply to an exchange of services between two EU citizens. Either the recipient or the provider of the service might even be a third-country national. But if both are third-country nationals the case does not fall within the scope of the freedom of services. Only the Member State national is entitled to rely on the free movement of service before a Court.[26] In this respect one could imagine an extension of the scope of the free movement of services in favour of third-country nationals, if the ECJ granted them the right to refer to the freedom of services. Such a development of the case law would not impose an additional burden on the Member States and would lead to more effectiveness in the enforcement of the freedom of services since a larger number of persons will be entitled to take up infringements. Although such an extension of the scope of the free movement of services towards third-country nationals might be quite sensible and tempting, this would infringe the Treaty since Art. 49 (2) ECT ex-

24 Case C-60/00, Carpenter [2002], not yet published.

25 Case 186/87, Cowan [1989], ECR 195.

26 *Randelzhofer/Forsthoff* in: *Grabitz/Hilf*, Recht der EU - Kommentar, Art. 49/50, para. 16.

plicitly offers the possibility to do so but through the instrument of legislation and therefore not through case law.[27]

A further aspect in this chapter on the freedom of services and third-country nationals concerns the posting of employees from third countries by undertakings for the provision of cross-border services. A firm which acts within the Internal Market may second its personnel to another Member State with a view to providing services there. Its personnel might however, not only be composed of EU citizens who anyhow enjoy the freedom of movement. In the *Vander Elst* case, the ECJ decided that Arts. 49 and 50 ECT preclude "Member States from requiring undertakings which are established in another Member State and enter the first Member State in order to provide services, and which lawfully and habitually employ nationals of non-member countries, to obtain work permits for those workers from a national immigration authority"[28]. In the present case a demolition business established in Brussels carried out a demolition of a building in France. It therefore sent to France several of its continuously employed Moroccan nationals who held Belgian work permits. The French authorities held that short-stay visa of the Moroccan workers was not sufficient to enable them to take up paid employment in France, they would have additionally needed French work permits. According to the ECJ such a request is contrary to Community law because it infringes the free movement of services.

Although the case law of the ECJ pointed the way, it did not solve all problems with regard to the posting of employees originating from third countries. The national administration has e.g. no guarantee from the Member State in which the undertaking is established that the third-country national is legally resident there and will return there after having completed the service. In order to clarify these practical problems linked to this topic the Commission made a proposal for a "Directive of the European Parliament and the Council on the posting of employees from third countries for the provision of cross boarder services"[29] which is currently under discussion. The Commission suggests among others to introduce an "EC service provision card" which would contain guarantees from the Member State in which the firm is established.

---

27 *Randelzhofer/Forsthoff* in: *Grabitz/Hilf*, Recht der EU - Kommentar, Art. 49/50, para. 21.

28 Case C-42/93, Vander Elst [1994], ECR I-3803, para. 26.

29 Commission proposal COM (99) 3 final COD99012, O.J. 1999 C 67, p. 17. Amended Commission proposal COM (2000) 271 final, O.J. 2000 C 311 E.

5. *Freedom of Capital*

In order to present the complete picture of the position of third-country nationals with regard to the Four Freedoms we will finally deal in brief with the freedom of capital. Art. 56 ECT prohibits all restrictions on movement of capital between Member States and between Member States and third countries. The scope of Art. 56 ECT is larger than the territory of the EU. Third-country-nationals can also rely on this freedom, some authors even pretend that it is not necessary for them to be established in the Community.[30] In any case, we might conclude that the freedom of movement of capital is guaranteed irrespectively of the nationality of the owner. To some extent the freedom of capital goes even further than the freedom of goods since capital – unlike products – does not need to overcome a barrier when it enters the EU. The image of the Fortress Europe is – at least with regard to capital – not true at all.

6. *Rights from the Four Freedoms on the Basis of International Agreements*

Until now we saw how a non-Member State national – no matter from which country he is – might benefit from the Four Freedoms. The EU has also signed a couple of agreements with some of these third countries whose nationals were granted additional rights and we will focus in the following on the most important ones.

a) *The European Economic Area Agreement and the EC-Swiss agreement on Free Movement of Persons*

The EEA Agreement which entered into force in 1994[31] has the purpose of creating a free trade zone between the EU and the EFTA Countries (Norway, Iceland, Liechtenstein). After having rejected the agreement in a referendum, Switzerland started bilateral negotiations with the EC, which lead to a separate agreement which has been in force since 2001. Both of these agreements grant EFTA and Swiss nationals almost the same rights of free movement within the EU as Community law grants to the nationals of its Member States. The nationals of these four signatory states have the same rights to work and to receive national treatment within the Member States as those guaranteed by the ECT to

30 *Ress/Ukow*, in: *Grabitz/Hilf*, Recht der EU – Kommentar, Art. 56, para. 73, *Kiemel*, in: *Groeben/Thiesing/Ehlermann*, EU-/EGV-Kommentar, Art. 73b, para. 13.

31 O.J. 1994 l 1/3.

EU citizens who are migrant workers, self employed or exercising the freedom of services.[32]

b) *The EC-Turkey Association Agreement*

The main sources of rights concerning Turkish nationals are the "Ankara" Agreement of 1963,[33] the Additional Protocol to the Association Agreement of 1970[34] and the Association Council's Decisions 1/80 and 3/80.[35] All of them are integral parts of the Community legal order.[36] The ECJ has without any doubt also played a decisive role in terms of developing the rights of Turkish nationals under these association agreements; its case law reflects nonetheless an ambivalent attitude since the ECJ interpreted some provisions rather restrictively.[37]

In the *Demirel* judgement, the Court denied direct effect to Art. 12 of the Association Agreement and to Art. 36 Additional Protocol both concerning the free movement of workers.[38] These provisions have merely programmatic character and are not sufficiently clear, precise and unconditional in order to be directly effective. The same is also true for Arts. 13 and 14 of the Agreement concerning the freedom of establishment and the freedom of services. Turkish nationals have therefore under EC law neither a right of establishment nor a freedom to provide services.[39]

Nevertheless, the standstill clause in relation to the freedom of establishment and to the freedom of services contained in Art. 41 (1) Additional Protocol is directly effective,[40] which prohibits Member States to tighten immigration con-

32 *Hedemann-Robinson*, "An overview of recent legal developments at Community level in relation to third-country nationals resident within the European Union, with particular reference to the case law of the European court of justice", 38 CMLRev. (2001), 537-538.

33 EEC-Turkey Association Agreement, O.J. 1964 L 217, entered into force as from 1.12.1973.

34 O.J. 1972 L 293, entered into force as from 1.1.1973.

35 Decision 1/80 on the development of the Association, Decision 3/80 on the application of the social security schemes of the Member States of the EC to Turkish workers and their families, both entered into force as from 1.12.1980.

36 Case 12/86, Demirel [1987], ECR 3719, para.7, Case C-192/89, Sevince [1990], ECRI-3461, para. 9.

37 *Hedemann-Robinson*, CMLRev (2001), 556.

38 Demirel, para. 25.

39 *Hedemann-Robinson*, CMLRev (2001), 545.

40 Case C-37/98, Savas [2000], ECR I-02927, para. 46 ff.

trols in relation to self-employed Turkish migrants. The Agreements do not grant Turkish nationals and their family members any rights of free movement between the EU Member States or any rights of residence, however, once a Member State has authorised the entry of a Turkish citizen and given him permission to engage in employment it necessarily has to grant an accompanying right of residence for the purpose of enabling him to exercise this employment right. Residence rights are also implicitly guaranteed for his family members.[41]

Moreover, Decision 1/80 provides several important employment rights with direct effect for Turkish nationals. Art. 6 for instance grants them rights in graduated form: after one year legal employment they only have the right to renew their working permit for another year with the same employer but after four years of legal employment they have free access in that Member State to any paid employment of their choice. In the *Sürül* judgement the ECJ confirmed that Art. 3 (1) of Decision 3/80 had direct effect and that therefore any discrimination in relation to social security for migrant workers and their families is prohibited.[42]

c) *Europe Agreements*

Since 1991, the EU has concluded Europe Agreements (EA) with Poland[43], Hungary[44], Romania[45], Bulgaria[46], the Czech[47] and Slovak Republics[48], Estonia[49], Latvia[50], Lithuania[51] and Slovenia[52]. These association agreements function as a first step towards the admission of these countries to the EU and are modelled upon the Four Freedoms. All of them contain provisions which concern the rights of their nationals living and working within the EU. However,

41 Sevince, para. 29, case C-355/93, Eroglu [1994], ECR I-5113, para.20, case C-210/97, Akman [1998], ECR I-7519, para. 24.

42 Case C-262/96, Sürül [1999], ECR I-2685.

43 O.J. 1993 L 347/2, entered into force as from 1.2.1994.

44 O.J. 1993 L 348/3, entered into force as from 1.2.1994.

45 O.J. 1994 L 357/2, entered into force as from 1.2.1995.

46 O.J. 1994 L 358/3, entered into force as from 1.2.1995.

47 O.J. 1994 L 360/2, entered into force as from 1.2.1995.

48 O.J. 1994 L 359/2, entered into force as from 1.2.1995.

49 O.J. 1998 L 68, entered into force as from 1.2.1998.

50 O.J. 1998 L 26, entered into force as from 1.2.1998.

51 O.J. 1998 L 51, entered into force as from 1.2.1998.

52 O.J. 1999 L 51/3, entered into force as from 1.2.1999.

Member States basically retain sovereignty over the question of migration, entry and stay in their territory.

In the area of employment the EAs contain only pretty modest provisions.[53] Subject to "conditions and modalities applicable in each Member State" the spouse and children of a migrant worker have a right to access the labour market of the host Member State as long as the migrant legally works and resides there. Therefore the last word in family reunion matters still remains with the Member States. The most important provision in the context of the freedom of workers are the non-discrimination clauses contained in the EAs. They prohibit the discrimination of Central and Eastern European (CEE) nationals as regards working conditions, remuneration or dismissal. In the *Pokrzeptowicz-Meyer* judgement the ECJ held that such a provision had direct effect and that a German provision which in a prior case had already been considered to be inapplicable because of its discriminatory character towards Community nationals, could not be applied to a Polish national either.[54] The non-discrimination clauses of the EAs establish in favour of legally employed CEE nationals a right to equal treatment as regards employment conditions of the same extent as that of Art. 48(2) ECT.

When it comes to self-employed workers, the EAs contain more far-reaching obligations. The Member States have to grant nationals and companies from CEE countries the right of establishment on the same terms as granted to host companies and nationals. In several recent judgements the ECJ gave direct effect to the provisions of the Polish, Czech and Bulgarian EAs concerning the freedom of establishment.[55] The rights of entry and residence are conferred, as corollaries of the right of establishment, on CEE nationals. The exercise of these rights may however, in some circumstances, be limited by national provisions of the host Member State. The EAs do not "preclude a system of prior control which make the issue by the competent immigration authorities of leave to enter and remain subject to the condition that the applicant must show that he genuinely intends to take up an activity as a self-employed person without at the same time entering into employment or having recourse to public funds, and that he possesses, from the outset, sufficient financial resources and has reasonable chances of success"[56]. Moreover, the freedom of establishment also contains the right to bring key personnel of CEE countries who may work in the branches registered in a Member State. This right has to be interpreted in a narrow way,

---

53 *Hedemann-Robinson*, CMLRev (2001), 571.

54 Case C- 162/00, *Pokrzeptowicz-Meyer*, ECR (2002), I-1049.

55 Case C-63/99, Gloszcuk [2001], case C.257/99, Barkoci [2001], case C-235/99 Kondova [2001], ECR I-6427, ECR I-6369 case C-268/99, Jany [2001].

56 Gloszczuk, para. 86.

since the Member States wished to reduce the mobility of CEE nationals into and within the EU to the minimum necessary to ensure the freedom of establishment.[57]

The above mentioned agreements show how international agreements between the Community and third countries may open gates to third-country nationals into the EU. A further source of law, the human rights, also secure their position within the Community.

7. Human rights – The Right of Asylum

The European Union Charter of Fundamental Rights was adopted at the Nice Summit in December 2000. Even though it has for now no binding legal force it is still worthy of analysis since it might in future become binding and may also be taken into account by the ECJ and thus, through the case law, have some effect.[58] Some of the Charter's rights are only intended for EU citizens others are granted to anybody and it would be a topic on its own to depict in detail which of these fundamental rights constitute additional benefits for EU foreigners. We will nevertheless briefly mention two articles which grant special protection to third-country nationals. Art. 18 deals with the rights of refugees, it reads "The right to asylum shall be guaranteed with due respect for the rules of the Geneva Convention of 28 July 1951 and the New York Protocol of 31 January 1967 relating to the status of refugees and in accordance with the Treaty establishing the European Community". Unlike many other articles of the Charter, Art. 18 is not derived from the ECHR or the ECT but directly refers to the UN documents. Art. 18 corresponds Art. 63 No 1 ECT, although the wording of the Charter uses "with due respect" to the Geneva Convention and to the Protocol whereas Art. 63 ECT entails the expression "in accordance with". Anyhow, the right to asylum must be exercised under the same conditions, as the EC has to exercise it when adopting refugee law which means in accordance with these two pieces of international law.[59]

Art. 19 of the Charter contains in its first paragraph the prohibition of collective expulsions and in its second paragraph the classic *non-refoulement* principle.

---

57 *Hedemann-Robinson*, CMLRev (2001), 576.

58 *Peers*, "Immigration, Asylum and the European Union Charter of Fundamental Rights", European Journal of Migration and Law (2001), 144.

59 *Peers*, EJML (2001), 162.

The Commission's Green Paper on a Community return policy on illegal residents[60] in the part "asylum and return" about accompanying rights also refers to the Geneva Convention, the Protocol and these Charter provisions. The Commission suggests an open co-ordination method for return issues relating to rejected asylum seekers, persons who have been under protection regime or illegal residents and underlines that human rights should be fully respected by such an eventual European return policy.

Having discussed the characteristics of the key constitutional provisions of EC Law relating to a Common European Immigration Policy and their effects on persons who are not nationals of a Member State, we will now, in a next step, examine the competence of the EU with regard to the development of an European Immigration Law.

IV. Competence to "Maintain and Develop the Union as an Area of Freedom, Security and Justice, in which the Free Movement of Persons is Assured" and Taken Measures

1. Introduction

With the entry into force of the Treaty of Amsterdam on 1 May 1999, the policies on immigration, visas and asylum as well as on other policies connected to the free movement of persons have become a full Community responsibility under Title IV. With a view to the progressive establishment of an "area of freedom, security and justice" (AFSJ), the ECT stipulates a number of measures that are to be taken by the Council within five years from the above date. Within these five years, we should *not* speak of *communitarization in the proper sense* of the competence brought under the remit of the ECT. We should rather refer to the procedural rules set out in Art. 67 of the ECT as a transitional regime of gradual communitarization,[61] which provides for a legal regime slightly different from that of "classic" Community law.

According to this Article, the Council shall, in most matters of Title IV – during the above five-year period – act unanimously on proposals from the Commission *or* on the initiative of a Member State; a method more closely related with intergovernmental forms of co-operation than with supranational legislation. After that period, the Commission will acquire sole right/the monopoly of initiative; it will however be obliged to examine any request a Member State makes

60 COM (2002) 175 final.

61 See *Hailbronner, K.* (fn. 7) p. 1053.

for a proposal to be submitted to the Council (Art. 67 (2)). With regard to the decision-making procedure, it is further laid down that the Council, acting unanimously after consulting the European Parliament, may take a decision with a view to making all or part of the areas covered by Title IV subject to the codecision procedure. As regards the procedures and requirements for the issue of visas by the Member States and rules on uniform visas, the Treaty provides for the codecision procedure to apply after the transitional period without the Council having to take a decision. And, there will then be a jurisdiction for the ECJ in Title IV matters, which currently is not the case.[62]

This *hybrid* form of legislative competence within the EU-context[63] is described by some commentator as being one of a *continuum*, in which the orthodox distinction between supranationalism and intergovernmentalism has been given up, but Member States still retain key powers and, in fact, impose legislation.[64]

As for the legal instruments applicable to Title IV, so-called *framework decisions* and *common positions*[65] add to the standard Community instruments of the Treaty. Framework decisions are aimed at providing for an approximation of laws and shall be binding in the Member States. Although similar, they do not have the same quality as directives, as there is no scope for them having direct effect and there is a unanimity requirement for their adoption (implementation, however, will take place on the basis of majority voting).

Within Title IV, a further special feature is the introduction of the open method of co-ordination. The idea lying behind this concept is to get away from hierarchical top-down structures and on to more co-operative methods.[66] In its communication of July 2001 on this issue, the Commission states as the key element of that method the approval by the Council of multi-annual guidelines for the Union accompanied by specific timetables for achieving goals which they set in the short, medium and long term. These guidelines are then to be translated into national policy where specific targets need to be set, which take into account national and regional differences. Such guidelines are initially proposed in the areas of management of migration flows, admission of economic migrants, part-

62 See *Hailbronner, K.* (fn. 7) pp. 1055 ss. for details on the current ECJ-regime applicable to Title IV measures.

63 See *Hailbronner, K.,* Asylpolitik in der Europäischen Union, 8 ZAR 2002, 259.

64 *Walker, N.*, lecture on the Institutional Structure of the Area of Freedom, Security and Justice, 02/07/2002, EUI, Florence.

65 The earlier joint positions

66 See COM (2001) 387 final.

nership with third countries and the integration of third-country nationals.[67] Instruments and methods proposed include the drawing up of National Action Plans, the development and evaluation of a Community Immigration Policy, involvement of the European Institutions as well as of civil society. Supporting measures by the Commission are deemed to be complementary to these methods.

A final institutional remark concerns the extent of applicability of Title IV in the Member States. There are exceptional regimes in relation to this Title in three countries; the UK and Ireland are not bound by Title IV, unless they decide to opt in to the measure in accordance with the procedure laid down to that effect in the Protocol annexed to the Treaty. For Denmark, this Title will not apply by virtue of the Protocol on its position, which is annexed to the Treaties.

In terms of policy, the special European Council meeting in *Tampere* of October 1999 played an important role. There, the political guidelines for the years to come in the AFSJ-field and especially in the field of asylum and immigration were adopted. The Presidency Conclusions to that Council Meeting are quite informative as to broad policy guidelines and to principles that should govern Title IV.

These guidelines are put in more concrete terms by a Communication of the Commission on a *Community Immigration Policy* [COM (2000) 757 final][68] which addresses the aforementioned issues and deals with the separate but closely related issues of asylum and immigration, emphasising that the zero immigration approach of the preceding 30 years was no longer appropriate and that channels for legal immigration to the EU were to be made available for labour migrants, thus introducing an authentic change of paradigm in European immigration policy.[69] Describing immigration as a multi-dimensional phenomenon with legal, social, cultural and economic impacts, it calls for the definition of an appropriate policy mix, thus mapping out a broad scope for the debate in the asylum and the immigration field that was soon followed by further proposals.

Finally, the six-monthly scoreboard reports[70] which are prepared by the Commission in order to review progress on the creation of an area of freedom, secu-

---

67 See fn. 13, pp. 6 s.

68 COM (2000) 757 final; Communication from the Commission to the Council and the European Parliament on a Community immigration policy.

69 For a critical view on the formulation of the new approach presented by the Commission see *Hailbronner, K.*, “Migrationspolitik und Rechte der Drittstaatsangehörigen in der Europäischen Union”, 3 ZAR 2002, 83.

70 See COM (2002) 261 final, COM (2001) 628 final, COM (2001) 278 final, COM (2000) 782 final and COM (2000) 167 final.

rity and justice in the European Union deserve a mention. They provide a very detailed and systematic overview of the measures within the first stage and their status of progress, thus representing a valuable complement to the political process to be initiated, continued or concluded wit reference to Title IV.

Having discussed some of the elements accompanying the legal provisions relating to the creation of an area of freedom, security and justice, we will now examine the provisions relevant for measures to be adopted in the field of legal and of illegal immigration.

2. *The Competence Issue – The Basic Question of Subsidiarity*

Before we start our analysis of the substantive provisions of that Title and the measures taken or proposed under it, we need to ask the question to what extent Community action is permissible, necessary and beneficial in that field. This leads us to a fundamental principle of EC Law, the principle of subsidiarity, which is set out in Art. 5 of the ECT.

Subsidiarity is often not explicitly mentioned in political discussions related to Title IV of the Treaty – some might say, because it is not as catchy a concept as it used to be back in 1992, when it was introduced with the Maastricht Treaty. However, its impact has, in fact, not lost any force yet, and, in the light of current discussions on the future of the Union, it becomes evident that a proper legal analysis of EC Law in any field cannot take place without having regard to this principle.

In this general context, *subsidiarity* implies the question whether, and if so, to what extent, competences exist at Community level to create rules dealing with issues such as immigration, be it legal migration or be it illegal immigration.

In general terms, the principle of subsidiarity is to be examined and evaluated in the context of the Treaty, where it heralds the group of fundamental principles of Community Law and in that way co-determines their scope and application.[71] The provision of Art. 5 ECT contains a duty to respect limits of competence, the core-principle of subsidiarity and the duty for the Community not to exceed the necessary extent of legislative activity, thus representing a *threefold limitation* of Community Law.[72] To put it in less abstract terms, before the Community can take action, the *three-level set of questions* that Art. 5 indirectly provides,

71 See *Calliess, C.*, Art. 5 EG-Vertrag in: *Calliess/Ruffert*, Kommentar zu EG-Vertrag und EU-Vertrag, p. 378 (380) at mn. 5 with further references.

72 See *Calliess, C.*, (fn. 71) at mn. 6, with further references.

need to be answered in an affirmative way; i.e. the *"can"*-question of para. 1 referring to the general admissibility of Community action in the field, the *"if"*-question of para. 2 that serves to determine the question if Community action in an area where it has no exclusive competence is desirable under the circumstances and the *"how"*-question of para. 3 dealing with the question how Community action needs to be designed in order not to go beyond what is necessary to comply with the objectives of the Treaty.[73]

Although these criteria do not appear all too permissive in nature, subsidiarity is indeed a *dynamic concept* that allows Community action within the limits of its powers to be expanded where circumstances so require, and conversely, to be restricted or discontinued where it is no longer justified.[74]

In *legal terms*, para. I of Art. 5 provides that the Community shall act within the limits of the powers conferred upon it by this Treaty and of the objectives assigned to it therein. This implies that a legal act to be decided by the EC not only requires a competence, but the *adequate/right* competence basis – a requirement relevant in the context of Council voting as well as with problems related to vertical competence conflicts.[75]

Having said that, there can be no doubt that the *Community has a competence* in the field of *immigration* (visas and asylum) and other policies related to the free movement of persons, as the heading of Title IV of the ECT clearly states. That is to say that the basic requirement of para. 1 is fulfilled.[76]

As to the *nature* of these *competences*, the Treaty only gives a hint in Art. 63 (we will come back to that provision at a later stage) to that effect by stating that measures adopted by the Council pursuant to immigration policy as well as to illegal immigration and illegal residence shall not prevent any Member State from maintaining or introducing in the areas concerned national provisions that are compatible with the ECT and with international agreements. This clause reflects the concession made to the Member States that were reluctant to give up parts of their sovereignty in immigration and asylum policy and – while not being easy to interpret – makes it quite clear that Community competences under Art. 62, the provision setting out the measures to be taken by the Council in or-

73 See *Calliess, C.*, (fn. 71), p. 380.

74 See Protocol on the application of the principle of subsidiarity and proportionality annexed to the Treaty of Amsterdam, recital 3.

75 *Calliess, C.*, (fn. 71), pp. 381-2, mn. 9.

76 See also COM (2001) 387 p. 5, which reads: "[...] the principle of subsidiarity […] is of particular relevance to the creation of an area of freedom, security and justice as is the need for solidarity among and between Member States and the European institutions in facing the transnational challenges presented by migration movements."

der to create an "area of freedom, security and justice" within five years after entry into force of the Treaty of Amsterdam (ToA) cannot be interpreted as an exclusive competence of the Community.[77] Member States may therefore pass new legislation or change existing laws as long as no Community legislation has been passed in this field.

As Community competences are non-exclusive in Title IV, EC action needs to comply with the requirement of Art. 5 para. II, which provides that such action is to be taken in accordance with the principle of subsidiarity if and insofar as the objectives of the proposed action cannot be sufficiently achieved by the Member States and, by reason of the scale or effects of the proposed action, can be better achieved by the Community.

The following guidelines which are set out in the *Subsidiarity Protocol* annexed to the ToA serve as important reference criteria for determining whether the above conditions are fulfilled, i.e.

— the issue under consideration has *trans-national* aspects which cannot be satisfactorily regulated by action by Member States;

— *actions by Member States alone or lack of Community action would conflict with the requirements of the Treaty* (such as the need to correct distortion of competition or avoid disguised restrictions on trade or strengthen economic and social cohesion) *or would otherwise significantly damage Member States' interests;*

— action at Community level would produce *clear benefits* by reason of its *scale or effects* compared with action at the level of the Member States.[78]

The importance of the subsidiarity provision in Art. 5 para. II will fully come to bear after the five-year transitional period applicable to most Title IV measures is over and the unanimity requirement which is typical for that transitional period set out in the Treaty is abolished. Then the principle of subsidiarity will serve as a genuine limitation clause for Community action, with particular relevance especially in the development of European (illegal) immigration policies.[79]

We find references to the principle of subsidiarity (and proportionality) in almost all the current (and preceding) Commission proposals in the field of immigration. This indicates a great awareness by the Commission of the sensitive na-

---

77 See *Hailbronner, K.*, "European Immigration and Asylum Law under the Amsterdam Treaty", CML Rev. 35 1998, p. 1047 (1051).

78 See Protocol (fn. 4) , recital 5.

79 *Hailbronner,* CML Rev. 35 1998, p. 1047 (1051).

ture of that field previously lying at the heart of the concept of national sovereignty.

Finally, Art. 5 para. III of the ECT, the "how"-provision concerning Community action, states that any action by the Community shall not go beyond what is necessary to achieve the objectives of the Treaty. Here again, we find guidance as to the precise meaning of these terms in the *Subsidiarity Protocol* annexed to the ToA. In its *number 6*, we read that "[t]he form of Community action shall be as simple as possible, consistent with satisfactory achievement of the objective of the measure and the need for effective enforcement [and that] [t]he Community shall legislate only to the extent necessary." This implies that – other things being equal – *directives* would have to be preferred to regulations and *framework directives* to detailed measures. Directives should, while being binding upon each Member State they are addressed to as to the result to be achieved, leave to the national authorities the choice of form and methods.[80]

Number 7 of the Subsidiarity Protocol provides with regard to the *nature and the extent of Community action*, that Community measures should – while securing the aim of the measure and observing the requirements of the Treaty – leave as much scope for national decision as possible and draws attention to the respect of well established national arrangements and the organisation and working of Member States' legal systems. Finally, it states that where appropriate and subject to the need for proper enforcement, Community measures should provide Member States with alternative ways to achieve the objectives of the measures.[81]

Title IV measures related to immigration have been proposed and adopted in more than one specific form. In the field of legal migration, most measures proposed have in fact been proposed as directives.

Having examined the mode of operation of the subsidiarity provision in Art. 5 ECT and concluded that the Community may take action in the AFSJ-field, we will now turn to the provisions of Title IV that represent the bases for several acts of Community law, proposed by the Community or the Member States or already adopted by the latter.

This next step will serve to clarify the specific Community competences/powers in the context of the AFSJ, which serve as a basis for action in the particular field of Title IV. We will therefore take a brief look at what the provisions of the Articles dealing with immigration within the EU-context set out in particular before we proceed to discuss the measures proposed or already taken.

---

80 Subsidiarity Protocol, no. 6.
81 Subsidiarity Protocol, no. 7.

3. *Legal Immigration*

The following constitutional provisions have served as a basis for a considerable number of proposals by the Commission in an area that could also be qualified as legal migration. It includes the traditional field of Community freedoms and related issues. Proposals cover – as indicated above – the issues of family reunion, long-term residents, economic migration, formats of residence permits, freedoms of EU citizens, short-term residence permits. They will be outlined in brief.

a) Art. 2 EUT

A general provision within the framework of the legal provisions relating to the AFSJ-branch of legal immigration is Art. 2 of the EUT That provision sets out in para. I the objective for the Union to promote economic and social progress and a high level of employment and to achieve balanced and sustainable development, in particular through the *creation of an area without internal frontiers*, and in para. 4 to maintain and develop the Union as an *area of freedom, security and justice*, in which the *free movement of persons is assured* in conjunction with appropriate measures with respect to *external border controls, asylum, immigration* and the prevention and combating of crime; those two paras thus being complementary to the ECT provisions of Title IV. And, in the last para, a – rather general – reference to the respect of the timetables, conditions and the principle of subsidiarity is made.

b) Art. 61 ECT

Legal immigration or migration has been an area dealt with in the framework of Community for a long time, however to varying degrees and with different effects on the persons concerned – mostly familiars of an EC or EU national sponsor. While we have seen the main lines of the development in traditional Community law in the previous section which dealt with the Constitutional Gates into the EU, we will now dedicate our attention to the analysis of the legal framework of Title IV. Firstly, the legal provisions that serve as the basis for Community action will be outlined, then we will turn to the measures adopted or proposed on the basis of them.

Art. 61 ECT sets out the tasks of the Community in the field of Justice and Home Affairs, transferred from the EUT into Community Law as Title IV of the ECT. The provision contains a programmatic obligation for the Council to adopt:

(a) measures aimed at ensuring the *free movement of persons*, in conjunction with directly related *flanking measures* with respect to *external border controls*, *asylum* and *immigration*, in accordance with the provisions of *Article 62(2)(in relation to the crossing of the external borders of the Member States) and (3) (freedom to travel for third-country nationals for maximum periods of three months)* and *Article 63(1)(a) and (2)(a),* and measures to *prevent and combat crime* in accordance with the provisions of *Article 31(e) of the Treaty on European Union* within a period of five years after the entry into force of the Treaty of Amsterdam,

(b) other measures in the fields of asylum, immigration and safeguarding the rights of nationals of third countries, in accordance with the provisions of Article 63 (measures on asylum, on refugees and displaced persons, on immigration policy and illegal immigration and illegal residence, including repatriation of illegal residents and finally measures defining the rights and conditions under which nationals of third countries who are legally resident in a Member State may reside in another Member State [...]).

These two paragraphs are of particular relevance in the area of immigration, as they provide a programmatic starting point. In fact, most measures in the field of legal migration do not make explicit reference to Art. 61.[82]

c) Art. 62 ECT

Art. 62 ECT is more specific than the previous provision of Art. 61. It contains, as to its substance, in (1) provisions *relating to the free movement of persons* within the EU area, in (2) rules aimed at the *harmonisation of border controls at external borders* and in (3) a provision relating to measures setting out the conditions under which nationals of third countries shall have the *freedom to travel* within the territory of the Member States during a period of no more than *three months*.

The five-year "deadline" for these measures to be adopted is of programmatic character.[83]

The measures proposed under this Article relate to the Schengen acquis – in fact, in the field of legal migration, there have not been too many measures proposed or adopted; mostly it will be measures related to visa formats [COM (2001) 577] and other visa related provisions, a neighbouring area of legal immigration.

---

82 See *Brechmann, W.*, Art. 61 EG, in: *Calliess/Ruffert* (Hrsg.), Kommentar zu EG-Vertrag und EU-Vertrag, p. 897, mn. 3.

83 See *Brechmann, W.*, Art. 62 EG, in *Calliess/Ruffert* (Hrsg.) p. 903 mn. 2.

The proposal for a regulation on uniform format for residence permits[84] [COM (2001) 157] would "communitarise" the 1997 Joint Action on residence permits, one of the few binding measures on immigration and asylum law adopted in the "Maastricht period" of co-operation in Justice and Home Affairs. This measure would be adopted on the basis of Art. 62 (2) (b) (iii).

Maintaining in substance most of the provisions, changes can be found on the one hand in updates and in the restructuring of provisions. On the other hand, implementing measures would be adopted by the Commission, replacing the Council's implementing powers under the current Joint Action, secondly, the Regulation would not apply to visas or to permits that are issued while an application for asylum or for residence permits is pending, but would cover all other types of residence permits, implying a much wider scope of application for the uniform residence permit than under current rules, and, thirdly, the rules of the EC data protection Directive would apply in the field of residence permits.[85]

d) Art. 63 (3) ECT

The provision most referred to in Commission proposals for legislation is Art. 63 (3) ECT. This provision sets out obligations in the areas of asylum, refugees and displaced persons and *immigration policy*, this third area now being of central interest. Under the heading of (3) the development of a comprehensive immigration policy at Community level has become possible. Such a policy can be developed in the field of legal migration under the competence heading of (a), i.e. *conditions of entry* and *residence*, and *standards on procedures* for the issue by Member States of long term visas and residence permits, including those for the purpose of *family reunion*. On its basis the following (proposed) measures were based.

aa) family reunification

In the field of family reunification, the most recent measure is a Directive from 2 May 2002.[86] The initial proposal dates from 1 December 1999.[87] The European Parliament, while supporting the general approach of that proposal, called

84 COM (2001) 157 final.

85 For details see *Peers* (fn. 13) 113.

86 COM (2002) 225 final, OJ 2002 C 203 E/136; Amended proposal for a Council directive on the right to family reunification/* COM/2002/0225 final – CNS 1999/0258 */ Official Journal C 203 E , 27/08/2002 P. 0136 – 0141.

87 COM (1999) 638 final; Proposal for a Council Directive on the right to family reunification / * COM/99/0638 final – CNS 99/0258 */.

for a restriction in its scope. That request was followed by an amended proposal on 10 October 2000[88]; however, the subsequent negotiations in the Council did not bear any fruit. The current proposal follows the Laeken European Council conclusions, incorporating compromises reached in the Council over two years of negotiation.

The new approach taken by this proposal focuses on flexibility as to the substance and the time frame of measures to be taken. While providing for room for manoeuvre for the Member States in areas where deadlock situations are likely to arise, exceptions to allow adjustment to the current legislation of certain Member States in limited cases is allowed for. A clause on some derogations has been inserted to inhibit new divergences between Member States from arising. The deadline clause provides for a review of the provisions of the implementation of the Directive in national legislation, with an eye on the rapid adoption of genuine "common rules" in the field.

The main changes necessitated by the new approach comprise: deletion of provisions relating to family reunification of Union citizens – there, a new proposal has been made to deal specifically with this group of people; specific exceptions for certain pieces of national legislation concerning the age up to which children may be reunified; possibility of checks on resources even after reunification; possibility for Member States to spread authorisations to enter for the purpose of family reunification depending on the reception capacity of the Member States concerned to a maximum of period of three years; introduction of long-term resident status for reunification candidates on the basis of the same criteria as the person with whom they are reunified; setting of an upper limit of five years' residence for the grant of autonomous status of family members.[89]

In recital (8), family reunification is characterised as a necessary way of making family life possible, by helping to create socio-cultural stability facilitating the integration of third-country nationals in the Member State, which also serves to promote economic and social cohesion as set out in Arts. 2 and 3 (1) (k) of the Treaty.

Recital (15) on its part contains a detailed reference to the principle of subsidiarity, stating why Community action is permissible and necessary[90] to achieve the

88 COM (2000) 624 final, OJ 2001 C 62 E/99; Amended proposal for a Council Directive on the right to family reunification (presented by the Commission pursuant to Article 250(2) of the EC Treaty)/* COM/2000/0624 final – CNS 99/0258 */; Official Journal C 062 E , 27/02/2001 P. 0099 – 0111.

89 See fn. 19, pp. 3 s.

90 "[...] [T]he objectives of the proposed action, namely the establishment of a right to family reunification for third-country nationals to be exercised in accordance with

objective of "establishment of a right to family reunification for third-country nationals to be exercised in accordance with common rules" on the one hand, while mentioning that the Directive would need to be confined to the minimum required to achieve the objectives set out and does not go beyond what is necessary for that purpose.

bb) long-term residents

The Commission, with respect to the status of third-country nationals who are long-term residents, has made a proposal based on Art. 63 para. 3 and 4 ECT. This legislation will provide, for the first time, a *common status* for long-term resident third-country nationals. This status would in substance entitle long-term residents to *equal treatment* with nationals in a number of areas – such as the right to reside, receive education and work as an employee or self-employed person, as well as the principle of *non-discrimination* vis-à-vis citizens of the State of residence – and to enhanced, though not absolute, protection against expulsion (Arts. 12 and 13).

cc) economic migration

Also based on Art. 63 para. 3 ECT is the proposal for a Directive on the conditions of entry and residence of third-country nationals for the purpose of paid employment and self-employed economic activities [COM (2001) 386][91], which relates to the ambit of economic migration.

The procedure for adoption of this proposal is laid down in Art. 67 of the Treaty. Again, exceptions as to the applicability of these measures in the United Kingdom, Ireland and Denmark are provided for.

The primary objective of this initiative is to determine a harmonised legal frame at EU level concerning the conditions of entry and residence of third-country nationals for the purpose of paid employment and self-employed economic activities and of the procedures for the issue by Member States of permanent permits.

---

common rules, cannot be sufficiently achieved by the Member States and can therefore, by reason of the scale and impact of the action, be better achieved by the Community. This Directive confines itself to the minimum required to achieve those objectives and does not go beyond what is necessary for that purpose."

91 COM (2001) 386 final, OJ 2001 C 332 E/248; Proposal for a Council Directive on the conditions of entry and residence of third-country nationals for the purpose of paid employment and self-employed economic activities/* COM/2001/ 0386 final – CNS 2001/0154 */ Official Journal C 332 E , 27/11/2001 P. 0248 – 0256.

Eventually, this proposal is to create a single national application procedure leading to one combined title, encompassing both residence and work permit within one administrative act, and will thus contribute to simplifying and harmonising the diverging rules currently applicable in Member States.

4. Illegal Immigration

a) The Basic Decisions

Illegal immigration is the area complementary to "legal migration" that the Community is to deal with in line with the relevant provisions of the Amsterdam Treaty and the Tampere Conclusions. While progress in the field of legal migration and of asylum law was faster to arrive, measures in this area have come to be proposed slightly later. The measures taken in this field include a Directive on the Mutual Recognition of Expulsion Decisions, one Directive relating to the Implementation of the Schengen Convention, as well as one Communication on Illegal Immigration and one Green Paper on a Common Return Policy. In this part we will mainly deal with *illegal immigration* but also point at the developments in *related areas* such as policy on borders, visas, implementation of Art. 62 ECT and conversion of the Schengen acquis.

The legal provisions setting out the framework for measures to be taken in the field of illegal immigration consist to some extent of the same Treaty Articles we have discussed above, but also contain the remaining third-pillar Articles of Title VI of the EUT.

While measures proposed in the area of legal immigration can be regarded as enabling provisions for migration, the proposals under this heading do have a potential to restrict immigration, thus contributing to the creation of a "Fortress Europe".

In its Communication on a Common Policy on Illegal Immigration from November 2001[92], [COM (2001) 672 final], the Commission has identified six areas for possible action with the aim of preventing and fighting illegal immigration. These areas cover visa policy; infrastructure for information exchange, co-operation and co-ordination, border management, police cooperation, aliens law and criminal law as well as return and readmission policy.

92 COM (2001) 672 final; Communication from the Commission to the Council and the European Parliament on a common policy on illegal immigration/* COM/2001/0672 final */.

The Commission is striving for synergies of national efforts by adding a European dimension to the issue. It proposes actions in and support of actions of countries of origin and transit, taking into account the EU policy on human rights.

Furthermore, the Commission stresses the importance of enforcement of existing common rules, whilst emphasising the need for the EU to strengthen its monitoring efforts as to the common standards for visa issuance and border controls.

In the field of administrative co-operation, the development of a network of liaison officers and the promotion of joint teams for border controls are put forward. The information needed in that field could better be gathered, analysed and disseminated in cooperation with a permanent technical support facility that would need to be established to co-ordinate efforts and to manage common databases for migration management.

The Early Warning System on irregular migration flows would serve as a model for the efficient use/utilisation of all modern technologies available, while a European Migration Observatory could play a facilitative role in the exchange of statistical as well as analytical data on migration and would therefore be an interesting option.

Another crucial aspect in this field of policy are sanctions against promoters of illegal immigration; while a further upgrade and harmonisation of sanctions already in place is put forward, particular emphasis is put on the severe punishment of criminal activities and the seizure of illegally obtained financial advantages, the latter being identified as a key factor in the field.

Undeclared work of illegal residents is also addressed in the Communication, being characterised as an area where further action is needed in order to diminish the attractiveness for employers and the pull factor for potential irregular immigrants.

The strengthening of police co-operation, leading up to an advanced role for Europol is identified as a necessary measure as well.

Finally, the development of a Community readmission policy is recommended to be pursued, as is the finalisation in due course of the current negotiations with third countries.

b) Art. 61 ECT

In Art. 61 (a) ECT, the catalogue of measures to be taken not only refers to legal migration movements, but also to illegal movements and the methods which the EU can use to deal with them. We have already seen that (a) also contains a reference to third pillar competences – the reference in that respect being therefore of declaratory nature.[93]

As to illegal immigration, it will especially be the *flanking measures* with respect to *external border* controls, asylum and *immigration*, in accordance with the provisions of *Article 62(2) (in relation to the crossing of the external borders of the Member State) and (3) (freedom to travel for third-country nationals for maximum periods of three months)* and Article 63(1)(a) and (2)(a), and measures to *prevent and combat crime* in accordance with the provisions of Article 31(e) of the Treaty on European Union within a period of five years after the entry into force of the Treaty of Amsterdam, that are of relevance – the design of the provision already indicates the link between free movement and security-related measures to safeguard the exercise of this right by preventing illegal activities in the field.[94]

The integration of the Schengen acquis into EU framework, provided for in the Schengen Protocol annexed to the ToA, is an essential but technically quite complex issue in that context – the instruments adopted under Title VI EUT will remain unchanged in their legal nature until their content is replaced by new measures under Title IV.[95]

c) *Art. 63 ECT*

The norm of Art. 63 (3) ECT is not only central with regard to legal but also to illegal immigration. In paragraph (3) (b) it sets out a competence in the field of immigration policy for the *areas of illegal immigration and illegal residence, including repatriation of illegal residents.*

The above mentioned Communication by the Commission on a common policy on illegal immigration [COM (2001) 672] was a first step in that field. Step by step this Communication is put in more concrete terms by the following measures.

---

93 See *Brechmann, W.*, Art. 61 EG, in: *Calliess/Ruffert* (Hrsg.), Kommentar zu EG-Vertrag und EU-Vertrag, p.897, mn. 3.

94 See *Brechmann, W.*, Art. 61 EG, in *Calliess/Ruffert* (Hrsg.), Kommentar zu EG-Vertrag und EU-Vertrag, p. 901, mn. 12.

95 For details see *Hailbronner, K.*, CML Rev. 35 1998, pp. 1059 ss.

aa) *Green Paper on a Community Return Policy on Illegal Residents*

The Commission Green on a Community Return Policy on Illegal Residents from 10th April 2002[96] approaches the issue of illegal integration in three sections, the first of which identifies *return* as an integral part of a comprehensive Community immigration and asylum policy, the second suggesting *approximation and improved co-operation on return* among Member States and the third one indicating the elements of a possible Common *readmission policy.*

The Green Paper builds on the elements defined in the Council's action plan following Conclusion No. 40 of the Laeken European Council calling for the integration of the policy on migratory flows into the European Union's foreign policy. As is stated in its foreword, it "[...] only intends to open a discussion on the return of illegal residents and should not be seen as an effort to cover all dimensions connected with the return of third-country nationals" and is as to its basic intention, in line with other Green Papers that in general strive to commence a broad debate on an issue in order to create a specific problem-awareness.

Some important issues being dealt with include the question of compatibility of a common return policy with the need for protection under international and European Law in the evolving European asylum system, the necessity for common standards for return procedures and the question whether they should be binding, the improvement of the Member States' services and the usefulness of a future financial instrument as well as the determination of the elements of a common readmission policy, that should encompass a balanced co-operation with the third countries concerned.[97] As to its *specific purpose*, the Green Paper describes the intention pursued as examining the complex return issues for people residing illegally in the EU and putting forward suggestions for a co-ordinated and efficient policy based on common principles and standards, and respectful of human rights and human dignity, the premise being that a return policy is needed in order to safeguard the integrity of the legal and humanitarian admission systems.[98]

In legal terms, reference is made to Art. 63 (3) b ECT and the Council competence emanating from this provision to adopt measures on illegal immigration and illegal residence including repatriation of illegal residents on the one hand and on the other hand to the Schengen *acquis* integrated into the European Un-

96 COM (2002) 175 final – Green paper on a community return policy on illegal residents/* COM/2002/0175 final */

97 COM (2002) 175 final, pp. 3 s.

98 COM (2002) 175 final, p. 6.

ion by the ToA, in particular Art. 23 of the Convention implementing the Schengen Agreement.

bb) Mutual Recognition of Expulsion Decisions

In the area of mutual recognition of expulsion decisions relating to third-country nationals, the proposal stage has been overcome and legislation been passed. Directive 2001/40[99] deals with the issues. It is based on Art. 63 (3) of the ECT and goes back to a French presidency proposal from mid-2000. Far from being uncontroversial, the final proposal was adopted after some changes were introduced following criticisms made by the European Parliament, which nevertheless still rejected the final version despite the changes made.[100]

cc) Carrier Sanctions

Following the second French proposal in the field of irregular immigration, the Directive supplementing the provision of Art. 26 of the Convention implementing the Schengen Agreement[101] (Directive 2001/51), was adopted by the Transport and Telecoms Council of 27/28 June 2001 and is due for implementation by 11 February 2003. The legal basis for this measure is Art. 61 (a) and Art. 63 (3) (b) of the ECT. A reference to the aim of the Directive – curbing migratory flows and combating illegal immigration – is found in recital 2, the Schengen acquis on which this measure is based and in full conformity with is mentioned in recital 6.

dd) Short-Term Residence Permit

A proposal for a Directive on the short-term residence permit issued to victims of action to facilitate illegal immigration or trafficking in human beings who cooperate with the competent authorities[102] [COM (2002) 71] was presented by the Commission in early 2002.

---

99 Council Directive 2001/40/EC, OJ 2001 L 149/34; Council Directive 2001/40/EC of 28 May 2001 on the mutual recognition of decisions on the expulsion of third-country nationals; Official Journal L 149 , 02/06/2001 P. 0034 – 0036.

100 See *Peers*, EJML (2001),p. 117.

101 Council Directive 2001/51/EC, OJ 2001 L 187/45; Council Directive 2001/51/EC of 28 June 2001 supplementing the provisions of Article 26 of the Convention implementing the Schengen Agreement of 14 June 1985, Official Journal L 187 , 10/07/2001 P. 0045 – 0046.

102 COM (2002) 71 final, OJ 2002 C 126 E/393; Proposal for a Council Directive on the short-term residence permit issued to victims of action to facilitate illegal immigration or trafficking in human beings who cooperate with the competent authorities/*

The legal basis chosen for this proposal is Art. 63(3) ECT, as for procedural requirements for adoption, it is again the procedure set out in Art. 67 of the Treaty which is central.

The purpose of the proposed Directive is to introduce a residence permit with the aim of enhancing measures to combat illegal immigration. The text is not intended to incriminate networks of organised crime or to arrange protection for victims or witnesses. The proposal does not regulate these aspects, even though they are to some extent related to the subject matter of the text.[103]

d) *Third-Pillar-Measures based on Art. 29, 30, 31 EUT*

With regard to illegal immigration, we also need to consider the provisions in *Title VI* of the EUT on police and judicial cooperation in criminal matters.

In that context, we find a competence for the Union in Art. 29 of the EUT to develop *common actions* among the Member States in the fields of police and judicial cooperation in criminal matters and by preventing and combating racism and xenophobia with the aim of providing citizens with a high level of safety within an area of freedom, security and justice – without prejudice to the powers of the European Community. The Union's objective in the context of illegal immigration consists in particular in preventing and combating *trafficking in persons*. In order to achieve that, closer cooperation between police forces, customs authorities and other competent authorities is provided in (sub)para. 1. This provision is of a general nature, the following ones specify what police cooperation (Art. 30) and judicial cooperation (Art. 31) should include.

Art. 30 lists a number of ways in which *police cooperation* can take place, mentioning in (a) operational cooperation in relation to the prevention, detection and investigation of criminal offences, in (b) the collection, storage, processing, analysis and exchange of relevant information (subject to the relevant provisions data protection), in (c) joint initiatives in training, the exchange of liaison officers, secondments, the use of equipment, and forensic research and finally in (d) the common evaluation of particular investigative techniques in relation to the detection of serious forms of organised crime.

In fact the Communication by the Commission on integrated management of external borders [COM (2002) 233] encourages measures of this type to be

---

COM/2002/0071 final - CNS 2002/0043 */ Official Journal C 126 E , 28/05/2002 P. 0393 – 0397.

103 See COM (2002) 71 final, pp. 7 s.

taken.[104] It gives an assessment of the current political and institutional environment and draws attention on the challenges to be faced by the Union in order to be able to fulfil the objectives of enforcing co-operation and developing an integrated strategy for the management of EU-external borders.

The current legal framework for the management of external borders is set out at the beginning of the Communication. It comprises the *common uniform principles* which are established by the *Chapter 2 of Title II of the Schengen Convention,* the *Common Manual for External Borders*[105] which lays down and spells out the detailed rules of that Convention; the new legal basis for these provision being Title IV of the ECT.[106] Art. 3 of the Convention contains rules as to the crossing of the external borders, Art. 5 lays down principles of Community legislation concerning foreign nationals' entry for periods not exceeding three months, Art. 6 determines the obligations of the Member States as regards checks and surveillance at external borders, those referring to checks of persons crossing the border legally (they bring along relatively extensive obligations for Member States[107]); rules directly (inseparably) linked to the provisions on the procedures at external borders relate to carriers liability (Art. 26) and the liability for assistance to unlawful immigration for lucrative purposes (Art. 27 of the Schengen Convention) – these two provisions are complemented by legislation subsequently enacted to prevent illegal immigration.[108] Art. 71.3 refers to the strengthening of checks on the movement of persons, goods and means of transport, "to combat the illegal import of narcotic drugs and psychotropic substances" and horizontal provisions such as the Schengen Information System (SIS)[109] which are also implemented at external borders. Access to all *"data*

---

104 COM (2002) 233 final; Communication from the Commission to the Council and the European Parliament - towards integrated management of the external borders of the Member States of the European Union/* COM/2002/0233 final */.

105 The Decision of the Schengen Executive Committee of 28 April 1999 adopting the Manual is in OJ L 239, 22.9.2000 (p. 317). It was given a European Union legal basis in accordance with Council Decision 1999/436/EC of 20 May 1999.

106 See Council Decision 1999/436/EC of 20 May 1999, OJ L 176, 10 July 1999.

107 Systematic checking of identities is compulsory, including in the case of EU citizens and beneficiaries of Community Law. Surveillance is exercised in the spaces located between the permitted passage points in order to dissuade persons from crossing the external border illegally. Member States have the obligation to ensure that the level of surveillance is equivalent all along their external borders.

108 Council Directive 2001/51/EC of 28 June 2001 supplementing the provisions of Article 26 of the Convention implementing the Schengen Agreement of 14 June 1985 (OJ L 187, 10.7.2001, pp. 45-46).

109 See Articles 92 to 101 of the Schengen Convention.

entered [in the SIS] *and the right to search such data directly"* for the *"authorities responsible for (...) border checks"* is regulated in Art. 101 (1) (a) of the Schengen Convention. The evaluation mechanism for the proper implementation of the common rules for crossing of external borders which is carried out by the Standing Committee on the Evaluation and Implementation of Schengen, now have a twofold basis – one in Art. 66 of the ECT, the other in Arts. 30 and 31 of the Union Treaty.

While in the operational context, measures such as the *exchange of liaison officers* (provided for in Art. 7 of the Schengen Convention[110]) [for purposes of assistance and permanent co-operation between Member States] and *bilateral police co-operation agreements* between Member States on the basis of Art. 47 of the Schengen Convention[111] are already in place, the Commission identifies a number of new priority projects in the field, classifying them into short term and medium term actions and indicating whether or not a Treaty amendment would be necessary for that purpose.

The central proposals include[112]:

- a common corpus of *legislation*, which would imply a recast of the Common Manual on Checks at the External Borders, the attribution of mandatory status to certain recommendations of the EU Schengen Catalogue of best practices, the production of a practical handbook for the use of border guards, the specification of the legal framework and practical procedures regarding "local border traffic" all of the former being envisaged as short-term measures, and, in the medium term (if necessary, following amendment of the Treaties, the specification of the institutional and legal framework of the staff of a future European Corps of Border Guards[113];
- a common *operational co-ordination and co-operation mechanism*, establishing an External borders practitioners common unit with a steering role in carrying out integrated risk analysis and projects on the ground, encouraging

110 Article 7 of the Schengen Convention was given a legal basis in Article 66 of the EC Treaty "to the extent that these provisions do not concern forms of police cooperation covered by the provisions of Title III of the Schengen Convention", by Council Decision 1999/436/EC of 20 May 1999 (OJ L 176, 10.7.1999).

111 The legal basis for this provision has come to be contained in Articles 34 and 30 (1) of the Treaty on European Union, in accordance with Council Decision 1999/436/EC of 20 May 1999. Article 47 of the Schengen Convention appears under "Police Cooperation", while Article 7 is under "Crossing external borders".

112 COM (2002) 233 final, pp. 22 ss.

113 COM (2002) 233 final, pp. 22 s.

convergence as to staff and equipment, exercising an inspection function and putting forward emergency operational measures in short term and, in the medium term, (without Treaty amendment) the exploration of the feasibility and relevance of a security procedure at external borders, consisting of establishing exchanges and processing of information and intelligence between the competent border authorities, possibly setting up contact points;[114]

- a common *integrated risk analysis*, including the establishment for these purposes of a common risk analysis matrix by the External borders practitioners common in the short term and the drawing up by that unit of conclusions for the deployment of personnel and equipment at external borders;[115]
- as to the development of *inter-operational personal and equipment*, a common basis for the training of border guards in the European Union should be developed, their use of mobile surveillance equipment could be encouraged – both in the short term, while a common radar or satellite-based external border surveillance network (drawing from the capacities of the Galileo system) could be established and a European border guards college on the basis of the national training institute networks could be considered in the medium term and without Treaty amendment;[116]
- with regard to *burden sharing* between the Member States and the Union, the organisation of the bases for Community financing of the policy on management of the external borders covered by Title IV of the Treaty (in the short term) and (most likely after amendment of the Treaties) the establishment of a European Corps of Border Guards the principal function of which would be the "common surveillance" of the most sensitive places (in particular maritime borders) and, also in the medium term, the establishment of a complementarity of action with the customs administrations to enhance efficiency in the community financing of the management of the external borders as far as possible according to the Treaties.

The provision of Art. 31 EUT sets out the details of common action on judicial and criminal matters, referring to (a) the facilitating and accelerating of cooperation in relation to proceedings and the enforcement of decisions; (b) the facilitating of extradition; (c) the compatibility in rules necessary for cooperation; (d) the prevention of conflicts of jurisdiction between Member States and (e) the progressive adoption of measures establishing minimum rules relating to the constituent elements of criminal acts and to penalties in the fields of organised

114 COM (2002) 233 final, p. 23.
115 COM (2002) 233 final, p. 23.
116 COM (2002) 233 final, pp. 23 s.

crime, terrorism and illicit drug trafficking. The provisions of (e) are especially important in the field of illegal immigration, as the phenomena dealt with there are often "bundled with" different forms of illegal immigration.

Within this legal framework just referred to, there are proposals for measures and measures already taken that deserve a mention. In particular we have a Communication on a common policy on illegal immigration, a Green Paper on a Community return policy for illegal residents, a Directive on the mutual recognition of expulsion decisions, a Directive on carrier sanctions (supplementing Art. 26 of the Schengen Convention); furthermore, a proposal for a Directive on the short-term residence permit for victims of action to facilitate illegal immigration or trafficking in human beings, and a Communication on the integrated management of the external borders of the Member States – to name only the central initiatives in that field.

5. *Accompanying Measures in the Field of Foreign- and Development Policy*

Accompanying measures in the field of Foreign- and Development Policy have come to be regarded as a crucial complement to the measures proposed in the field of EU (im)migration policy. While not dealing with immigration in the strict sense, their importance for an effective immigration policy at the European level has been stressed on more than one occasion. In fact, the Treaties contain quite a number of provisions enabling the Union to take action in the field; action that has already been proposed by the Seville Council especially with regard to future agreements with third-countries. These provisions will be outlined in brief and then we will focus on the Council proposals.

a) Introduction

The Seville Council last June dedicated considerable efforts to the field of asylum and migration in the European context, which is reflected in the fact that 14 out of 59 paragraphs of the Seville Presidency Conclusions deal with aspects related to the Asylum and Immigration.[117] While reference is made to the timetable of measures, *general principles* of EU migration policy, of combating illegal immigration and of the necessity of a gradual introduction of coordinated, integrated management of external borders,[118] a central issue of these Conclu-

117 See Presidency Conclusions SN 200/02 11 EN Presidency Conclusions – Seville, 21 and 22 June 2002, points 26 to 39.

118 See points 26 to 32.

sions lies with the intention of the European Council to *integrate immigration policy into the Union's relations with third countries.*[119]

A targeted approach to the problem of illegal immigration with the use of all appropriate instruments in the context of the European Union's external relations – i.e. the aforementioned instruments of the EC and the EU Treaties – is proposed as a constant long-term objective for the EU in point 33 of the Conclusions in order to tackle the root causes of illegal immigration. It is closer economic cooperation, trade expansion, development assistance and conflict prevention that are identified as effective means of promoting economic prosperity in the countries concerned, thus reducing the underlying causes of migration flows. In particular, the European Council urges for a *clause on joint management of migration flows and on compulsory readmission in the event of illegal immigration* to be included in any future cooperation, association or equivalent agreement concluded by the EC or the EU with any other country.[120] That way, the EU is introducing a new *"stick and carrot – method"* in relation to third countries. While the Union stresses the importance of ensuring the *cooperation* of countries of origin and transit in joint management, in border control and on readmission and declares its readiness to provide technical and financial assistance to the countries concerned[121] (carrot) it also intends to draw up a (kind of) *"black list"* that is to contain (following systematic assessment) all those countries not cooperating in combating illegal immigration, inadequate cooperation by a country being a reason for the Union not to establish any closer relations with it[122] (stick). If such an insufficiency of cooperation persists with that one Member States despite the application of existing Community mechanisms, the Council may unanimously find that that (third) country has demonstrated an unjustified lack cooperation in joint management of migration flows and, in accordance with the relevant Treaty provisions, adopt measures or positions under the provisions concerning Common Foreign and Security Policy (CFSP) of Title V EUT or under other European policies, while honouring the Union's contractual commitments and not jeopardising development cooperation objectives.[123]

Beside the economic aspects of the issue, which clearly aim at streamlining the Union's asylum and immigration system, also a reference to fundamental rights can be found in the Seville Presidency Conclusions. Point 29 sets out the principles for action by the Union in the field, declaring that the legitimate aspiration

119 Points 33 to 36.
120 Point 33 of the Seville Presidency Conclusions.
121 Point 34.
122 Point 35.
123 Point 36.

to a better life needs to be reconcilable with the reception capacity of the Union and its Member States and that immigration must pass through the legal channels provided for it; "the integration of immigrants lawfully present in the Union entails both rights and obligations in relation to the fundamental rights recognised within the Union; combating racism and xenophobia is of essential importance here"[124]; and further, that in accordance with the 1951 Geneva Convention, it is important to afford refugees swift, effective protection, while making arrangements to prevent abuse of the system and ensuring that those whose asylum applications have been rejected are returned to their countries of origin more quickly.

b) *Legal framework*

Title XX of the ECT deals specifically with Development Cooperation and contains a number of provisions to that effect.

Art. 177 ECT heralds these provisions and sets out the general *objectives* of Community policy in the field of development cooperation. The objective of fostering economic and social development of the developing countries contained in para. 1, I is a well-suited basis for the accompanying measures referred to above in the field of immigration.

Art. 178 sets out an obligation for the Community to take account of the objectives referred to in the preceding provision when implementing policies that are likely to affect developing countries. This provision establishes a *link* between Development Cooperation and Title IV measures, especially those related to immigration; as immigration policies are very likely to (also) affect developing countries, the Community will need to take account of the objectives set out in Art. 177 ECT.

Art. 179 contains an obligation for the Council (while acting in accordance with Art. 251 – the co-decision procedure) to take measures that are necessary to further the objectives referred to in Art. 177 – provided that these measures as to their central purpose essentially serve the objectives of Art. 177.[125]

Art. 180 in its first paragraph sets out an obligation for the Community and the Member States to coordinate their policies on development cooperation and to consult each other on their aid programmes, including in international organisations and during international conferences, providing for the possibility of un-

124 Point 29.

125 See ECJ Case C-268/94 (Portugal/Council), ECR [1996] I-6177, no. 39

dertaking joint action. In the second paragraph it provides a right for the Commission to take any useful initiative the coordination referred to in paragraph 1.

Finally, *Art. 181* contains a provision entailing an obligation for the Community and the Member States to cooperate – within their respective spheres of competence – with third countries and with the competent international organisations; there, the arrangements for Community cooperation may be the subject of agreements between the Community and the third parties concerned, which shall be negotiated and concluded in accordance with Art. 300, while Member States will still remain competent to negotiate in international bodies and to conclude international agreements. Art. 181, therefore constitutes an important basis for the *modes of elaboration of* any *agreement* concluded between the Community and third countries with a view to complementing the measures in the field of immigration.

The legal basis for the conclusion by the Community of so-called *association agreements*, i.e. agreements that involve reciprocal rights and obligations as well as common action and special procedure, is set out in *Art. 310* of the ECT. Therefore, this competence norm will be central for the Community when concluding agreements of association or cooperation with clauses on the joint management of migration flows, as envisaged in the Seville Presidency Conclusions,[126] to which reference will be made below again.

All the above provisions refer to external action by the Community and are of central importance when the deployment of a comprehensive strategy in the field of immigration and asylum in cooperation with third countries, and, in particular developing countries, is at issue. They might be regarded as *external* complements to (or: complementary external components of) EU immigration policy.

The provisions on a Common Foreign and Security Policy contained in Title V of the EUT, on the other hand, could then be referred to as *internal* complements to (the complementary internal components of) that policy, insofar as they refer to the security of the Union, security being regarded as a key-condition for the Community freedoms to be operable and for migration to be governed by a stable framework.

Art. 11 of the EUT contains the *objectives* of the CFSP to be defined and implemented by the Union – here, we are in the field of public international law. The elements in paragraph 1 – safeguarding the common values, fundamental interests, independence and integrity of the Union in conformity with the principles of the United Nations Charter (para. I); strengthening the security of the

126 Conclusions of the Spanish Presidency, Seville, 21 and 22 June 2002, p.10, no. 33.

Union (para. II), of promoting international cooperation (para. III) and of developing and consolidating democracy and the rule of law and respect for human rights and fundamental freedoms (para. IV) – are relevant to any measure taken under the Third Pillar (public international law) with a view to enhancing security within the territory of the Union; that might well include measures against illegal immigration, trafficking in human beings.

The *methods and instruments* by means of which these objectives should be pursued are set out in *Art. 12* EUT which mentions the definition of principles and general guidelines for the CFSP; the decision on common strategies; the adoption of joint actions, the adoption of common positions and the strengthening of systematic cooperation between Member States in the conduct of policy.

V. European Immigration Policy Based on the Model of Freedom of Goods

From the above it became quite clear that at the moment the EU cannot be described as a real fortress. Firstly, this is because there are a lot of open gates for *legal* immigration into the EU, which can be passed by the "community link", on the basis of special agreements with third countries or for reasons of humanity (asylum, refugees). And second there seem to be a lot of loopholes in the walls of the fortress with regard to *illegal* immigration. The EU is insofar not able to close the loopholes and to safeguard the fortress efficiently.

With regard to the future it seems therefore necessary, that Europe becomes a kind of "Open Fortress": In order to fight illegal immigration, Europe has to become a fortress, well guarded and without loopholes. This is the precondition for open gates concerning legal immigration. Establishing this kind of controlled legal immigration is for several reasons of importance for the EU: While Europe's population is growing older and many EU Member States are experiencing a continued shortage of labour in a number of sectors and at different skill levels, an increasing number of people have in recent years wanted to migrate to Europe either on a temporary or on a permanent basis. Insofar the EU has interests of its own. Moreover the EU has a certain ethical responsibility – flowing from its values [Art. 6 (1) EUT] – to open a gate for asylum-seekers, refugees, displaced persons and those in search of temporary protection as well as family members coming to join migrants already settled in the EU.

To a certain extent the mentioned aspects of a future immigration policy correspond with the model (outlined at the beginning) of the freedom of goods: The strong walls of the fortress, which serve the aim of preventing illegal immigration, are similar to the quite efficient system of the customs-union as designed in

Art. 23 (1) and 27 ECT. By Art. 23 (2) and 24 ECT is ensured that once a foreign product has legally (customs are paid; all due import duties are fulfilled) passed the common external boarder and entered the Internal Market of the Community it is treated exactly the same way as if it has been produced within the EC. By virtue of Art. 23 (2) ECT any third-country-product is consequently treated as an EU-product, that profits without any difference from the free circulation in the Internal Market. Since the Internal Market according to Art. 14 (2) ECT is based on the Four Freedoms, the non-discriminatory-principle (Art. 28 ECT) is applicable on the third-country product. Exactly this model might be a guideline for the framing of a transparent Immigration Policy: If a person has legally passed the gate into the EU, he or she participates in the Internal Market. With regard to Art. 14 (2) ECT and the freedom of persons, he or she has not only the right of free circulation in the EU, but also the right to be treated like an EU citizen, the non-discriminatory-principle as laid down in Art. 39, 43 and 49 ECT becomes applicable. The third-country-national takes part in the Internal Market like an EU citizen, he has all economic rights guaranteed by the Four Freedoms, including the connected family rights and social rights. Already now – as the mentioned ECJ-decisions with regard to European-Agreements and Association-Agreements have shown – the non-discrimination-principle applies under certain conditions on third-country nationals. This means at the same time that the third-country-national cannot enjoy the rights of EU citizenship as laid down in Art. 17-21 ECT. Moreover, since the Art. 23 (2) ECT-Model applies only for the entry into the Internal Market, a third-country-national who is unemployed (and therefore cannot rely on the Four Freedoms) has – after a certain time-period of job seeking – the obligation to leave the EU, except when he has an asylum or refugee status.

It is quite interesting, that the above mentioned aspects and (planned) measures in the context of EU-Immigration-Policy already correspond to a large extent to the outlined model. This counts for the rules on family reunification as well as for some social rights. Actors at the EU-level now seem to be determined to treat immigration and asylum matters as priority issues, dedicating a great deal of efforts to develop a new consistent and effective policy in the field, paying due respect to the multi-dimensional nature of the field with its legal, social, cultural and economic impacts. Clear principles in economic and in human rights respects seem to be present in most measures proposed or already adopted. There is a good chance that at the end of the 5-year transitional period after the entry into force of the ToA, the full programme of measures will have been achieved and Title IV will have become – to the extent possible – fully communitarised.

Of course it is necessary to put the model in more concrete terms. For example it is to be decided under which conditions a third-country-national is allowed to pass the gate into the EU. This is not as easy as it is with Arts. 23 (2), 24 ECT. With regard to the national labour markets there might be immigration-quotas as well as restrictions with regard to the free circulation in the Internal Market; with regard to asylum- and refugee-status there have to be developed common guidelines and criteria. For example there may be time limits with regard to the free circulation in the Internal Market, especially at the moment the third-country-national is unemployed. Next question to be answered is, who should decide on the conditions for entry, the EU or Member States? As we have seen from the above outlined aspects, European Immigration Policy is a complex subject and a big challenge for the EU and its Member States. But in order to establish a transparent and coherent system for the developing Immigration Policy all arising questions should be answered on the basis of the model that refers, after the entry into the EU (based on Art. 23 (2) ECT), to the well established principles of the freedom of persons. In this context these principles are not necessarily direct applicable to third-country nationals, they could also be a guideline for the community legislator in his efforts to establish a transparent and coherent system for European Immigration Policy.

DISCUSSION

The discussion was started by Mr Weber, who asked whether it was possible to compare free movement of persons with free movement of goods. He stressed that the Right of free movement of persons is more related to the subjects of international Human Rights. Mr. von Hoffmann agreed that the issue of immigration had to be seen in the light of Human Rights obligations. Mr. Calliess replied that he chose the comparison of free movement of goods with free movement of persons as a theoretical concept. The juridical model of the free movement of goods would be a very open as well as a simple one and could thus be a kind of archetype for a Right of free movement of third-country nationals. The model of free movement of goods as it is stated in the ECT is a juridical idea how the EU can pave the way for third-country nationals to move within or in the territory of the European Union.

Ms. Apap did not agree that in practice the model of free movement of goods can be applied to the free movement of persons as the latter, due to the complexity of the human factor, the social attachments a person develops to the territory they are on, human rights issues, etc. cannot viewed in pure "commodity" terms.

Regarding the *Carpenter* case, Ms. Langenfeld mentioned the Principle of Subsidiarity as it is codified in Art. 5 ECT and asked what role this principle can play in EU immigration policy, regarding that the admission of migrants more or less belongs to the field of intergovernmental co-operation between the Member States.

Mr. Calliess replied that the importance of the subsidiarity provision in Art. 5 (2) ECT will fully come to bear after a five year transitional period and the unanimity requirement set out in the ECT is abolished.

Mr. Weber stated that it would be less necessary to harmonize immigration policy, than the policy of the labour market. It would make no sense to harmonize the immigration policy of the Member States because of the Principle of Subsidiarity.

Ms. Oellers-Frahm – being an international public lawyer – quoted that one also has to consider international treaties and agreements, which provide for rights to immigrants though not being harmonized on the European level.

Next, Mr. Werner mentioned that when discussing the problems of immigration between the EU Member States, the differences between theory and practice has to be considered. In fact there would not be so many movements of third-country nationals from one EU Member State into another. He took as an example a Turk, living in Munich and usually having no need to move to Frankfurt or to another Member State, once his centre of life is established in Munich. Considering this, the need to establish a Right of free movement for third-country nationals was not obvious. Mr. Weber replied, that the reason for the low migration movements of third-country nationals were, that this freedom is not granted to this group. This point was later agreed by Mr. von Hoffmann.

Ms. Medved stated that there is a need to establish a right of Free Movement for Third-country-nationals. Although movement of third-country-nationals may not be high, there have been some cases of such movements recently reported from Sweden to the United Kingdom. The reason was mainly that highly qualified immigrants could not find appropriate jobs in Sweden or even remained unemployed. This in turn made the Swedish pay more attention to the problem of insufficiently used immigrants' skills potential as well as discrimination in the labour market

According to Ms. Oellers-Frahm, questions about the considerations of provisions in the field of International Law in EU immigration policy, Mr. Calliess agreed that the European Community has obligations deriving from international treaties such as the European Convention on Human Rights and the Geneva Convention on Refugees. The WTO treaty however, would not play an important role regarding the here discussed topic as the Right of free movement of persons is hardly regulated in WTO law.

II. IMMIGRATION AND LABOUR MARKET

Anastasios Bisopoulos[1]

IMMIGRATION AND LABOUR MARKET POLICIES IN THE EUROPEAN UNION:

WHAT PROSPECTS AND WHAT POLICIES?

A CHALLENGE EUROPE IS FACING TODAY

I. Introduction

Immigration has become an important but controversial issue in the EU. Some blame it for unemployment and increasing inequality but wiser policy makers see that it can contribute to easing the problems from Europe's ageing population. Both approaches may exaggerate to some extent but such conflicting attitudes to immigration need to gradually converge into a coherent perspective and the EU is already advancing fast in this direction.

Immigration is a recurring theme in economic development, which appears under different conditions. Eventual gaps in this debate need to be filled in order to provide orientations for the current and future social policies. This paper will attempt to examine some of the current challenges related to immigration. The workshop to which this paper was presented was an very fruitful opportunity to exchange ideas with the participants and to think of the most appropriate replies to the challenges of immigration. The paper cannot present the full picture of this complex policy debate where every detail matters. It will focus on critical aspects that require further analysis. Radical answers to the challenges ahead cannot be conceived before further research underpins the efforts and the achievements so far.

II. Main Principles

Since 1997 the European Union has embarked in a major effort to increase employment. Full employment, combined with stable economic growth, should be reached by the year 2010. However, even if this target is fully met, the ageing of the working population in Europe will cause a shrink in total employment and a

1 The content of this paper is the responsibility of the author and does not reflect the opinion of the European Commission.

reduction in the growth potential of the economy. Managing migratory flows might represent one solution. There are parallel and to some extent overlapping ways to keeping the growth potential of the economy for instance by increasing productivity through technology. This paper will try to see aspects of the debate on the demographic change mostly relevant to immigration.

The main argument of the paper is that if Europe manages to deal effectively with immigrants and immigration flows it will increase its ability to deal with the ongoing and the future economic and social transformations.

Immigration offers many potential benefits to the economy, but those are not going to appear automatically. Migrants need to actively participate in the recipient economy for these benefits to be reaped. Experience of EU countries indicates that often the potential offered by the migrants' population is not realized and immigrants remain for long in the margins of the labour market and aggravate existing problems. It is worth noting that many second-generation immigrants in EU countries end up more "marginalized" than their parents. Immigrants need to be integrated in the society by actively participating in the existing adaptation systems. Failings in their integration may have unwanted consequences in the future.

Successful integration of immigrants in the society is a prerequisite for both social cohesion and economic efficiency. Integration strategies should combat social exclusion and discrimination and promote full access to education and training. Learning from existing good practice as well as taking into account the impact on countries of origin are important principles to be taken into account.

The impact of immigration in the countries of origin is important but often it is given less attention. The remittances transmitted by the immigrants to their countries of origin often represent considerable amounts.[2] However, the correct estimation of these amounts is difficult. It usually comes from the statistics on balance of payments in the hosts and the countries of origin. There are also several unofficial methods for the transfer of funds by the immigrants that are never reported officially.

The main immediate effect from remittances is that they considerably improve the living conditions in the immigrants' families. Often such transfers are invested in housing or in the services sector. The extent to which immigration and remittances contribute to the development of both the host and the countries of

---

2 In 1999 such transfers for Morocco represented 21% of goods and services exported. Djajic. (1986) as reported in Cahiers francais 307, mars-avril 2002.
As the Economist reported (2.11.02) Albania is receiving from remittances amounts which correspond to 75% of its exports on goods and services.

origin need to be better documented especially if immigrants move permanently. Therefore immigration needs to be examined also in conjunction with development aspects in both the host and the countries of origin.

To that end a very recent Communication indicates that the Commission during the 2003 review of the strategy documents linking the EU to third countries is going to examine immigration as a priority issue with possible increase of funding for related activities such as the combat of illegal immigration.[3]

III. Some of the Key Questions

It is one thing to recognise the importance that immigration can play in Europe's destiny but quite another to classify the numerous problems, and to attempt resolving some of them. The European Union is working to establish a more coherent framework on this issue and it is hoped that a more comprehensive picture will emerge.

Immigration, however, will probably stay at the forefront of the political debate in the years to come. There are so many pressing questions not easily answered which will need to be researched, discussed, and agreed upon amongst the Member States before a common understanding emerges.

How best would Member States estimate their needs in immigrant workers and what would be the impact of immigration in the actual structure of their labour markets?

Which are the most appropriate policies or measures for the management of immigration flows as well as for the economic assimilation of immigrants and their offspring?

What are the links between immigration and undeclared work and how can we reduce illegal work among immigrants?

What are the actual short and long term effects of immigration on the countries of origin and how could we help immigrants to increase their contribution to their countries of origin?

These are just a few of the questions that need to be considered. What is more difficult is that such questions cannot be easily analysed as separate issues. Whether someone is looking for the reasons for immigration or its impact on the societies concerned, the economic, social or political aspects seem inseparable.

---

3 Agence Europe, 3.12.02.

To put it differently, the impact of immigration on economic development cannot be separated from aspects of human rights or asylum, from political and economic development in the countries of origin or from social cohesion and the future of welfare state in host countries.

Migration is not a new phenomenon but recent trends show that although the EU still hosts a migrant population relatively smaller than the one in the US, the growth rate in the flows has been significant, especially for some countries. These growing flows, combined with the challenges posed by an ageing population and concerns about skills shortages, direct the debate to the expected benefits. The expected benefits of migration, particularly in the European labour markets, and how those benefits could be harnessed better will help in answering some of these pressing questions.

IV. What Benefits from Immigration?

Migration offers potential benefits under a variety of profiles, ranging from the fiscal side, to creating a demand stimulus, increasing availability of goods and possibly stimulating the spread of knowledge developing new competitive advantages. As an increase in the labour supply, and a relief to shortages in particular sectors, its impact is particularly visible in the labour market. This is an area on which extreme positions on the consequences of migration have been voiced, and where reviewing and reassessing available evidence can enrich the debate. On balance empirical assessments find that the negative impact of migration on existing workers is minimal if at all existent. It might be noticeable, however, for well-defined groups such as the recently settled and less skilled immigrants. At the same time, the evidence does not leave space for complacency as it shows that reaping the full benefits of increased migration crucially hinges on addressing issues of inclusion and economic integration.

Although some of the less skilled may lose from immigration, natives benefit from it because there are production complementarities between immigrant workers and natives. Immigrants are often willing to work on jobs that have become unpopular with natives allowing them to investigate opportunities in another part of the job market. Even where that is not the case, immigrants may increase productivity of the native workers. They free up their time and allow natives to devote themselves to activities where they are most productive.

Immigrants can lower prices of several goods and services benefiting the economy. They help with household work, with care of children and the elderly and with agriculture. Their impact in construction work is important particularly their contribution to keeping housing and construction work prices at reasonable level. However, their potential is not fully exploited and they are vulnerable to cyclical fluctuation in the economy as the next brief examination of their position in the EU labour markets suggests.

V. The Position of Non-EU Nationals in the Labour Market

As the chart below shows, non-nationals are at a disadvantage with respect to national EU citizens in terms of employment rate (52% compared to 64%). In Greece, Spain and Italy, however, the employment rate of non-EU nationals is above the one for EU nationals. In these countries non-EU nationals are concentrated in low-skilled sectors such as agriculture and construction.

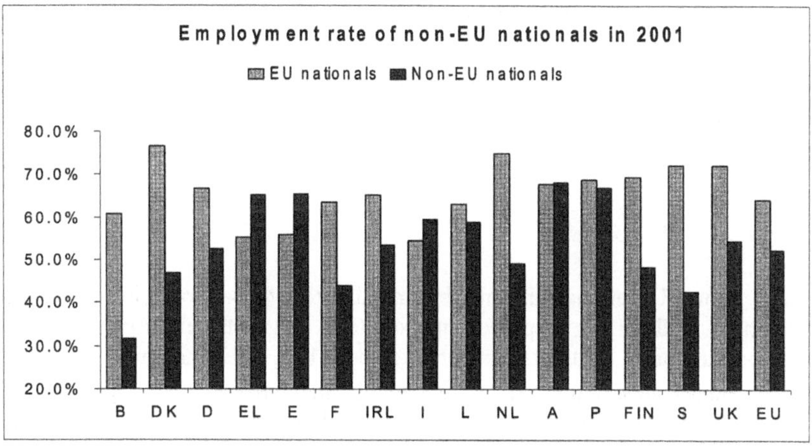

Source: *LFS, Eurostat*

In contrast, non-EU nationals are more disadvantaged in employment terms in Denmark, Sweden and Belgium, with employment rates at about 30 percentage points below their EU national counterparts. Moreover, non-EU nationals find it harder to find work in Belgium, France, Finland and Sweden where their unemployment rates are substantially higher than for EU nationals.

These gaps tend to close with permanence in Member States, but this type of evolution and its differences across countries might be influenced by different legislative frameworks, particularly on incentives for the regularisation of illegal immigrants.

In the next table, for the year 2001 when considering employment performance by skill levels, low-skilled non-EU nationals appear to have comparable employment rates to EU nationals (45% versus 50%), while much higher gaps characterise the high skilled (66% versus 83%).

	B	DK	D	EL	E	F	IRL	I	L	NL	A	P	FIN	S	UK	EU
	Employment rate for high skilled (having completed tertiary education)															
Non-EU nationals	49.4%	54.5%	64.5%	68.5%	74.5%	57.2%	67.6%	63.9%	71.0%	68.2%	79.9%	95.0%	58.9%	55.0%	74.8%	65.8%
EU nationals	84.4%	87.9%	84.0%	79.3%	76.1%	80.1%	86.3%	81.6%	84.5%	87.2%	86.6%	89.8%	85.7%	83.7%	88.2%	83.3%
	Employment rate for low skilled (less than upper secondary education)															
Non-EU nationals	26.8%	44.7%	45.6%	63.7%	62.2%	38.8%	33.4%	57.3%	55.5%	40.0%	58.5%	66.7%	37.6%	35.6%	33.5%	44.9%
EU nationals	41.6%	59.6%	44.8%	47.6%	51.1%	47.2%	49.0%	44.3%	50.7%	62.3%	45.2%	67.8%	49.6%	56.6%	52.8%	49.2%
	Percentage of employees of working age in fixed-term contracts															
Non-EU nationals	18.5%	18.6%	17.0%	21.8%	58.2%	20.8%	4.5%	11.2%	7.5%	32.4%	8.8%	55.6%	32.5%	35.3%	17.9%	20.2%
EU nationals	8.6%	9.3%	12.2%	12.3%	31.2%	14.7%	3.6%	9.5%	4.2%	13.8%	8.1%	19.7%	17.8%	13.9%	6.3%	13.0%

Source: *LFS, Eurostat*

Finally, non-EU nationals are more vulnerable to cyclical conditions as a large proportion of them are employed in fixed-term contracts. In 2001, about 20% were on fixed-term contracts compared to about 13% of EU nationals.

As the tables have indicated, current employment patterns of migrants show lower employment rates than those for nationals in most Member States – particularly for high skilled workers, pointing to problems of integration of those workers in our productive systems.

In order for Europe to take advantage of the benefits in terms of effective labour supply and productivity that migration offers, a range of options needs to be considered. For instance migrants' needs in acquiring skills complementary to those they hold (such as language) and information on local labour markets can be addressed. Furthermore, existing migrants often enter low value added and non-dynamic sectors, where barriers of entry and capital needs are low. Measures to encourage skills upgrading and reinforce entrepreneurship for migrants and nationals in those sectors should be considered as aiming towards raising productivity and furthering integration. Finally, the role played by existing migrants community as a vehicle for integration of new migrants should be considered.

VI. Taking Advantage of the Benefits of Migration

Despite the potential that migration offers in terms of relieving pressures and constraints on the labour market and contributing to productivity growth, these benefits are not automatic. How to take advantage of the potential offered by migrants is therefore a central policy question. As the available evidence shows, migrants often have lower employment rates than nationals and significant differentials, sometimes persistent over time, characterise their wages. These different performances might reflect either discrimination or different endowments of crucial assets for the successful integration into the labour market. Lack of qualification seems indeed to explain a large part of this gap.

The prioritisation of the policy options is important and politically sensitive. One is to apply selective policies for entry into the country or at least incentives for high skilled migration. An increasing number of Member States is following this approach, though its results might fall short of expectations due to the comparative size of skilled and unskilled flows. A second type of policy option focuses, in contrast, on favouring the integration of migrants in the labour market by helping them building up host-country specific human capital, as well as acquiring information on local labour markets. Both these policies are equally important and can be implemented simultaneously if necessary. However, some political parties tend to focus more on one or the other of the approaches with controversial results. Elements from both options are useful and the socio-economic complexities of immigration does not allow for single-minded solutions.

A central element for both economic and social integration is the acquisition of language, particularly in economies increasingly characterised by service activities which largely rely on interpersonal communication. The benefits of pursuing such policies of integration in the labour market and of putting in place appropriate educational systems for the needs of new migrant communities are also to be assessed against a background of underperformance of second generation migrants. This can be explained by problems of exclusion. Living in neighbourhoods characterised by high migrant concentration can be linked to underperformance of national young generations, due for example to low quality of schooling and more generally of infrastructure.

VII. Labour Market Needs and Immigration

The European Employment Strategy can be very effective in dealing with labour market shortages in areas where significant unemployment still exists despite the efforts in the European Union since 1997. Immigration can play a role in this context, especially as the broader results of the Strategy might take time to materialise. As a Commission's communication states, while migration cannot provide the answer to the demographic decline or skills gaps in the EU, well-designed economic migration can make a contribution to solving future labour shortages, increasing employment and economic growth.[4] Indications in this sense are also confirmed by the Communication on an open method of coordination for the community immigration policy. The admission of economic migrants for economic purposes should, as far as possible, be done in partnership with the country of origin and within the framework of the European employment strategy. In this sense Member States will need to ensure that the procedures in place to implement the European employment strategy are suitable to deal with the contribution that migrants can make to the labour market. In parallel the fight against illegal immigration needs to be intensified. To that end migration flows should be managed in accordance with the law and in cooperation with the countries of origin.[5]

Finally, the links between immigration and enlargement should be studied further as both are crucial for the development of social and labour market policies. A Commission's study found that migrant inflows from the CCs will be limited. It estimated that some 335.000 persons expected to immigrate from the CCs during the enlargement process. However, this estimation did not include Turkey.[6]

VIII. Facing the Main Challenges

Business leaders regularly report their increasing difficulties to fill job vacancies in their businesses with the appropriate personnel. Labour shortages and skills gaps are often the result of the ongoing structural reforms in the European economy. They represent wasted opportunities for growth even when they are not noticeable at the aggregate level (shortages in the context of unemployment). Addressing them would increase the overall efficiency of the system as well as possibly having a stabilising effect on the business cycle.

---

4 (COM (2002) 416 final).

5 See Part III of the Seville European Council conclusions, on Asylum and Immigration.

6 The Impact of Eastern Enlargement on Employment and Labour Markets in the EU Member States – DIW report, 22.5.2000 http://europa.eu.int/comm/dgs/employment_social/key_en.htm.

The emergence of these shortages could become more widespread in the future, particularly due to the evolution of labour supply, as made clear by existing forecasts on the demographic evolution. Demographic trends such as Europe's ageing population also represent a challenge for the sustainability of the current pension systems.

From the '90s several EU Commission initiatives have started to deal with the complex problems which immigration brings. On labour shortages, one Communication from the Commission is of particular importance. It attempts to use the main instruments of the open method of co-ordination in migration. This method had a profound influence on policy-making at the national level in policy areas outside the "aquis communaitaire". Labour market policy is one area where the European Employment strategy is the most successful implementation example of this method. Migration needs to be seen, however, in the framework of a broader strategy encompassing:

- mobilising the labour force by promoting participation particularly for groups such as women and older workers, as agreed at the Laeken European Council.
- increasing mobility within the Member States with a comprehensive strategy centred on increasing occupational mobility, as well as geographic mobility and improving the quality of information on mobility and individual sectors, as emphasised by the "*Commission's Action Plan for skills and mobility*".[7]
- enhancing investment in human capital with a wide spectrum of policy tools (in order?) to lead to a general upgrading of qualifications to support productivity growth, international competitiveness, the reduction of disparities between regions and social cohesion in the enlarged Union.
- targeting members of the migrants communities already established in Europe e.g. second and third generation migrants. Integration implies that immigrants participate in occupational and regional mobility as well as in training and education including special training where needed. In this way they will enhance their contribution to productivity growth. Integration of members of the immigrants' communities in Europe should have important benefits both for a more efficient working of the labour markets and for social cohesion. The ESF will have a significant role to play with National programmes as well as with Community initiatives. Important gender and

7 [COM (2002) 72 final]. The implementation of the new regulation "1408" should facilitate this mobility in the case of migrant workers.

age dimensions might be involved in the activation of these groups of workers.

IX. Additional Migration

However, labour mobilisation might not be the only answer to the emerging job vacancies and skills gap, particularly in the short term. Additional migratory flows, particularly by high skilled individuals with critical competencies, could play a crucial role in removing bottlenecks. Member States are already recurring to this type of migrants and these flows should be encouraged. The possibility of offering an extension of their stay to students from third countries should be particularly considered.

The possibility of favouring short-term migration for the purpose of facing cyclical labour gaps should also be considered and reports in the press indicate that during the Greek presidency of the European Council in the first semester of 2003 there will be relevant initiatives. This type of immigration could concern workers with a variety of skills and skill levels. Care should be taken to discuss such policy developments with the social partners to facilitate social acceptance. There is an objective basis for taking such measures as the effects of immigration on wage and employment of national workers are limited and overall positive.

Two issues related to short term migration deserve further consideration: the analysis of trans-frontier mobility within trans-national firms regarding third-country nationals and how legal short term immigration might contribute to the fighting against undeclared work.

X. Assessment of Past Experience With Migratory Flows

The complexities and the peculiarities of migration ask for elaborate policy mixes and ample implementation experience. Such experience exists in the European Union, with Germany offering a lot of comprehensive good practice on immigration matters.

An assessment of this experience and the extent to which it has contributed to the shape of the social and economic outlook of recipient countries – as well as that of the countries of origin- is the basis of future policy orientations.

In particular, factors underpinning the successful integration of migrants need to be explored. They include the entrepreneurial successes of immigrants, their ability to generate jobs, their degree of economic integration with the rest of the population and the nature of their links with countries of origin. Furthermore, past experience with the encouragement of temporary flows should also be assessed as well as the link between illegal immigration and the shadow economy. Finally, such an assessment should keep in mind that future migratory flows could be different in qualitative terms from the past ones. Limitations on entry for economic migrants and emphasis on family reunion entry might have selected a migrant population with different characteristics (in terms of education, labour market participation etc.) from the ones which a managed approach to economic migration could obtain.

XI. Some Replies to the Challenges

The demographic developments in our societies have already started to have an effect, but as time goes by they will become more visible. A more balanced and forward looking approach to immigration is needed to face the economic implications of the socio-democratic changes.

Immigration alone cannot provide a solution for all the challenges raised by the demographic change. Promoting labour participation, increasing productivity through investment in human capital and increasing the share of investment abroad in the context of an ageing population will remain priorities for the EU in order to reach its objectives of increased employment, social cohesion and economic growth. However, there is a growing recognition that immigration is likely to contribute positively to such objectives, provided it is properly managed.

The current EU framework already offers a diversity of instruments (e.g. coordination of immigration policies, European Employment Strategy, anti-discrimination package, social inclusion process, extension of Regulation 1408/71 to third-country nationals) that directly affect the situation of immigrants.

A balanced policy mix must continue to be developed in order to improve employment and social integration of immigrants and their offspring. This requires continuous vigilance in front of the challenges so that:

- immigration is better taken into account under the European Employment Strategy
- the existing and improving legal framework facilitates the migration flows required for the development of the EU economy.
- greater attention is given to settled and arriving immigrants under social inclusion, social protection and anti-discrimination policies. More immigration will require more efforts at integration.

- the social partners integrate immigration in their dialogue
- education policies are revisited to take better account of the changing profiles of the school population
- the structure and management of public finances is reviewed to take account of the growing importance of immigration
- the EU structural funds take full account of the challenge of immigration in terms of jobs and social inclusion
- external policy and in particular development policy address the implications for the countries of origin in order to achieve an equitable sharing of costs and benefits of immigration.

The opening of new legal channels for the entry of a variety of economic migrants would be a necessary part of a future oriented strategy for growth employment and sustainable social protection. But the economic and social benefits of immigration remain predicated on achieving a substantially higher degree of successful integration of migrants.

As the press reports at the time of drafting the final version of this paper, the Presidency of the EU in the first semester of 2003 has announced that it will take on board immigration as one of its main issues of its agenda. The links between immigration and growth, the integration of legal immigrants and the fight against illegal immigration will be amongst the main priorities of the EU Presidency. To this end and on the basis of the Seville Conclusions the Presidency indends to pursue an integrated strategy for immigration which will take into account most of the challenges presented in this paper. It is expected that the European Council in Thessaloniki 2003 will, among other issues, examine the results of the implementation of the Seville Conclusions. Therefore it is expected to be a landmark event on the matters of immigration.

Selected References

European Commission, Employment in Europe. The reports of the recent years. Particularly the 2002 report.

The Impact of Eastern Enlargement on Employment and Labour Markets in the EU Member States – Final Report, 22/05/2000, http://europa.eu.int/comm/dgs/employment_social/key_en.htm.

COM/2002/416 final, 17-7-2002. Communication from the Commission to the Council, the European Parliament, the Economic and Social Committee and the Committee of the Regions – Taking stock of five years of the European Employment Strategy.

COM (2002) 72 final , 13-2-2002. Communication from the Commission to the Council and the European Parliament on a Commission's Action Plan for skills and mobility".

COM/2001/0387 final, 11-7-2001, Communication from the Commission to the Council and the European Parliament on an open method of co-ordination for the community immigration policy.

Les Cahiers français, no 307, Mars-avril 2002, Les migrations internationales.

To BHMA, 29-12-02, Greek Newspaper.

DISCUSSION

Ms. Medved began the discussion. She raised the question in how far the EU has bilateral agreements (partnerships) with countries of origin of economic migrants, compensating them for the "Brain Drain" and how the EU Commission views the latter concept in this context. Mr. Bisopoulos reported apart from the ongoing discussions in the WTO on the trade in services – immigration is concerned in Mode 4 of these discussions – technical assistance for these countries was in fact mainly provided by EU partnerships. He stressed that in this context the EU was the biggest donor in the world and provides far more assistance than the US. However, the latter publicized its donations more than the EU did and therefore received more public attention. In addition, higher wages motivated more skilled migrants to emigrate to the US instead of Europe.

Mr. Münz then made several clarifying remarks regarding the statistics and figures Mr. Bisopolous had used to illustrate the relation of the European to the US net migration rate over the last decades. He reported that although the US was trying to enforce exit controls on other countries, they were completely unwilling to do exit controls itself. Therefore, the US had no idea how many people emigrated from their country. Consequently, the figures given by the US as migration rate in fact only indicated the gross immigration to the US.

Hereon, Ms. Medved asked for Mr. Münz's estimation for the US net migration rate. He replied that it could only be traced back after a census, but assumed that the real net migration would be some 20-30 % below the given figures. Hence, the discrepancy in immigration between the US and Europe was much smaller than it looked in the statistics.

Additionally, Mr. Münz remarked that US and EU statistics were based on different systems. The US counted only Green Card holders and refugees as immigrants, whereas the great number of former immigrants were nationalized. Furthermore a student or an employee, for example, who stayed with an H1B-Visa for 4-6 years would not appear in US immigration statistics. The EU, not collecting migration data of its own, would have to rely on the figures provided by the Member States, whose statistical systems differ from each other and from that of the US. He illustrated this by giving an example from Germany: in German statistics even Polish seasonal workers who only came over to work for some 90 days are counted as immigrants, and later on as emigrants, while the US does not count seasonal workers at all. He concluded that therefore the given EU migration rates could only be compared to the US data with caution.

Mr. Münz added that, depending on the employment level and the age structure some European countries had more alternatives to make up for the expected decline of the labour force by bringing in more women in and by extending the employment rate or the working age. Others had fewer alternatives because they already had high labour force participation rates and would therefore have to rely on foreign labour. Therefore, according to Mr. Münz, immigration policy was more important to countries that already had high labour force participation rates, e.g. Switzerland and the Scandinavian countries in contrast to e.g. the Greece and Italy where the labour force participation rates are rather low. He stressed that due to these differences there could be no "one-size-fits-all"-migration and recruitment policy for all individual Member States.

Mr. von Hoffmann then brought up the question when exactly the decline of labour force, predicted by Mr. Bisopoulos in his speech, would occur. He stated that the present discussion concerning this critical "Day X" was too abstract. A fixed date should be predicted to put pressure on the political establishment responsible for adequate counter measures. Mr. Münz, having been a member of the "Süssmuth Commission" (an ad hoc commission set up by the German government to develop new immigration concepts), agreed that indeed many political decisions were short sighted, for the next 2 years at the most, with an eye on the next elections, a method which might have severe consequences in this case. He added that the coming decline of the labour force would occur at different times in the individual Member States, depending on the respective demographic situation. Some countries would have to face the problem earlier, e.g. Italy and Greece, because the fertility rate was already very low in these countries, and there still was the big "Baby Boom Generation" growing older. Therefore, individual solutions for each country were necessary. However, the problem still concerned all of Europe.

Furthermore, European countries had to realise that sooner or later they would become competitors on a world market of professional migrants, Mr. Münz continued. They already were in a competition with the US and Canada that they had not taken up yet. But this would be realized soon. Then appropriate measures would have to be taken to fight Germany's/Europe's negative image among highly skilled migrants. While refugees would like to come over any time, enjoying Europe's typical social benefits, those economic migrants were rather attracted by the American melting pot and American Dollars. In his opinion, this image problem will have to be addressed soon by the European Member States.

Joanna Apap

SHAPING EUROPE'S MIGRATION POLICY:

A COMPARATIVE ANALYSIS OF MEMBER STATES' "GREEN CARD" LEGISLATION:

A COMPARISON OF STRATEGIES IN GERMANY, SWEDEN, THE NETHERLANDS AND THE UK

I. Introduction: An Historical Overview

During the 1990s, Justice and Home Affairs moved, in an unexpected way, to centre stage in the European debate. Concern had been growing about immigration policy since the Maastricht Treaty institutionalised the third pillar of the European Union. This concern had been stimulated by several factors – the persistence of irregular migration and tragic incidents, such as the one in Dover in July 2000 in which 58 Chinese nationals lost their lives trying to enter illegally into the United Kingdom, the need for immigrant workers in some sectors, and the spectre of an ageing European population. More generally, the Treaty of Amsterdam, since its entry into force in 1999, represents a major development in overall Justice and Home Affairs policy, and the implementation of the treaty provisions in Justice and Home Affairs was described as the next major EU initiative after the single currency.

Moreover, the Conclusions of the European Council in Tampere (15th and 16th October 1999) gave an additional push for the adoption of the measures considered necessary for the realisation of an area of freedom, security and justice, reaffirming traditional and integrating new principles in these fields.

In fact, the debate at European level on immigration and free movement had commenced in the early 1980s and developed in the run-up to the Schengen Agreement of 1985. A general formula was agreed in the Single European Act Art. 7a (Art. 14), which stated:

> "The internal market shall comprise an area without internal borders in which the free movement of goods, persons, services and capital is ensured in accordance to the provisions of this Treaty."

This Article gave rise to different interpretations of who has freedom of movement rights, and on the methods, including the compensatory measures involved, of implementing free movement of persons. The Single European Act did not clarify the question of the institutional framework of the compensatory measures for free movement of persons. Whilst the programme of the Commission in this area had to be carried out according to Community standards and by the Community method, some Member States considered that only the intergovernmental method was acceptable in matters at the core of national sovereignty. Progress has been made, however, in that Member States have agreed on a common approach to foreigners' rights.

Omissions and ambiguities in the Single European Act led to conflict between the Commission and certain Member States on the competence of the Community Institutions with the result that Member States decided policy by the intergovernmental method; a good example of the latter was the Schengen Agreement of 14 June 1985, followed by a Convention of 19 June 1990. Various episodes of the conflict about competence even provoked disagreement between Community Institutions. Worn down by these disputes and the systematic blocking by the Council of Ministers, the Commission for the most part conceded the intergovernmental method in the field of Justice and Home Affairs, in the hope that a pragmatic stance would make progress possible in this sensitive field. The European Parliament suffered most because it was for the most part excluded from the decision-making process.

The Maastricht Treaty signed in 1992 gave comfort to the partisans of the intergovernmental method over those who were in favour of a more communitarian/supranational approach. The new Title VI called Cooperation in the fields of Justice and Home Affairs was nothing other than the formalisation of very slightly modified intergovernmental cooperation. The policy sectors covered by Title VI were referred to simply as "matters of common interest" (Art. K.1). This weak statement of intent was scarcely developed by Art. K.3, which only stated that "Member States shall inform and consult one another within the Council with a view to coordinating their action". There was no clarification of whether Justice and Home Affairs cooperation is intended to provide for and/or encourage *legislative initiatives*, or whether practical, *operational cooperation* was the objective (Den Boer, 1996). Rather than a clear distinction between supranational or intergovernmental cooperation, the Third Pillar occupied (and, what remains of it, still occupies) a halfway house, struggling to reconcile two very different institutional patterns, neither with primacy.

In the Maastricht Treaty, Member States seemed happy to have included a reference to the principle of subsidiarity (Art. 3b [now Art. 5]). It reads that the EC shall act:

> "... only if ... the objectives of the proposed action cannot be sufficiently achieved by the Member States and can therefore, by reason of the scale or effects of the proposed action be better achieved by the Community."

With the Amsterdam Treaty (1998); the transfer of competence of the third pillar towards the first pillar seemed impressive: all the matters listed under Art. K.1 of the Maastricht Treaty were transferred to Pillar 1, except for the police and judicial cooperation in penal matters which remains in the third pillar. The new Title IV "Visas, asylum, immigration and other policies related to free movement of persons", which brings together the most important provisions, is subject to a special institutional mechanism providing for derogation on numerous points from the supranational approach (Art. 67) and allowing for a transition period – 5 years after the entry into force of the Treaty before majority voting is introduced. Policy towards third-country nationals until Amsterdam was one clear example of the limits of European integration. Amsterdam tries to address the various lacunae by assigning to the Community objectives to be achieved within a fixed timetable. Parliament may eventually be involved if the Council of Ministers accepts the co-decision procedure. Furthermore, the transfer of competence to the 1st Pillar implies recognising the authority of the European Court of Justice (ECJ) in the new areas of Community competence.

II. Supranational and National Competencies and the Status of Third-Country Nationals

In the provisions of the Treaty of Amsterdam, third-country nationals have finally found their place in Community law. Certain categories of third-country nationals already benefited from the protection of Community law. These are:

- members of the family of an EU national;
- nationals of states connected to the EU by an association or cooperation agreement;
- workers of a company on whose behalf they carry out services in another Member State (according to the Vander Elst principles).

These three categories of third-country nationals were privileged – the provisions of Community law did not cover other third-country nationals until the entry into force of the Amsterdam Treaty.

The heading of the new Title IV is significant. It does not mention a common immigration policy, but provides a partial inventory of elements of such a policy: "visas, asylum, immigration and other policies connected with free movement of persons". Whereas Art. K.1.3 of the Maastricht Treaty aimed at "immigration policy and policy with regard to third-country nationals" before listing "measures concerning immigration policy within the following areas". In three sectors (Art. 63.3), the more detailed specification of these sectors and the level of competence accorded to the EU in migration matters do not live up to the statement of the intent to introduce a comprehensive and coherent immigration policy. Also the second subparagraph of Art. 63 indicates that:

> "Measures adopted by the Council pursuant to points 3 and 4 shall not prevent any Member State from maintaining or introducing in the areas concerned national provisions which are compatible with this Treaty and with international agreements."

The tendency in recent years by the Member States to interpret restrictively the competencies of the European Union contributes to a genuine doubt about when the European level of decision-making applies. Only recourse to Art. 308 (ex Art. 235) of the Treaty makes it possible to avoid a purely intergovernmental approach, by transferring the provisions concerning immigration policy from the third to the first pillar (Hailbronner, 1998).

Despite the significant progress that the Treaty of Amsterdam represents for the European Union, it is only the beginning of a move towards a genuine European immigration policy. It remains uncertain whether, at some time in the future, it will become a supranational competence. Art. 61 stipulates that the Council will adopt «within a period of five years after the entry into force of the Treaty of Amsterdam the measures aiming to ensure free movement of persons in compliance with Art. 14 »; this illustrates the resistance of the Member States to further European integration in this field. Art. 14 is a re-statement of Art. 7 A of the (1986) Single European Act, which instituted an area without internal borders and with free movement of persons by 1st January 1993. The Treaty of Amsterdam complements the Single Market by security and justice supports for free movement. The compensatory measures intended to complement free movement of persons, alluded to in the Single European Act, became explicit in Art. 61 (a) (Amsterdam Treaty).

III. The Current Post-Amsterdam Debate

In March 2000, a very controversial report of the United Nations based on demographic considerations was published (UN Secretariat ESA/P/WP.160). Resting on the analysis of the current population trends in the world and projections for the period 1995-2050, this report pleaded for "replacement immigration" in order to compensate for the inevitable population decline in Europe and in other parts of the world. According to this report, the number of immigrants necessary to avoid a *decline of the total population* of the EU in the 50 years ahead is approximately comparable with the immigration rate of the 1990s, i.e. average annual net migration of 857000 persons. However, the report stipulates that, in order to prevent a *labour force decline*, the number of migrants entering each year should double.

The "provocative" observations of the report stimulated an intense public debate in the European press on this question, but they also contributed to re-open the issue on immigration in the European institutions and Member States at a time of reflection on how to implement the new Amsterdam provisions.

One of the first post-Amsterdam initiatives proposed by the Commission on the ground of migration is the draft Directive on the right to family reunification, submitted to the Council on 1 December 1999, but which has not been approved yet. This initiative is the first of a series of draft Directives on the admission of third-country nationals for various purposes, which represent the "communitarisation" of the draft Convention on the admission submitted by the Commission to the Council before the entry into force of the Treaty of Amsterdam. This project was followed by a draft Directive on the status of third-country nationals who are long-term residents in the Union, presented on 13 March 2001.

A proposal for a Directive dealing with the conditions of entry and residence of third-country nationals for the purpose of paid employment and self-employed economic activities has been published on 11 July 2001, the same day as the publication of a Commission Communication on an open method of coordination for the Community immigration policy. Furthermore, the Commission has prepared a draft Directive on the admission of third-country nationals for study and vocational training purposes. Two other directives approved by the Council, respectively in June and November 2000, are closely connected with the questions of migration, but deal more specifically with the fight against discrimination, racism and xenophobia.

With respect to the fight against illegal immigration and to the management of migratory flows, a particularly important instrument is the framework-decision of the Council on the fight against the trafficking of human beings which entered into force on 1st August 2002. In addition, a Communication proposal from the Commission to the Council and to the European Parliament covering the common fight against illegal immigration has been prepared and this was followed up by a Council Action Plan on fighting illegal immigration. Several proposals have also been submitted by the Member States, which share with the Commission a right to take initiatives in this field (Art. 67.1 ECT). The French Presidency, in particular, presented several initiatives in the second half of 2000 covering primarily the means of preventing and of fighting illegal immigration. The initiatives that have been approved by the Council comprise:

- the definition of the assistance at the entry, residence and the irregular stay,
- a Framework Decision on the reinforcement of the penal framework for the prevention of facilitation of unauthorised entry and the stay of third-country nationals;
- a draft Directive relating to the harmonisation of the legislation of the Member States as regards liabilities imposed to the carriers for the territory of the Member States of the nationals of third countries stripped of the documents required to be allowed there; and
- a draft Directive relating to the mutual recognition of the orders of expulsion.

Moreover, the French Presidency was particularly active to revive the general debate on immigration which had been started by the above-mentioned report of the United Nations: discussions on this subject were held at the informal ministerial meeting in Marseilles (in July 2000) and at three conferences on Co-developments and Migrants (6-7 July), on Illegal Migration Networks (20-21 July) and on the Integration of Immigrants (5-6 October).

The Commission intervened in this discussion in November 2000 with a Communication analysing the state of the debate on immigration. In this Communication on a Community immigration policy, the Commission states as a starting point that "there is a growing recognition that the "zero immigration" policies of the past thirty years are no longer appropriate" in the current economic and demographic context of the European Union and of the countries of origin, and argues for a "new approach" of immigration, according to which channels for legal immigration should be made available, especially for labour migrants.

However, the Communication clearly distances itself from the adoption of a policy of replacement migration as proposed by the UN report on Replacement Migration as a possible scenario to counteract demographic decline. The Commission believes that "while increased legal immigration in itself cannot be considered in the long term as an effective way to offset demographic changes, since migrants once settled tend to adopt the fertility patterns of the host country".

Nevertheless, it considers that many "economic migrants have been driven either to seek entry through asylum procedure or to enter illegally. This allows for no adequate response to labour market needs and plays into hands of well organised traffickers and unscrupulous employers". It stresses the need for an approach "based on the recognition that these migratory pressures will continue". Moreover, it stresses the fact that "the opening up of channels for immigration for economic purposes to meet urgent needs for both skilled and unskilled workers has already begun in a number of Member States".

In this context, the Commission underlined the need to have a "proactive" immigration policy, i.e. a policy which instead of focusing on vain attempts aiming to prevent and stop immigration by creating a "Fortress Europe", would try to control immigration according to needs of the European labour market (see the proposal of Directive of 11 July 2001).

Moreover, the Tampere Council itself stressed the need for an "approximation of national legislations on the conditions for admission and residence of third-country nationals, based on a shared assessment of the economic and demographic developments within the Union, as well as the situation in the countries of origin" (paragraph 20 of the Presidency conclusions).

The Commission does not propose any quota system on a European scale, which would be "impracticable", but rather some "indicative targets", a system based on periodic reports of the Member States, re-examining the impact of their immigration policies during the past period and making projections on the number of economic migrants they would need in future (including their qualification levels). These indicative objectives would not only take into account the labour market needs of each Member State, but also take into consideration the agreements in place with the countries of origin of the migrants, the public acceptance of additional migrant workers in the country concerned, the resources available for reception and integration, the possibilities of cultural and social adaptation, etc...

This process should take into account the development of the general employment situation in the EU, and in particular the progress achieved in the implementation of the European Strategy for employment, defined by the European Councils of Luxembourg (1997) and Lisbon (March 2000). The mechanism proposed by the Commission therefore leaves the last word on the admission of the migrants to the Member States, but the various migration policies will however be coordinated at European level.

It is obvious that the approach defended in these texts represents a clear rupture with former immigration policies on EU-level. The question is to know if Member States will follow the Commission on this way, considering the sensitivity of the question at the national level as well as the differences of approaches and policies in this field.

In presenting its proposals, the Commission intends to establish a coherent framework that would determine the basic conditions and procedures to be applied. This framework approach would be based on the following principles:

- The granting of a work permit should be simple, rational, flexible, on the basis of verifiable and objective criteria, delivered within a short time and the procedure should be transparent.

- Applicants should preferably have an employment contract or a recruiting promise. However, this should not be an obligation.
- Member States should have the possibility of establishing quotas responding to their specific needs.
- The response on the request for the work permit should be delivered in a 180-day maximum delay (although this period is certainly not optimal for industry).
- The reason for refusals should be clear.
- The work permit should not be limited to only one employer, but should be related to the sector of specialisation of the migrant worker or even to the region of his/her residence for a 3-year duration, with a possibility of prolongation.

The question of competence to grant or refuse a permit arises then: according to the principle of subsidiarity, this one should be delegated to the Member States. This will give more coherence between the employment and immigration policies.

The objective would be to give a secure legal status for temporary workers who intend to return to their countries of origin, while at the same time providing a pathway leading eventually to a permanent status for those who wish to stay and who meet a certain number of criteria.

The proposal for a Directive of 13 March 2001 on the status of third-country nationals who are long-term residents supplements the other initiatives. The idea is a differentiation of the rights according to the length of stay. The principle that the length of residence has an influence on the rights of persons has a long tradition in the Member States and is referred to in the Tampere conclusions. Within five years, they will be allowed to move freely on the territory of the Union with the aim of seeking employment in another Member State.

Migration alone is unlikely to be the answer to Europe's demographic problem. Policies for legal migration of labour can also be coupled with other less politically sensitive ways which could reduce the governments' costs of an ageing population, such as increasing labour force participation among older people and women (OECD, 2001).

IV. A Comparison of Strategies in Germany, Sweden, the Netherlands and the UK to Promote Selective Labour Migration of Third-Country Nationals

In the countries, there are clear signs that they recognise a labour shortage, particularly in specialised sectors. The four countries have tried to develop attractive packages to attract specialised labour. However, in all four cases, prior to granting the necessary permits for skilled candidates from outside the Union, it is normally necessary to show that attempts have been made to fill the position from the resident and European Economic Area (EEA) labour markets. These attempts should include advertising and the local employment service, which will run searches using the European Employment Services placement network (EURES). Usually the training of existing employees should also have been investigated.

In this section, I attempt to answer the following questions:

- Which are the main legal provisions governing the entry and residence of foreigners under the new evolving schemes?
- What are the main aims of the new provisions on employment of third-country nationals?
- What are the criteria for eligibility?
- How is the country making the scheme attractive both to the employers and to the potential employee?
- Which is the competent authority issuing/dealing with such permits?

1. Germany

In Germany, the law of 9 July 1990 governs the entry and residence of foreigners. The Ordinance Governing stays for Employment Purposes was adopted on 18 December 1990 and is the main regulatory text for recruitment of foreigners.

Over the last 2 years it was recognised that despite the general policy to limit immigration of unskilled workers, there is, however, a distinct need for qualified workers in specific areas of industry, particularly IT companies. By a decision of the Federal Government on 1 August 2000, the Green Card regulation, which is made up of ordinances regulating residence and work permits, was introduced to admit IT specialists for businesses and to address the emerging need for specialists in other industries. This marked the beginning of a new policy to regulate migration. These ordinances allow companies to employ up to 20,000 IT experts from non-EU states, to which end a fast-track procedure is applied. The foreigners concerned are also given more favourable conditions in terms of foreigners law.

According to this regulation (2000), foreign experts who have been promised or granted authorisation to work are given a residence permit for a maximum of five years – together with their spouses and minor children, as the case may be.

Apart from applications from abroad, young and upcoming foreign IT experts who have successfully obtained a degree in the field of information and communications technology, from university or higher technical colleges may also benefit from the Green Card regulation. The receivers of the Green Card could also change employers once in Germany.

This Green Card mechanism is modelled on the US green card. To qualify, the applicants must fulfil the following criteria:

- successfully obtained a degree in the field of information and communications technology, from university or higher technical colleges may also benefit from the Green Card regulation, *or* received a job offer with a gross salary of at least DM 100,000 (51,200 €),
- reside outside the European Union or the EEA, and
- have a good grasp of the German language or be able to speak English well.

On 3 August 2001, Germany's interior minister, Otto Schilly, announced an overhaul of the German immigration regulations. This revision of the regulation is designed to relax the rules for immigration for skilled staff, especially those in the IT and telecomm industries. However this was counterbalanced with a tightening of regulations for unskilled workers as well as a proposal to introduce tougher measures for asylum seekers and those under deportation orders.

The main points of this revision of the German Green Card system are as follows:

- immediate permanent residency for IT professionals and other highly skilled staff with valid job offers (to replace the 5 year Green Card).
- Points-based system for skilled immigrants without job offers (similar to the Australian system).
- immediate granting of a work permit for dependants of skilled immigrants.
- combined residence and work permit.
- automatic one-year residence permit for graduates of German universities (to be extended if the applicant finds work in this time).
- compulsory integration courses for new migrants.

The competent authority dealing with all immigration aspects is the Independent Commission on Immigration set up by the Federal Minister Schilly in September 2000. This will eventually become a Foreigners' bureau at the Federal level

Between August 2000 and August 2001 – one year since the commencement of the green card programme, 8,556 foreign computer experts have come to Germany and become green card holders so far, below the expected number of 10,000 for the planned first green card-year. Among the green card holders, Indians account for one-fifth, totalling 1,782. Some 14 percent, and 1,198 computer experts are from the former Soviet Union countries. In the third place are experts from Romania, amounting to 736. The government decided to launch the Green Card project to make up for the domestic shortfall of computer personal. Germany had some 75,000 vacant computer positions before the launch of the project.

2. *UK*

The Highly Skilled Migrant Programme (HSMP)

The Home Secretary David Blunkett announced that one of his priorities was to introduce a scheme for independent migration to the UK (Green Cards). This scheme has been put in practice since 28th January 2002 and it resembles the Australian "points based" migration scheme.

This scheme proposes a new category of permits which will allow certain individuals to be granted a permit in their own right without the need for there to be a supporting employer, provided that the individual *meets three out of the four criteria set out below.*

Their leave will be for one year in the first instance, extendible by a further three years providing the criteria continue to be met. The scheme is a pilot one, lasting for twelve months in the first instance. To qualify for it one does not need to have a concrete offer of employment.

To get a "full" work permit, one needs to score 75 points or more by meeting three of the four following criteria:

- hold a PhD or equivalent qualification;
- have five years recent graduate experience (or three years if a PhD is held), two years of which should have been at senior level;
- have been earning at least £40,000.00 (64,000 €) in the previous year or an adjusted salary which was equal to the top 5% of the wage earners in the country in which the last employment took place (the amount which is

equivalent to the top 5% of salary differs from country to country – lists explaining such can be downloaded from the British Home Office website);
- be able to demonstrate a significant achievement in their field.

The sectors experiencing labour shortages in the UK are IT, health (doctors and nurses), higher education academic staff. For one to have one's application considered, one must complete the HSMP form and the 1M2A entry form.

The foundation of the UK immigration law continues to be the Immigration Act of 1971. However, the work permit regime was subjected to a thorough review announced in November 1999 of the UK Immigration and Asylum Act 1999 (c33) – 3/4/99 main provisions.

The dependents of work permit holders are entitled to remain in the UK during the period for which the permit is valid, providing they can be supported without recourse to public funds.

The competent authority in charge of issuing such permits is the Immigration and Nationality Department of the British Home Office. The Home Office/ FCO Joint Entry Clearance Unit administers entry clearance.

3. *The Netherlands*

The Netherlands has experienced sustained growth over the past few years partly due to its favourable position within Europe and its flexible labour force. It remains an attractive country for investment and for foreign nationals to work.

Due to a recent acknowledgement by the Netherlands authorities of the shortages in some types of IT and Telecomm skills, work permit applications can be made for relevant IT/Telecomm positions without showing details of the above detailed recruitment search.

The Law governing legal residence in the Netherlands is the recent – Vreemdelingenwet (Aliens law) of 2000 which came into force on 1 April 2001. Art. 13 is the most important in this respect.

Unfortunately, the application process for Netherlands work permits often means that candidates cannot even visit the Netherlands to attend meetings while the Netherlands work permit application is being processed.

To be suitable to hold a Netherlands work permit, the candidate should be a professional and have the skill set necessary to fill a post that has already been unsuccessfully advertised in the Netherlands, or which is subject to recognised shortages. There is a legal requirement that the candidate is between 18 and 45 years of age, however it is unlikely that a candidate below 23 would have attained a skill set necessary to fill a professional position.

For nationals of all other countries not exempt from requiring a residence visa, the candidate should apply for a residence permit (MVV), which is the authorisation for temporary stay, at the Netherlands Embassy in their normal country of residence before a work permit application is made. The candidate is then prohibited from travelling to any Schengen state until a decision is made on the application.

It is important to note that on the contrary to the two previous schemes, a Netherlands work permit is employer-specific. If a candidate has a permit to work for one company, and they want to work for another Dutch company, this would not be possible – unless/until the new company has obtained another work permit. The employer also has to guarantee a salary above the minimum wage.

Unless the candidate is exempted from the MVV requirement (i.e. is a national of: Norway, Iceland, Liechtenstein, Switzerland, Japan, New Zealand, Australia, Canada or the United States), the first stage of the process involves the candidate making an application for a temporary residence permit (MVV) through his/her local Netherlands embassy. The application goes then to the Regional employment board (RBA) who approve it initially and pass it to the national employment board (AFB) who make the final decision, taking into account the national and EU labour markets. When the work permit is approved, the residence permit is issued by the embassy and the candidate may travel to the Netherlands and start work.

One attractive aspect of employing foreign nationals in the Netherlands is that many *will qualify to receive 35% of their income tax free.* The effect of this is to make the overall tax burden similar to that faced in the UK.

The Dutch Embassy has to obtain approval for the issuance of a temporary residence permit from the immigration authorities in the Netherlands. It is important that one applies for the temporary residence permit at least three months prior to one's intended stay in the Netherlands. The Netherlands Embassy has to obtain approval for the issuance of a temporary residence permit from the immigration authorities in the Netherlands. It is important that one applies for the temporary residence permit at least three months prior to one's intended stay in the Netherlands.

After 3 years in the Netherlands on a work permit, it is usually possible for an individual to have free access to the labour market. Thereafter they are free to take up any lawful employment and no longer require an employer-sponsored work permit.

If one is working and holding a valid work permit and holds a temporary residence visa (MVV) for 5 years, then one can automatically gain permanent residency in that country.

The competent authority is the Immigration and Naturalisation Service (IND) in the Ministry of Justice

4. Sweden

Swedish regulation on employment of third-country nationals and labour related immigration has traditionally been restrictive. One task of migration policy is however at times to enable migration to supply additional labour to the national labour market. National regulations as well as international agreements on the free movement of persons may help to even out imbalances of labour supply and demand in the labour market. Among those seeking to move to the EU, there are many that are mainly looking for work. In Sweden, it is believed that the forthcoming enlargement of the EU will alter the balance of labour supply and demand, which need to be taken into consideration. In a longer perspective, the ageing population in Europe will require additional labour force.

The principles for labour immigration, mainly regulated in the Aliens Ordinance and only to a lesser degree in the Aliens Act, are based on a government bill of 1968. It was then established that as a general rule, it should not be possible in the Swedish labour market to use foreign workers to regulate the demand for labour. This should be done instead mainly through labour market policy measures such as training of the unemployed, relocation within the country etc.

Residence permits purely for labour market reasons are granted in principle to other non-Swedes only if the need for manpower cannot be satisfied within Sweden or the EU/EEA. In 2000, 433 permanent residence permits were granted for labour market reasons. The largest groups for such permits were citizens from China, Russia and the United States. In addition, about 19,400 temporary work permits were granted in 2000. This represented a considerable increase from 15,000 the previous year. These permits are mainly granted with reference to temporary shortages of labour force and international exchange. Permits are granted mainly to experts and key people in industry, research, culture and sports in the cases where it is not possible to find equivalent competence in Sweden or within the EU/EEA area.

People in the professions and self-employed business people may also be granted such permits, if they fulfil certain conditions. In addition, a far greater number of work permits for limited periods are granted for such people as fitters, various specialists, artists and sportsmen.

For all categories of employment, the permit may only be granted on condition that there is an offer of employment and housing arranged beforehand. The permit must be issued before entry into Sweden. Permits are granted for the duration of between 1 day (e.g. artists and athletes) and up to 18 months regarding labour shortage and up to 48 months regarding international exchange.

The Migration Board (Mv) – which is the competent central authority in aliens affairs – handles and decides on work permit cases and permits regulated in the EEA agreement. The Board determines whether the applicant may have other reasons than labour market reasons for being granted or refused a residence permit (e.g. family ties). The Labour Market Board (AMS) carries out a labour market examination and the Migration Board must in principle consult with the county employment boards in all cases. AMS may also issue general guidelines. Before AMS issues guidelines the labour market parties (employers and employee organisations) must be given the opportunity to state an opinion.

Group of persons concerned

Applicants in the cases related to job finding can be divided into different groups.

- If the work is part of an international exchange between e.g. an international company or similar, the applicant is entitled to stay in Sweden for a maximum of four years. Since April 1, 2002, a specialist employed by an international organisation and travelling to and from Sweden for definite periods of time will not need a work permit if his/her stay does not exceed 3 months each time. However a residence permit needs to be granted before the person can take up employment.
- Permits can also be granted to persons for a maximum of 18 months altogether if the employment is due to a temporary labour shortage.
- Also can be mentioned the group of persons who participate in an organised exchange programme within the framework of different countries (trainees).
- One can also mention work permits for seasonal employment, which can be granted for three months at the most.

Procedures (differences between applications lodged from abroad and applications filed by foreigners already present in Sweden)

The initial application should be submitted to a Swedish embassy or consulate in the country of origin or the country of domicile. The permit thus must be granted before entry in to Sweden. To obtain an extension of the permit one must show that he/she still is employed.

One also has the possibility to change the status of the permit while being in Sweden; i.e. from permit for studies to permit based on an offer of employment.

Prerequisites

To obtain a work permit the applicant must:

- have a written offer of work and employment in Sweden within the above-mentioned categories,
- be guaranteed a minimum salary of SEK 13.000 = 1,311.64 EUR (15,740 € annually), per month before tax or a salary in accordance with a Swedish collective wage agreement,
- have arranged accommodation in Sweden before entry.
- be prepared to leave Sweden if the contract expires.
- have the approval of the National Labour Market Board.

To make the package more attractive, as in the case of the Netherlands:

- the tax reform lowering marginal taxes continues,
- employer-related bureaucracy is being simplified, and
- benefits (board and lodging) received by household employees are favourable.

Legal remedies

In the event that the Migration Board is considering expelling someone, their need of a lawyer is assessed and a decision is taken in this respect. It is always up to the Migration Board to decide whether legal aid should be provided or not.

It should be noted that a decision to deny an application of work permit cannot be appealed against if the decision is not connected to a decision of expulsion.

V. What Can One Deduce From the Above Four Cases?

As we can see from the four cases above, the policy evolution in these countries is certainly pointing towards an explicit recognition of shortages of specific skills in the labour markets. Germany and the UK seem to favour the Australian system of points, which would lead to a relatively more independent status for the potential candidate. Those applicants who score sufficient points – on the basis of an accumulation of the criteria to be met, will have a permit in their own right independent of the employer, which allows them the possibility of changing employment.

Sweden and Netherlands have both reviewed their regulations related to the employment of foreigners to make the labour market more accessible to persons with required skills. However, they emphasise that their policy remains restrictive, even though they could also be moving towards the "green card system" and their priority is to first recruit their own nationals, other EU/EEA citizens or third-country nationals already residing on their territory. On the other hand, both these two countries promote interesting expatriate tax status to attract potentially suitable candidates.

In these four countries, policies for entry and residence seem to place a lot of emphasis on the need of the applicant to be integrated. The four countries recognise that the greater the possibility of integration and eventual accumulation of rights, the more they would manage to attract the specialised labour they require. They recognise that integration is promoted if the family of the worker can join the applicant and if the applicant can obtain more secure residence rights after a certain period of time on the territory, with a possibility to naturalise if s/he so wishes. Apart from offering a structured package of rights, which eventually could bring the status of the specialised third-country national workers very close to that of EU citizens, language courses and information about the host country's culture are also offered.

Studies have shown that the greater the integration of the persons participating in the host country's labour market, the more beneficial it is for the economy of that country.

It would be interesting to compare the situation in North Europe with the type of labour demands in South Europe.

VI. The Paradox Between the Debate About a More Open Immigration Policy for Labour Reasons and the Provisions Underway for Freedom of Movement of Workers From the CEECs

A clear demonstration of the Member States' reserve, particularly towards migration of lower-skilled persons, is the attitude towards the separate but related question of the extension of freedom of movement for the workers coming from the Central and Eastern European countries (CEECs) after enlargement.

On this topic, which one cannot develop fully here, a plethora of studies and reports have already been produced, presenting rather different (and sometimes contradictory) figures, forecasts and scenarios.

The German government for instance, proposed a seven-year transitional period before extending the right to freedom of movement for the workers to the nationals of the CEECs, although the Commission had submitted an "information Note" in March 2001, which concluded that there would be no spectacular increase in East-West migration and that the overall impact on the European labour market would be limited, even if certain Member States could be affected more than others.

This document suggested five possible options to deal with this issue:

- a total closure of the Community labour market for a limited period to the workers of the CEECs;
- a complete liberalisation from the adhesion onwards;
- three intermediate approaches: a quota system; a safeguard clause and a flexible system of transitional schemes.

The option retained ultimately by the Commission envisages a general transitional period of five years, with a possible individual extension by each Member State for a period of maximum two years. However, after the first two years, an automatic review is envisaged, resting on a report submitted by the Commission to the Council: at that moment, it would be possible to decide to shorten or raise the transitional period, while leaving to the Member States the possibility of maintaining a more restrictive procedure if they wish to. The discussions on the question remain open and the result of the debate will depend without any doubt on the overall agreement on the package deal of adhesion.

One must bear in mind that the end of the Cold War precipitated a new liberalised era for the free movement of persons: not only between Eastern and Western Europe, but also within Central and Eastern Europe itself. Open borders policy within CEE has helped to break down stereotypes and hostilities in the region, as between Poland and Russia, has helped foster contacts between national minorities, such as between Hungarians in Ukraine, and has generated spheres of economic activity and cooperation within the region. The EU accession of Baltic and Central European States threatens this. In February 2000 the Czech Republic announced visa regimes for citizens of the Ukraine, Russia and Belarus, with Slovakia following suit. In September Estonia introduced full visa regimes for Russian citizens, following the termination in March of the two countries agreement on simplified border crossings. Lithuania has warned that it may have to rule out its agreement allowing for visa free travel of Kaliningrad citizens by 2003. And while the implementation of the Schengen acquis creates tensions along between candidate countries and their eastern neighbours, candidate countries will only be able to reap the benefits of freedom to take up employment in present member countries after a "transition" period of several years.

It is clear that the present implementation of the Schengen criteria will have an adverse effect on the free movement rights of citizens along the EU's future border: both in the freedom to travel and the freedom to reside and work. Meanwhile the question of whether visa regimes could have the effect of not curbing crime while making travel and work difficult for most normal citizens remains unanswered. Moreover, the new security agenda in the wake of September 11th will in all likelihood make the process of obtaining a Schengen visa even more difficult, and could exacerbate existing tendencies in the lack of transparency in the administration of visas. Increasingly the obtaining of a visa could become a privilege, not a right. Keeping in mind that the border regions are not only linked through economic ties, but often of family and national identity- as with the Russian population living on both sides of the Narva-Ivangorod border between Estonia and Russia – it is clear that a hostile visa regime could infringe on the basic rights of citizens.

These opposing tendencies have highlighted an existing contradiction in the EU's eastern policy. On the one hand EU external relations have focused on encouraging cooperation between the EU and its future Eastern neighbours, on the other, the logic of EU enlargement and the demands made on candidate and accession countries to adopt the Schengen criteria lead to an exclusionary situation on the EU's future border. The incorporation of Central European and the Baltic States in to the EU has the marked potential of drawing new dividing lines across Europe: undoing the progress which has been achieved over the last decade.

One must not forget either that the future members of the EU have also started to experience similar demographic problems as the current EU members. Therefore, they too will be thinking of participating in a controlled open immigration policy addressing their own needs.

VII. A Common European Policy on Immigration: The Way Forward

The topic of immigration is very sensitive, as it has an impact on a wide range of areas (social, cultural, economic and legal). It is therefore difficult to reach an agreement on this debate. Although the latest developments and the partial change of attitude on European level can give rise to moderate optimism on the future of a European policy on immigration, the following main points remain highly controversial.

The EU should publish a declaration espousing the principle that the territory of the EU is a common immigration area, which needs to be endorsed by the Member States.

Europe should not back into the future. If we really want to stop the "zero immigration policies" of the early 1990s, which did not work well or address the current demographic situation and labour market needs, then we should not be afraid to declare our objective of defining Europe as an area of immigration. We need to bear in mind that the definition of an area of immigration does not necessarily involve the granting of free and generalised access to the labour markets, as the examples of the United States and Australia show. However, it would probably be the first step towards a clear and coherent policy of management of migratory flows, which should supplement the measures intended to fight against illegal immigration, smuggling and the draft of human beings.

The European Union must grant rights to third-country nationals, who reside legally in one of the Member States, that are "as near as possible" to those enjoyed by EU citizens.

The importance of fair treatment of third-country nationals has been underlined by the European Council in Tampere, in which the need for an "approximation of the legal status of third-country nationals to that of the Member State's" was acknowledged (paragraph 21), and the objective that "long-term legally resident third-country nationals be offered the opportunity to obtain the nationality of the Member State in which they are resident" was endorsed. However, EU immigration policy has not, so far, incorporated steps to ensure that migrants benefit from comparable living and working conditions to those of nationals. We must think very clearly before defining a status for long-term third-country nationals which falls short of the objectives set out in Tampere as otherwise we risk institutionalising discrimination.

By Way of Conclusion...

It is undeniable that the EU is advancing towards a common migration procedure. However the question is to know when and, one could add, how, such a system will be set up. Although the Treaty of Amsterdam, the Vienna Action Plan and the Tampere Conclusions fix precise deadlines for the adoption of the majority of the measures, this process knew some delays and encountered a number of difficulties. One can only hope that the new attitude towards the immigration of third-country nationals combined with the new competencies of the Community in the field of immigration will reflect the "good intentions" expressed in several documents and action plans in policies that would be at the same time concrete, effective and human.

References

den Boer, M. (1998), Taming the Third Pillar: Improving the Management of Justice and Home Affairs Cooperation in the EU, IEAP, Maastricht.

European Commission (2000), Communication from the Commission to the Council and the European Parliament on a Community Immigration Policy, Brussels, 22 November.

European Commission (2001), Proposal of Directive concerning the status of third-country nationals who are long term residents of 13/3/2001 (COM 2001/127 final).

European Commission (2001), Proposal for a Council Directive on the conditions of entry and residence of third-country nationals for the purpose of paid employment and self-employed economic activities (COM (2001) 386 final).

European Commission (2001), Communication from the Commission to the Council and the European Parliament on an open method of co-ordination for the Community immigration policy, 11th July (COM (2001387final).

European Council (1997), "The European union today and tomorrow: To adapt the European Union in the interest of its citizens and prepare it for the future, general Framework for a draft revision of the treaties", published by the Secretariat-General of the Council under the title An Intergovernmental Conference for the amendment of the treaties, the Irish presidency's Six-month period, Compilation of texts, Luxembourg, Office for Official Publications of the European Communities, p. 32.

Federal Ministry of the Interior (2000*),* Policy and Law Concerning Foreigners in Germany, Berlin, August.

Glover S./Gott, C./Loizillon, A./Portes, J./Price, R./Spencer, S./Srinivasan, V. and *Willis C.* (2001*),* Migration: an economic and social analysis. Research, Development and Statistics Directorate, Home Office, London.

Hailbronner, K. (1998), "European Immigration and Asylum Law under the Amsterdam Treaty", CMLR, 35, 1047-1067.

IOM (1998), Migration Potential in Central and Eastern Europe, IOM, Geneva.

IOM (2000), World Migration Report *2000*, IOM, Geneva.

Ministry of Foreign Affairs, Sweden (2001*),* Sweden in 2000 – A Country of Migration Past, Present, Future, Department for Migration and Asylum Policy, Stockholm.

OECD (1991), Migration: The Demographic Aspects, Organisation for Economic Cooperation and Development, Paris.

OECD (1998), Ageing Populations: The Social Policy Implications, Organisation for Economic Co-operation and Development, Paris

OECD (1999), Trends in International Migration, Organisation for Economic Cooperation and Development, Paris.

OECD (2000), Trends in International Migration, Organisation for Economic Cooperation and Development, Paris.

OECD (2001), Migration Policies and EU Enlargement: The Case of Central and Eastern Europe.

Salt, J. (2000), Current Trends in International Migration in Europe, Council of Europe, Strasbourg, November.

Van Het Loo, M./DeSpiegelaire, S./Lindstrom, G./Kahan, J. and *Vernez, G.* (2001), A Comparison of American and Dutch Immigration and Integration Experiences: What lessons can be learned?, The Hague, WRR Working Document W 120, May.

DISCUSSION

Mr. Werner referred to Ms. Apap's remarks to the German green card model by stating that the conditions to achieve a green card in Germany were extraordinarily easy. The applicant needed a job in Germany and a diploma in an IT-subject; there was no need of a language test and no point system.

Ms. Langenfeld referred to Ms. Apap's idea of granting third-country nationals the same rights as EU nationals. According to her, from the moment the immigrant was accepted after a certain period of time, he should be granted the same social rights as EU nationals. The granting of political rights is, however, a very different issue. Ms. Apap agreed and added that on the local level too there were considerations in granting political rights, especially because immigrants pay taxes and should therefore be able to influence at least local decisions.

Ms. Langenfeld mentioned that the question of whether third-country nationals should be granted political rights on a local basis is controversially discussed throughout the European Union. In her opinion the simple fact that people are living in a state would not be a sufficient reason to grant voting rights. This question has already been decided by the Federal Constitutional Court of the FRG. Mr. Münz added that trade union rights for third-country nationals was not seen as a problem throughout the European Union.

Ms. Medved commented that although in the Swedish system of immigration the labour-testing is rather strict, there were, nevertheless other ways for competent employees to get labour permissions in order to avoid labour testing, e.g. if corporate investments were concerned. Insofar theoretical and practical situations differ.

With regard to the issue of approaching third-country national's rights to EU citizen's rights Ms. Medved remarked, that proceeding from Tampere Presidency Conclusions and more specifically the European Commission's proposals on a Community immigration policy not only socio-economic rights are meant, but also political rights in order to create a "civic citizenship" are implied. Mr. von Hoffmann pointed out that this issue would rather be decided by majorities and was more a political question, as no government would grant political rights to third-country nationals, if not favoured by the citizenship.

Ms. Medved added that some of the acceding countries (Estonia, Hungary, Slovenia) introduced electoral rights on a local level for EU citizens, on the basis of the argument that EU law demanded this change. Slovenia also introduced them for "third" country nationals.

Mr. Münz mentioned that the German green card system did not follow the American green card system at all, but was so called in order to make it popular and gain electoral support. He stated that there was a consensus in the present discussion of this forum insofar as political rights should be granted as far as possible to third-country nationals. But in fact most immigration countries would not do that; instead they encourage the immigrants to nationalise. For example in the US the government took away some immigrant's rights in the 1996 Welfare Reform, which led to much higher naturalisation rates. Although this was not, in the opinion of Mr. Münz, the aim of the legal reform, it has been a quite effective way to speed up naturalisation.

Ms. Apap emphasised that foreigners wanted to be part of the country, even if they had not yet decided to stay forever, but for a period of e.g. five years. They didn't even have the right to vote and thereby take part in shaping their surrounding conditions. By being granted the same rights, third-country nationals should also undertake the same duties as nationals and thereby be nationalised.

Mr. von Hoffmann stated that there were two possible approaches in order to determine immigration: which is best for the economy of the host country, or which is the best for the immigrants. Ms. Apap held that immigration was also in the host country's interests, especially regarding demographical aspects.

Mr. Bisopoulos added, agreeing with Mr. Münz, that the main issue was efficient integration in the labour market as well as inclusion into society. The question was, which way was the best way to achieve integration. In his opinion this was naturalisation.

Ms. Medved concluded that taking into account this consideration, most European States would have to change their philosophy and see naturalisation as the first step to successful integration and not, as it now appears to be the case, as the crowning touch of successful integration.

Heinz Werner

THE INTEGRATION OF FOREIGN WORKERS INTO THE LABOUR MARKET:

AN EU PERSPECTIVE

I. Introduction

According to OECD data there are about 20 million foreigners in Western Europe. About 40% of them are employed. Many of those non-nationals live there for quite some time. Experience demonstrates that with increasing duration of stay a large proportion of the foreign workers and their families will remain permanently. Therefore, their integration is an important issue. Integration issues may gain increased importance for three reasons: firstly, because of the existing migration pressure (from third countries and EU-enlargement), secondly, because of the ageing of the population in Europe, and thirdly, due to a need for more skilled immigration in many European countries.

Participation in the labour market is central to the overall integration into the host society. In the following the state of labour market participation of nationals and non-nationals (EU- and non-EU nationals) will be presented. Before doing so two questions will dealt with first: What is integration? and Why is integration necessary? After that some labour market indicator will be chosen to show the labour market position of EU and non-EU nationals in the countries of the European Union.

II. What is Integration?

Integration can be understood as a process and at the same time as a state. The integration process proceeds in the direction of a desired state, i.e. the achievement of successful integration. The integration process has proceeded successfully if, with respect to participation in social areas of the receiving country, differences between comparable groups of nationals and foreigners/ethnic minorities no longer exist. Important areas for integration are housing, education, and work. The pre-requisite for the successful integration of a person is legal security/legal equality for the migrants.

But opportunities must not only be the same in law for nationals, non-nationals and members of ethnic minorities, but conditions must also be the same in actual practice. In competitive societies, equality before the law rarely suffices by itself to ensure that people with different cultural backgrounds can take advantage of society's opportunities on equal terms. Therefore, disadvantaged persons must be assisted or enabled to compete on comparable terms with those nationals with similar characteristics.

Gainful employment is an important component of society and in the life of each individual as it is necessary for one's livelihood and determines status in society. With regard to the labour market a successful integration would have to show the same employment structures between comparable groups of nationals and foreigners e.g. in unemployment, earnings, employment rate. The pre-requisite for this is the same access to occupation/work, including the existence of certain preconditions which enable the foreign workers to practise an occupation on the same terms as nationals, such as access to the education systems and to training schemes, housing or social security. These areas are not independent of each other and can influence each other.

III. Why Integration Efforts?

For a number of European countries the presence of a more or less large number of foreign employees and their dependants is a fact to which the countries must adjust. With the increasing duration of residence a return to the country of origin becomes increasingly less probable. Seen against this background, the most comprehensive integration possible of the foreign workers and their dependants becomes necessary on humanitarian, social and economic grounds.

- On humanitarian grounds, because the people have lived and worked in the country for some years and have made a contribution to the development of the receiving country. If they decide to remain in the country permanently, it must be made possible for them to take part in the life of the society of the receiving country as equals, like nationals of the receiving country.
- On social grounds integration is necessary because discrimination against certain groups can lead to their marginalisation. This in turn can lead to socially undesirable behaviour, which is expressed, for example, in the form of criminal activity or social unrest.
- From an economic point of view successful integration is necessary because discrimination in the labour market has the effect that the human resources (in this case the foreign workers) are not employed in accordance with their qualifications, which means their inefficient use. As a result, productivity potentials are not used, and avoidable costs are incurred.

IV. Non-National Workers in the EU

The foreign labour force reaches more than 8 millions in the European Union. Three quarters of them live in the larger countries Germany, France and the UK. The proportion of the non-nationals in relation to the total labour force varies considerably from country to country (Table 1). The highest percentages can be observed in Luxembourg, Austria, Germany and Belgium. Since the early 80s the number of foreign workers increased in nearly all Member States. But their shares remained more or less the same as the national labour force increased as well.

Only about 3 million of the foreign work force are from other EU countries. This means, that at community level, less than 2% of the EU workforce live in another Member State.

TABLE 1: FOREIGN WORKERS IN EU STATES BY CITIZENSHIP 2000

Percentage of total employment

	Third-country nationals	EU nationals
EU-15	2,9	1,8
B	1,8	5,7
DK	1,7	0,9
D	5,5	2,8
EL	3,5	0,2
E	0,9	0,4
F	3,0	2,3
IRL	0,5	2,9
I	0,9	0,1
L	3,9	37,0

	Third-country nationals	EU nationals
NL	2,0	1,6
A	7,7	1,7
P	1,7	0,3
FIN	0,8	0,2
S	2,1	2,2
UK	2,4	1,6

Source: Eurostat (2001): Labour Force Survey 2000.

Note: The number of the non-nationals is influenced by the naturalisation legislation. Where the granting of citizenship is possible after a short period of time and is made easy, the naturalised part of the foreign workers "disappears" and can be found among the nationals. Countries like NL, S, B, DK or France have high rates of naturalisation. Germany, until recently, had comparably low rates of naturalisation. This has changed now with the new naturalisation law in force.

V. Measurement of Integration Into the Labour Market

Integration into the labour market means a process in the direction of the same gainful employment structures for foreign economically active persons/ethnic minorities as for national employees. Similar gainful employment structures signalise successful integration. Applied specifically to labour market conditions this means that at the end of the integration process no more differences should be found between comparable groups of nationals and migrants in employment participation (activity rate), in unemployment or income, etc.

As integration means a process in the direction of a desired state (same employment structures), integration could be measured by the deviation (or similarity) of employment structures between the foreign and national workforces. In the most simple case of measurement the labour market indicators (e.g. activity, unemployment, incomes) for national and foreign gainfully employed persons can be juxtaposed and compared. Indices could also be calculated which, for example, indicate the degree of deviation.

A great problem is the delimitation of a comparable national group: in order to be able to assess the degree of integration, comparable groups of nationals and foreigners/ethnic minorities must be juxtaposed. The national contrast group must, in its characteristics, as far as possible be identical with those of the foreign/ethnic minority group. The most important characteristics concerning the labour market are age, sex, qualifications, occupation, economic sector and region.

Integration also has a time-related aspect. The personal situation and the situation of the successive generations change in the course of time. If one wants to measure integration by way of indicators, the situation is compared at a particular point in time. Individual integration processes showing different developments, at the time of the measurement can be at different stages of integration. These measurements are then added up and standardised at a given point in time (e.g. by the formation of ratios). The difference in the time sequence and between the generations is, therefore, blurred since only one mean value is retained at a point in time. Behind this average value, considerable differences e.g. of nationality/country of origin etc., can continue to exist. A more detailed breakdown, as far as this is statistically possible, could make these differences visible.

Because of the time dimension of integration, the degree of integration can only be correctly determined in the time sequence, which is with the help of a longitudinal survey. The individual development of the immigrants and that of the following generations within the society of the receiving country would have to be followed up and compared with the national population. This is, for example, possible with a retrospective survey during which the stages of integration are individually surveyed on the basis of past development up to the time of the survey.

The measurement of integration in the form of indicators is therefore not unproblematic.

There is also no single indicator, which depicts the stage of integration reached. Only by simultaneously looking at several indicators can an overall picture be obtained. Assessment of the indicators must not be carried out schematically on the basis of one figure. Behind the one figure in each case other processes can be hidden which are attributable to differences in the functioning of the labour markets from country to country. Nevertheless, some indicators are to be presented below which can be seen as pointers to the level of integration of the foreign workers into the labour market.

To assure cross-country comparability the following indicators are based on the annual Labour Force Survey of Eurostat. The EU Labour Force Survey uses a harmonised questionnaire for all countries involved. Thus it is a valuable source of information on the EU as a whole or for individual EU countries as it provides data on a comparable basis. Due to limitations of the survey the availability of data is limited. Three labour market indicators are chosen which allow an assessment of the labour market position of nationals and non-nationals in EU countries: the unemployment rate, the employment rate and the self-employment rate.

VI. Some Indicators for the Measurement of Integration Into the Labour Market

1. Unemployment rate

Unemployment has an unfavourable effect on the integration of foreign workers. Repeated or lengthy periods of unemployment lead to de-skilling and involve the risk of marginalisation. Table 2 shows that in all countries the unemployment rates for foreigners are considerably higher than the one for nationals. It usually is double the unemployment rate for nationals. It is worth noting that – as a rule – the unemployment rate for EU nationals living in another Member State is situated between the rate for third-country nationals and the national population. Reasons for the better position of EU citizens (as compared to third countries) could be their longer residence period, better knowledge of the language and their better qualifications and skills. A further reason may be that EU citizens in case of unemployment can go back to their home country and return whenever they want – due to free movement of labour regulation. The latter possibility does not apply to third-country nationals. Therefore, they tend to stay in the host country, even when without work. It should be mentioned that the overall rate of unemployment of foreigners conceals marked differences according to nationalities. For certain nationality groups the unemployment rate is much higher than for others.

TABLE 2

Unemployment rates in EU States 1983 – 2000					
Year	Nationals	Non-nationals	of whom		Total
			EU nationals	Third-country nationals	
Austria					
1983					
1987					
1995	4,1	6,8	1,2	7,6	4,4
2000	4,3	8,8	3,4	9,9	4,7
Belgium					
1983	10,8	21,9	19,3	26,0	11,7
1987	10,2	24,8	21,8	32,8	11,3
1995	8,2	23,5	17,5	36,7	9,4
2000	5,8	15,6	9,1	30,8	6,6
Germany					
1983	6,1	11,3	9,7	11,9	6,5
1987	6,4	12,5	9,7	14,0	6,9
1995	7,5	15,1	9,4	17,6	8,2
2000	7,5	12,9	7,3	15,5	8,0
Denmark					
1983	9,8	19,0	8,1	24,8	9,9
1987	6,0	15,2	11,3	17,0	6,2
1995	6,8	18,1	7,2	26,5	7,0
2000	4,3	9,9	1,9	13,6	4,5
Spain					
1983					
1987	20,8	15,4	10,6	20,0	20,8
1995	22,9	22,8	19,4	24,7	22,9
2000	14,1	16,0	9,5	18,9	14,1

Unemployment rates in EU States 1983 – 2000					
Year	Nationals	Non-nationals	of whom		Total
			EU nationals	Third-country nationals	
Finland					
1983					
1987					
1995	17,1	26,3	24,1	27,3	17,2
2000	11,0	29,3	9,9	33,2	11,2
France					
1983	7,5	14,6	11,4	15,1	8,0
1987	10,2	19,0	11,8	25,1	10,8
1995	11,3	21,7	10,5	29,3	11,9
2000	9,6	20,9	9,7	28,0	10,3
Greece					
1983	8,1	14,5	4,8	16,6	8,1
1987	7,5	16,4	9,0	18,2	7,6
1995	9,2	13,8	8,2	14,6	9,3
2000	11,3	11,6	13,9	11,4	11,3
Ireland					
1983	15,0	21,0	22,1	16,2	15,2
1987	18,3	23,0	23,7	19,9	18,5
1995	12,0	18,1	19,1	14,1	12,2
2000	4,3	6,2	6,4	5,9	4,3
Italy					
1983					8,6
1987					10,9
1995	11,9	12,9	9,3	13,9	11,9
2000	10,9	12,2	9,1	12,9	11,0

Unemployment rates in EU States 1983 – 2000					
Year	Nationals	Non-nationals	of whom		Total
			EU nationals	Third-country nationals	
Luxembourg					
1983	2,9	3,9	3,9	4,0	3,2
1987	2,2	3,0	2,9	5,5	2,5
1995	2,5	3,6	3,5	5,5	2,9
2000	1,6	3,4	2,8	8,4	2,4
Netherlands					
1983	11,4	24,5	16,1	27,8	11,9
1987	9,4	25,0	14,5	31,5	10,0
1995	6,5	23,6	11,0	33,3	7,2
2000	2,6	6,7	3,1	9,0	2,7
Portugal					
1983					
1987	7,6	14,1	5,6	16,2	7,6
1995	7,3	12,2	9,9	14,5	7,4
2000	4,0	9,1	16,5	7,6	4,1
Sweden					
1983					
1987					
1995	7,7	19,7	14,5	24,7	8,2
2000	5,1	14,6	6,1	22,0	5,5
United Kingdom					
1983	11,1	14,0	11,2	15,8	11,2
1987	11,0	13,2	12,4	13,7	11,1
1995	8,6	14,4	11,2	17,0	8,8
2000	5,4	10,1	6,7	12,2	5,6

Unemployment rates in EU States 1983 – 2000					
Year	Nationals	Non-nationals	of whom: EU nationals	of whom: Third-country nationals	Total
EU					
1983	8,7	13,9	11,8	14,8	8,9
1987	10,6	15,5	12,1	17,9	10,8
1995	10,5	16,7	10,8	20,2	10,8
2000	8,2	13,6	7,6	16,9	8,4

Note: unemployed 15-64 years of age related to labour force 15-64 years of age.

Source: Eurostat Labour Force Survey.

The generally higher unemployment among women is more pronounced among females from outside the EU (Table 3). But in some countries, however, the unemployment rate for EU nationals is close to that of the indigenous work force or even below (in D, DK, E, F, IT, S).

TABLE 3

Unemployment rates for females in EU States 1983 – 2000					
Year	Nationals	Non-nationals	of whom: EU nationals	of whom: Third-country nationals	Total
Austria					
1983					
1987					
1995	4,7	7,8	1,0	8,9	4,9
2000	4,1	9,1	5,2	10,1	4,6

Unemployment rates for females in EU States 1983 – 2000					
Year	Nationals	Non-nationals	of whom		Total
			EU nationals	Third-country nationals	
Belgium					
1983	16,9	32,6	31,5	34,5	17,9
1987	16,5	36,5	34,8	43,1	17,7
1995	11,0	31,5	24,4	48,0	12,3
2000	7,8	16,4	11,7	31,2	8,3
Germany					
1983	7,1	14,3	11,8	15,2	7,6
1987	7,5	15,1	12,0	17,1	8,0
1995	9,3	14,9	9,4	17,5	9,7
2000	8,1	11,6	7,6	13,5	8,3
Denmark					
1983	10,5	17,9	17,7	18,0	10,6
1987	7,0	18,6	15,6	19,8	7,2
1995	8,4	21,5	3,8	30,8	8,6
2000	5,0	4,0		5,1	5,0
Spain					
1983					
1987	28,3	14,6	8,2	18,9	28,3
1995	30,6	27,0	26,1	27,6	30,5
2000	20,6	18,1	11,1	21,0	20,5
Finland					
1983					
1987					
1995	16,2	30,4	57,8	24,1	16,3
2000	11,8	29,8		32,3	12,0

Unemployment rates for females in EU States 1983 – 2000					
Year	Nationals	Non-nationals	of whom		Total
			EU nationals	Third-country nationals	
France					
1983	10,1	19,3	16,8	19,6	10,5
1987	13,1	23,6	15,0	34,9	13,5
1995	13,6	24,4	11,8	35,3	14,2
2000	11,6	25,6	11,8	35,7	12,3
Greece					
1983	12,1	18,2	11,1	20,2	12,2
1987	11,6	21,3	7,4	24,8	11,7
1995	14,0	18,2	8,8	20,4	14,1
2000	16,9	17,6	21,0	17,3	16,9
Ireland					
1983	15,9	24,3	25,6	18,6	16,2
1987	19,0	26,7	27,6	21,9	19,2
1995	11,9	19,2	19,5	17,7	12,1
2000	4,1	7,0	8,2	4,6	4,2
Italy					
1983					14,3
1987					16,8
1995	16,3	22,8	15,0	27,1	16,3
2000	14,9	21,1	18,9	21,6	14,9
Luxembourg					
1983	4,2	6,9	6,8	7,0	5,1
1987	3,5	4,3	4,0	10,2	3,8
1995	3,8	5,3	5,3	6,1	4,4
2000	2,4	4,0	3,4	9,4	3,2

Unemployment rates for females in EU States 1983 – 2000					
Year	Nationals	Non-nationals	of whom		Total
			EU nationals	Third-country nationals	
Netherlands					
1983	13,4	29,5	20,1	34,2	13,8
1987	13,5	36,6	26,9	42,2	14,0
1995	8,2	24,3	14,8	32,3	8,7
2000	3,3	8,8	4,9	11,7	3,5
Portugal					
1983					
1987	9,9	19,1	53,3	17,5	9,9
1995	8,0	20,3	15,0	24,8	8,1
2000	5,0	10,8	26,1	8,1	5,1
Sweden					
1983					
1987					
1995	7,1	15,6	12,5	19,0	7,4
2000	4,6	13,0	2,9	23,4	5,1
United Kingdom					
1983	9,8	10,2	7,4	12,5	9,9
1987	10,5	10,9	8,6	12,3	10,5
1995	6,8	11,8	8,2	15,1	7,0
2000	4,8	8,1	6,5	9,2	4,9
EU					
1983	9,8	16,0	13,4	17,1	10,8
1987	12,5	17,5	14,1	20,4	13,3
1995	12,3	17,2	11,3	21,1	12,5
2000	9,7	13,9	8,4	17,2	9,9

Note: unemployed 15-64 years of age related to labour force 15-64 years of age.

Source: Eurostat Labour Force Survey.

If one splits up the ages into under 25s (young people), the differences between the rates are even more marked (Table 4). The young foreigners reach considerably higher unemployment rates as the comparable national age group. This is to be understood as a clear signal for the education and labour market policies that there is a need for corrective measures to be taken!

TABLE 4

Youth unemployment rates in EU States 1983 – 2000					
Year	Nationals	Non-nationals	of whom		Total
			EU nationals	Third-country nationals	
Austria					
1983					
1987					
1995	5,3	10,4	2,6	10,8	5,9
2000	5,7	11,2	11,7	11,2	6,3
Belgium					
1983	22,4	39,0	34,5	46,7	23,9
1987	19,6	41,9	39,4	48,7	21,4
1995	19,7	42,7	33,3	55,3	21,5
2000	14,4	24,9	14,9	43,4	15,2
Germany					
1983	10,1	18,2	16,7	18,8	10,6
1987	6,9	15,4	10,6	18,0	7,5
1995	7,3	15,7	9,1	17,8	8,5
2000	8,1	11,8	8,5	12,8	8,5
Denmark					
1983	18,8	22,5	11,0	29,4	18,9
1987	8,8	18,1	9,7	20,8	8,9
1995	9,8	14,3		18,2	9,9
2000	6,6	11,0		12,0	6,7

Youth unemployment rates in EU States 1983 – 2000					
Year	Nationals	Non-nationals	of whom		Total
			EU nationals	Third-country nationals	
Spain					
1983					
1987	43,5	26,5	12,3	49,8	43,5
1995	41,8	36,1	16,2	45,6	41,7
2000	25,5	25,9	8,6	29,7	25,5
Finland					
1983					
1987					
1995	41,6	8,6		9,6	41,2
2000	28,2	42,1		45,3	28,4
France					
1983	19,1	30,0	22,9	30,7	19,8
1987	22,8	34,0	22,1	46,0	23,4
1995	26,5	38,1	20,4	46,3	27,1
2000	20,2	32,7	17,3	37,9	20,6
Greece					
1983	23,0	26,7		33,3	23,1
1987	24,9	29,8	44,4	27,1	25,0
1995	28,2	17,7	18,8	17,6	27,9
2000	30,1	18,6		18,6	29,5
Ireland					
1983	21,0	32,5	34,7	24,3	21,3
1987	25,8	33,3	34,8	24,7	26,0
1995	18,9	24,3	23,8	26,3	19,0
2000	6,3	8,4	8,7	7,9	6,4

Youth unemployment rates in EU States 1983 – 2000					
Year	Nationals	Non-nationals	of whom: EU nationals	of whom: Third-country nationals	Total
Italy					
1983					28,9
1987					33,7
1995	32,8	29,1		32,9	32,8
2000	31,5	30,8	38,8	29,9	31,5
Luxembourg					
1983	6,1	8,3	7,8	9,1	6,7
1987	5,0	6,1	5,8	13,9	5,4
1995	6,1	8,5	7,4	21,0	7,2
2000	5,0	7,5	6,4	14,2	6,4
Netherlands					
1983	20,4	37,2	23,6	40,3	21,0
1987	16,1	38,9	24,9	47,8	16,8
1995	11,5	26,9	17,9	30,7	12,1
2000	5,0	10,9	6,9	11,8	5,3
Portugal					
1983					
1987	17,5	17,0	19,3	16,4	17,5
1995	16,0	13,8	19,6		16,0
2000	8,1	21,1	31,5	16,4	8,4
Sweden					
1983					
1987					
1995	19,0	17,6	24,0	12,5	19,0
2000	9,0	22,7		28,9	9,5

Youth unemployment rates in EU States 1983 – 2000					
Year	Nationals	Non-nationals	of whom		Total
			EU nationals	Third-country nationals	
United Kingdom					
1983	20,2	22,0	21,1	22,4	20,2
1987	16,2	15,9	13,2	17,3	16,2
1995	15,3	22,6	24,1	21,5	15,5
2000	11,8	19,0	12,1	22,5	12,1
EU					
1983	17,2	24,7	21,5	25,9	19,6
1987	19,4	22,7	18,0	26,0	21,6
1995	21,2	20,6	15,4	22,5	21,2
2000	16,0	16,5	11,1	18,3	16,1

Note: unemployed 15-64 years of age related to labour force 15-64 years of age.

Source: Eurostat Labour Force Survey.

The situation has not improved for foreign workers since the early 1980s. In particular, the unemployment rates for young foreign people have remained frighteningly high. In Germany the unemployment rate for foreign young people fell up to 1990 but has increased dramatically since then. This fall can be explained by the fact that, as a result of demographic developments and the extended duration of education, fewer young Germans entered the labour market through the so-called dual vocational training system. Thus more places/apprenticeships were available to foreign young people. But as the economic situation deteriorated the apprenticeship system also came under pressure and less young people were taken on as trainees. However, foreign youth are more affected by the reduction of training places than their German counterparts. This may have consequences for the future labour market position of young migrants: if they remain unskilled their risk of becoming unemployed will be higher.

How can these differences in unemployment between nationals and foreigners be explained? The following reasons can be put forward.

The foreign workers were, and still are in some countries such as Germany, to a high degree employed in the manufacturing industry or the building sector. Employment in these sectors is generally declining. Moreover, these sectors are undergoing a restructuring and rationalisation process which requires better qualifications on the part of those employed there. Foreign workers often work in jobs not requiring any qualifications. Such jobs are increasingly being lost in the course of rationalisation and restructuring. Redundancies and unemployment of the less qualified workers, including many foreigners, are the result. Access to further training and retraining is more difficult for them because foreign workers usually do not have a good educational basis and also because of language deficiencies.

In the case of foreigners, massive losses of industrial jobs are only partly compensated for by employment in the tertiary sector. In the case of more demanding jobs or those closer to the customers, such as consulting/sales, they encounter competition with the national employees. As regards the establishment of businesses or self-employment, foreigners are usually short of financial capital.

But even if one compares nationals and foreigners who have the same characteristics such as qualifications, age and sex, the unemployment rate of foreigners is higher than that of nationals. A "residue" of unemployment remains which cannot be accounted for by other features (apart from nationality). This residue, can only be related to nationality, but does not necessarily have anything directly to do with the nationality. It can, for example, involve discrimination due to prejudices regarding ethnic origin.

This discrimination against foreign workers occurs, for example, in the recruitment and selection processes of the companies. National workers tend to follow formal application routes, whereas foreigners look to a greater extent for work through a network of friends and relatives. Thus they do not make use of certain application procedures.[1]

The labour market problems of the foreign workers are greater during a recession: the less qualified persons (including many foreigners) are affected to a disproportionate extent by redundancies. For new recruits, the companies can select from a larger pool of persons looking for work. This larger pool not only consists of workers who have become redundant, but also of new additions to the labour market, such as young people having completed training or women who want to take up employment after a period of occupational inactivity. When they

1 The ILO carried out a number of studies in various countries which should measure the degree of discrimination in the course of the recruitment process: For the same vacancy a national and a foreigner/person from an ethnic minority "apply". They pretend to have the same qualifications. In general the refusal rate for foreigners/ethnic minorities was considerably higher than for the nationals.

have a greater choice the companies prefer, all other conditions being equal, to take on national workers or experienced workers (and not new school-leavers).

The position of many low-skilled migrant workers may become more difficult in the course of the globalisation of the economy. The current globalisation of the world economy is characterised by the large-scale introduction of new information technology. It enables rapid exchange of, access to and processing of data. Information technology requires new skills and the updating of knowledge. The less qualified, among them many migrants, who do not have the qualifications required or are difficult to retrain, risk falling further behind in terms of position in the labour market.

It would be interesting to show the unemployment rate for naturalised persons and foreigners. If one assumes that the naturalisation decision indicates a better basis for integration and the intention, as a matter of principle, to become integrated into the society of the receiving country, the unemployment rate for naturalised former foreigners would have to be lower than that of the foreign workers.

The EU Labour Force Survey does not allow to differentiate between naturalised and native nationals, but the foreign-born population is counted. As a proxy for naturalisation the numbers of the foreign-born can be taken and unemployment rates can be calculated. As a rule, foreign-born nationals have a lower unemployment rate than the foreign population, the exceptions being Germany and Sweden. As far as Germany is concerned, it should be stated that many of the foreign-born nationals consist of people of German origin from Central and Eastern Europe and the former Soviet Union. After entering Germany they obtain German citizenship although very often they possess all the characteristics of some other "typical" immigrants, such as language deficiencies, different cultural backgrounds, inappropriate qualifications and skills. This explains why their unemployment rate is above the rate of the foreign labour force. A similar phenomenon can be seen in Sweden as it is relatively easy to obtain Swedish citizenship.

Granting citizenship does not automatically abolish all the barriers to employment in the host country. In principle naturalisation facilitates integration. But equality before the law (and naturalisation means – legally spoken – equal opportunities) does not automatically lead to the same labour market position for naturalised migrants and the native population. However, it should be stated, that equal opportunities are a prerequisite for successful integration.

2. *Female employment rate*

Gainful employment seen in itself is an integration factor and is the basis for covering the cost of living. It also facilitates personal contact and social relationships. Employment behaviour is, in the most simple case, expressed by the activity rate. This relates the working population (= persons in employment + unemployed persons) to the population of the same basic total group e.g. age group. For our purpose the employment rate – that is the relationship of employed persons to the corresponding population of working age – is better suited. The employment rate refers to a positive sign of integration (having a job). It excludes the unemployed, who were unsuccessful (could not find a job). Unemployment has already been dealt with in a previous chapter. The employment behaviour and labour market integration (having a job) is thus expressed in the employment rate. The employment rates vary between nationals and foreigners. However, they have the tendency to converge in the course of time. Therefore, one can regard the employment rate as an indicator of integration: the closer the employment rates of the nationals and foreigners have converged, the more similar is the employment behaviour, and the further the labour market integration has progressed. However, it is not the overall rate, but the activity rate of women which is to be considered. To explain this choice some general remarks on international migratory processes and on female employment activity are necessary.

It is true that foreign women have greater difficulties in finding a job than national women or foreign men. Their unemployment rate is, generally, above the total rate for foreigners and considerably higher than the unemployment rate of the national women. While the male employee often has established contacts through his working environment and socialisation processes thus become possible in the receiving country, this is difficult for foreign women. Their access to the labour market is therefore not easy. It is made even more difficult due to language deficiencies, lack of qualifications and cultural distance from working life. These factors represent an obstacle to integration. Once in the labour market the foreign women – even more than the foreign men – can be found in the less attractive, badly paid jobs which are also unstable (highly dependent on the economic cycle, with limited contracts, dismissal at any time etc.). Periods of employment and unemployment alternate.

The special employment problems of foreign women are reflected in different employment rates in comparison with the national women. In the course of time the employment rates between foreign and national women should converge, which would mean a step in the direction of integration. The difference between the two employment rates can therefore be regarded as an indicator of integration or non-integration into the labour market.

In table 5 the employment rates of foreign women and national women are shown. The employment rates of foreign women were, across the board, considerably below those of national women. Compared over time no major convergence has taken place. These deviations indicate a lack of integration of foreign women. If one makes a comparison with women from EU countries their activity rate is often close to that of national women, in some cases even above. This may be linked to the fact that, on average, women from EU countries stayed in the country for a longer time than women from third countries and that their skills are better.

TABLE 5

Employment rates for females in EU States 1983 – 2000

Year	Nationals	Non-nationals	of whom		Total
			EU nationals	Third-country nationals	
Austria					
1983					
1987					
1995	59,2	59,1	60,4	58,9	59,2
2000	59,8	58,5	63,2	57,4	59,7
Belgium					
1983	37,5	22,9	25,6	19,0	36,4
1987	38,8	21,6	26,2	12,1	37,5
1995	47,1	26,0	34,5	14,2	45,4
2000	53,6	34,5	43,5	18,9	51,9
Germany					
1983	45,3	43,9	50,0	41,9	45,2
1987	49,1	41,8	51,4	37,1	48,5
1995	56,5	43,1	55,6	38,5	55,3
2000	59,2	43,9	56,9	39,4	57,8

Employment rates for females in EU States 1983 – 2000					
Year	Nationals	Non-nationals	of whom		Total
			EU nationals	Third-country nationals	
			Denmark		
1983	64,5	50,1	47,2	50,9	64,3
1987	71,3	56,4	69,2	52,5	71,0
1995	67,7	37,9	53,3	31,2	67,0
2000	72,9	48,9	69,8	44,7	72,1
			Spain		
1983					
1987	26,6	32,5	31,8	33,0	26,6
1995	31,2	35,5	33,3	37,2	31,2
2000	40,2	46,9	46,4	47,2	40,3
			Finland		
1983					
1987					
1995	58,2	45,9	33,0	48,3	58,1
2000	65,4	43,4	63,0	41,8	65,2
			France		
1983	51,6	33,9	34,8	33,8	50,5
1987	51,0	32,6	47,7	21,2	49,8
1995	53,1	35,4	54,0	25,2	52,0
2000	56,1	36,1	56,6	26,4	54,8
			Greece		
1983	34,5	27,3	36,6	25,3	34,4
1987	36,4	29,0	30,1	28,7	36,3
1995	37,9	46,1	48,5	45,4	38,0
2000	41,1	46,0	39,2	46,7	41,3

Employment rates for females in EU States 1983 – 2000					
Year	Nationals	Non-nationals	of whom		Total
			EU nationals	Third-country nationals	
Ireland					
1983	33,5	30,5	30,7	29,4	33,4
1987	33,3	28,9	30,3	23,8	33,1
1995	41,5	36,1	37,4	31,8	41,3
2000	53,5	49,8	52,2	45,4	53,4
Italy					
1983					34,0
1987					34,7
1995	35,6	38,1	51,8	32,5	35,6
2000	39,3	40,5	41,9	40,1	39,3
Luxembourg					
1983	35,8	46,3	41,1	56,0	38,6
1987	38,2	50,9	52,1	35,0	41,8
1995	38,7	48,5	49,9	34,2	42,2
2000	46,7	54,6	56,6	40,8	50,0
Netherlands					
1983	34,8	24,7	35,8	20,7	34,5
1987	43,1	20,7	27,2	17,6	42,4
1995	54,3	30,1	48,3	21,5	53,2
2000	64,5	43,5	64,7	34,5	63,4

Employment rates for females in EU States 1983 – 2000					
Year	Nationals	Non-nationals	of whom		Total
			EU nationals	Third-country nationals	
Portugal					
1983					
1987	49,6	29,8	5,1	34,2	49,5
1995	54,4	28,0	24,9	31,7	54,3
2000	60,3	62,0	40,1	67,2	60,4
Sweden					
1983					
1987					
1995	73,6	50,8	64,4	40,5	72,4
2000	70,8	52,1	69,7	39,3	69,7
United Kingdom					
1983	51,6	47,2	55,2	42,2	51,4
1987	56,8	48,3	56,5	43,9	56,3
1995	62,0	49,0	60,9	40,8	61,4
2000	65,2	51,5	61,0	46,1	64,5
EU					
1983	47,2	39,5	44,8	37,4	44,0
1987	46,7	38,8	47,4	33,2	44,3
1995	50,0	41,6	53,3	35,7	49,6
2000	54,3	44,4	56,5	38,9	53,8

Note: employed persons 15-64 of age related to population 15-64 years of age.

Source: Eurostat Labour Force Survey.

3. *Self-employment rate*

A further indication of the integration of foreigners/ethnic groups into the labour market can be the percentage of foreign self-employed persons among economically active foreigners. The decision to take up self-employment can as a rule only be made after a certain knowledge of the local labour market has been obtained, which presupposes a certain familiarity with local conditions. Self-employment also tends to suggest the intention of staying permanently in the receiving country. The possibility of a foreigner setting up business indicates a certain freedom of access to this part of the labour market in the receiving country. As a matter of principle, free access to the labour market has an integration-promoting effect.

Access of foreigners can be restricted if the practice of certain forms of self-employment is linked to the nationality of the country of residence. Access can also be restrictive as a result of the requirements for admission to certain forms of self-employment being difficult to fulfil by foreigners. Thus for example, the running of a tradesman's business in Germany is tied to the "Meisterprüfung" (master tradesman's examination). The latter presupposes a final examination in a recognised occupation. This precondition cannot be fulfilled by foreigners who have not passed through the German vocational training system. About two thirds of young Germans pass through this vocational training system as compared to one third of young foreigners. The training takes three years as a rule. Nevertheless, the percentage of self-employed foreigners can, with a certain justification, be regarded as an indicator of integration into the labour market.

According to the labour force survey by the Statistical Office of the European Communities (EUROSTAT) the percentages of self-employed persons among the foreign economically active persons show a converging tendency (Table 6).

TABLE 6

Self-employment rates in EU States 1983 – 2000					
Year	Nationals	Non-nationals	of whom		Total
			EU nationals	Third country nationals	
Austria					
1983					
1987					
1995	11,4	5,6	22,9	3,2	10,8
2000	11,2	4,7	11,2	3,3	10,5
Belgium					
1983	15,0	11,7	13,6	8,6	14,7
1987	15,4	13,7	14,8	10,1	15,3
1995	15,3	16,4	17,2	14,0	15,4
2000	13,7	13,4	13,1	14,3	13,6
Germany					
1983	9,3	4,7	8,6	3,2	9,0
1987	9,3	6,7	9,5	5,0	9,1
1995	9,5	8,2	12,9	5,8	9,4
2000	9,8	8,7	12,8	6,5	9,7
Denmark					
1983	11,6	7,5	13,4	3,7	11,6
1987	9,2	7,3	6,4	7,7	9,2
1995	8,3	9,9	10,0	9,8	8,4
2000	8,0	6,8	11,2	4,5	8,0
Spain					
1983					
1987	23,5	24,1	28,7	19,2	23,5
1995	21,7	26,3	32,6	22,5	21,8
2000	18,0	17,8	31,6	11,0	18,0

Self-employment rates in EU States 1983 – 2000					
Year	Nationals	Non-nationals	of whom		Total
			EU nationals	Third country nationals	
Finland					
1983					
1987					
1995	14,4	7,5	14,9	4,2	14,3
2000	12,6	12,9	14,9	12,4	12,6
France					
1983	13,4	4,8	13,8	3,4	12,8
1987	13,0	7,0	6,4	7,6	12,7
1995	11,7	8,9	8,8	9,0	11,6
2000	10,0	9,4	10,3	8,6	10,0
Greece					
1983	36,6	23,3	25,2	22,9	36,5
1987	35,5	25,3	29,0	24,4	35,4
1995	34,1	12,8	23,8	11,0	33,8
2000	32,2	8,5	12,8	8,2	31,3
Ireland					
1983	21,3	20,1	20,3	19,1	21,3
1987	21,8	22,8	22,3	24,6	21,8
1995	20,7	22,7	22,9	22,2	20,8
2000	16,5	15,9	17,7	11,9	16,5
Italy					
1983					23,9
1987					24,4
1995	24,5	21,7	26,4	20,4	24,5
2000	23,7	19,3	26,1	17,9	23,6

Self-employment rates in EU States 1983 – 2000					
Year	Nationals	Non-nationals	of whom		Total
			EU nationals	Third country nationals	
Luxembourg					
1983	11,0	5,7	8,2	2,4	9,4
1987	10,9	5,5	5,2	9,8	9,2
1995	12,2	6,5	6,5	6,0	10,0
2000	10,2	6,5	6,6	6,2	8,7
Netherlands					
1983	9,6	5,6	9,1	3,9	9,5
1987	10,2	8,4	9,7	7,4	10,1
1995	11,6	7,9	8,6	7,1	11,5
2000	10,1	8,8	11,5	7,0	10,0
Portugal					
1983					
1987	27,3	15,3	42,2	8,0	27,2
1995	25,8	34,9	33,8	36,0	25,8
2000	20,3	11,7	9,1	12,1	20,2
Sweden					
1983					
1987					
1995	11,3	9,8	7,9	11,9	11,3
2000	9,9	9,1	7,3	11,0	9,8
United Kingdom					
1983	10,1	12,6	13,0	12,4	10,2
1987	12,4	15,9	15,1	16,4	12,5
1995	13,0	13,7	15,2	12,4	13,0
2000	10,9	12,2	12,7	11,8	10,9

Self-employment rates in EU States 1983 – 2000					
Year	Nationals	Non-nationals	of whom		Total
			EU nationals	Third country nationals	
EU					
1983					14,2
1987					15,9
1995	15,2	9,9	12,9	7,9	15,0
2000	13,8	10,0	12,6	8,4	13,6

Note: self-employed related to all employed persons.

Source: Eurostat Labour Force Survey.

But there are striking differences between countries and between EU and Non-EU nationals. In general self-employment for non-nationals is on the rise and, in some countries, reached the same level as for nationals, e. g. in D, F, UK. Self-employment is in general more frequent among the EU citizens. However, a word of caution: the circumstances of the development of self-employed activity and the type of companies must be taken into account. Were the foreigners "forced" into self-employment due to the poor labour market situation? What income can be realised with it and how viable are the companies? In order to answer these questions more research is necessary.

4. Other indicators

As already mentioned during the discussion on the indicators of integration into the labour market there is no single indicator which reliably reflects the degree or the rate of integration into the labour market. Only by simultaneous consideration of several indicators can an overall picture be obtained. Each of the indicators mentioned so far describes a particular partial situation in the labour market. Besides the indicators of integration into the labour market so far mentioned one can imagine others (without any empirical evidence of them being provided here):

(1) For the integration of migrants their economic success is important. Integration can only be successful if material equality between nationals and foreigners (or ethnic groups) is achieved under otherwise equal conditions. An important

prerequisite for this is equal pay for equal work, as well as equal work in the case of equal qualifications between nationals and foreigners. The same earnings of nationals and foreigners with otherwise identical characteristics is an indicator of integration into the labour market.

(2) The degree of employment of nationals and foreigners in atypical forms of employment can be compared. Examples of such forms are contracts of employment for a limited period, as well as involuntary part-time work and manpower hire arrangements.

For employers, the use of atypical forms of employment are attractive because in that way they can adjust personnel to fluctuating production requirements. From the point of view of employees, atypical forms of employment are not always automatically the worse alternative compared with normal contracts of employment. In part, they correspond to their interests. This applies, e.g. in the case of women with children who wish to have part-time work or in the case of schoolchildren and students who are not interested in permanent work. In most cases, as a result of the employment situation, persons looking for work as a rule have no alternative to atypical employment.

Atypical forms of employment are often part of the so-called secondary labour market, and therefore reflect a precarious situation for employees in the labour market. If foreign employees are found in such employment to a disproportionately high extent this would be an indication of inadequate integration into the labour market. There are indications that foreigners can be found to a disproportionately high extent in so-called precarious employment.

(3) Training represents a decisive factor for integration into the labour market. As a rule education/training promotes access to employment and makes equality of opportunity possible with regard to incomes and choice of occupation. Success or lack of success at school not only determines later opportunities in the labour market, but leads to social behaviour which can influence the course of life positively or negatively (marginalisation, criminality). The proportions of the second and third generations of foreigners which pass through the various levels of the education/training system are an important indicator of integration into the education system and the society of the particular country.

VII. Concluding Remarks

It can be stated that the labour market position of non-nationals is less favourable than that of the indigenous labour force. This statement applies in particular to third-country nationals but not always to citizens from EU Member States. Employment difficulties cumulate for certain groups of persons e. g. women, young people, less qualified. The figures are particularly worrying for young people.

The differences between nationals and non-nationals (esp. from third countries) did not level off over time. With decreasing overall unemployment the joblessness for foreigners also came down. But the relational differences remained.

Foreign workers are more affected by an economic downturn. The same applies to restructuring and rationalisations. The industrial sector, which still employs many foreigners, sheds labour. Re-employment in the expanding services sector or participation in re-training schemes are often difficult due to insufficient knowledge of the language or the lack of basic qualifications.

With on-going globalisation and further technology advances higher skills become an essential ingredient of employability. The continuing unfavourable labour market situation of non-nationals is mostly due to their unsatisfactory skills. For example, the share of foreign workers with low skills did not change over time in Germany. With 60% (Turks 70%) it is double the percentage as for the nationals.

What is particularly alarming is the fact that for young foreigners the situation is not much different and did not improve much over time. This is especially true for young Turks in Germany. Worrying is also that participation in education, for example in the dual system of vocational training in Germany, did not increase.

It has to be emphasised that intensive integration efforts will still be necessary in the future – particularly for young people. Education and training will play a crucial role. To young migrants and their parents it must be made clear how important qualifications and skills are for their future vocational life. It is in the interest of the host society (skill gaps) and of the young people themselves to undertake efforts in education and training.

Immigration and integration can not be separated. They are the two sides of the same coin. Successful integration is only possible if the inflows can be controlled as well. An uncontrolled and massive entry makes integration efforts more difficult and creates competition between the indigenous population and foreigners on the markets for labour and housing, for example. The indigenous population would also not accept the excessive strain on the educational and social systems and the ensuing high cost. Therefore, the traditional immigration countries such as USA, Canada, Australia or countries with high shares of foreign workers such as Switzerland have been very careful to control immigration in line with the economic situation and the acceptance by their population.

Sources – summarised, revised and up-dated for this conference from:

Werner, H./König, I. (2001): Integration ausländischer Arbeitnehmer in die Arbeitsmärkte der EU-Länder – Ein europäischer Vergleich, IAB-Werkstattbericht Nr. 10, www.iab.de.

Kiehl, M./Werner, H. (1998): The labour market situation of EU and of third-country nationals in the European Union, IAB-Topics No. 32.

DISCUSSION

Mr. von Hoffmann started the discussion by stating that the results of the report made him thoughtful as to the efficiency of recruitment of foreigners in order to solve the ageing problem in a country, since the situation on the labour markets seemed to be very uncertain for non-nationals. Mr. Werner sought a response to this fact for the territory of Europe in a change of the economical situation. Low-skilled "Gast" worker who were brought in earlier to expand the industry were no longer of importance for the present economy. Hence, some skilled migration would be desirable. The speaker added that the rules for "Gast" workers had probably not been selective enough.

Mr. von Hoffmann rose the question if there could be a possibility to help the second generation of Turks to find an occupation. Mr. Werner noted, that equal rights – eventually naturalisation – were the basis for overall integration including integration to the labour market. He then stated, that though naturalized, foreigners often suffered greater unemployment rates than nationals.

Mr. Bisopoulos referred to the self-employment of non-nationals, which had been mentioned by Mr. Werner as one of the clues showing the degree of integration. Up to his personal experience, migrants are often forced to be self-employed since they cannot find any other occupation. Although there are many examples of successful immigrant entrepreneurs, he asked if self-employment of immigrants really advances their integration in the labour market. Mr. Werner admitted that no indicator on its own depicted integration at a whole and he concurred Mr. Bisopoulos with the necessity to consider the viability of an enterprise. However, he underlined that self-employment demonstrated an access to the market and therefore still could be seen as an important indicator relating to the degree of integration.

Ms. Oellers-Frahm marked that statistics on unemployment of young people and women shown by the speaker during his report, made it clear that these worries had to be examined closely when talking about the family reunification, since they arise out of it. Mr. Werner entirely agreed. In his attitude, the success of young people depends inter alias on aid to parents since German part time schools are not sufficient supportive on the integration point.

Ms. Langenfeld focussed the participant's attention on the difficulties of integration of Turkish people in Germany, stemming among others from differences in religion. This kind of problems are especially important in the public education context in case that e.g. Muslim pupils are not willing to participate in sport education, education on sexual matters etc. Quite obviously it could be maintained that orthodox have more problems to integrate than non-religious people.

Mr. Werner consented that religion may play a role in integration matters. Especially among Turkish migrants, he noticed a strong polarization of some people being well-integrated and some not integrated at all.

Ms. Langenfeld noted a strong distinction between the integration ability among different minorities: Spanish as well as Yugoslavian minorities seem to be very successful, whereas Italian minorities at least partially are not. Concerning the Turks, she identified two different groups, one of which becomes isolated, while the other becomes more and more integrated. The crucial question should then be how to help this first part, since it should not be contemplated about new immigration until the already migrated population has been fully integrated.

Mr. Werner made the observation that while the unemployment rate of the Portuguese was very low, that of Italians was very high. Nonetheless he persisted to be very cautious when generalizing the integration ability of one minority.

An explanation of the unwillingness to integrate was sought by Ms. Langenfeld in the mistrust of parts of the Italian population towards the state and its authorities as well as the lack of deeper interest in educational matters. Mr. Werner identified one reason for the low unemployment rate of Portuguese migrants in their attitude towards the employment, since it played a very important role for them. He maintained his statement by showing that unemployment rates of Portuguese migrants are very low also in France and even Portugal.

Ms. Fernando presumed that for successful integration other motives than only economical must exist. She gave an example of Vietnamese people who knew there would be no possibility to go back to their origin and so were very motivated to integrate.

The discussion was concluded by Mr. Bisopoulos who emphasised the importance of the helping emigrants to integrate in the host country.

III. INTEGRATION

SANDRINE VAN DER VELDE*

THREE PARADOXES IN THE COMMUNITY RIGHT TO FAMILY REUNIFICATION FOR MIGRANT WORKERS

A common feature in European migration politics, which may even be true for politics in general, is that it is characterised by a lack of – economically – logic based thinking, and rather "inspired" by psychological considerations. Therefore it is often difficult to explain certain processes or developments in migration law. As AG Mancini mentioned in the *Migration Policy* case: "in order to understand the reasons behind these proceedings there is no alternative but to leave the realm of logic and venture into the realm of psychology."

In this paper, I would like to focus on one particular aspect of European migration policy, namely the right to family reunification. Notwithstanding the initial economical characteristics of European integration, this subject has been on the agenda of the European Union since its very beginning, and yet no legislative act covers this right for all legal residents within the European Community. I will outline the history of the right to family reunification, in particular of third-country nationals and show the difficulties and controversies of its development, which is characterised by the several paradoxes, which will form the thread of this presentation.

In doing so, I will always keep in mind the heart of the subject under discussion, which is the (third-country national) migrant workers. They are individuals, looking for a way to lead a satisfactory life, from both an economic and sentimental perspective. I believe that these are the same perspectives Member States consider in their legislative process. Since the current conference has already put ample emphasis on the economic (and demographic) side of the spectrum, I will be more concerned with the more "sentimental" aspects of the Member States' and the EU's decision-making within the field of migration policy.

Finally, I will also try to give an explanation for the paradoxical development. This requires to "venture into the realm of psychology" of politicians, as well as into sociological and political considerations. As a lawyer, I am possibly less qualified to do so than many of the readers. What I can hope to do is give you food for thought on the subject and initiate a meaningful discussion for which I would be very grateful.

---

* Many thanks to professor G. De Búrca.

I. The Principle of Family Reunification

First of all, I would like to go back to the very basis of European integration, where the free movement of persons is concerned. Regulation 1612/68 about the free movement of workers within the Community already stresses the importance of the right to family reunification. It mentions that "Whereas the right of freedom of movement, in order that it may be exercised, by objective standards, in freedom and dignity, requires that (...) obstacles to the mobility of workers shall be eliminated, in particular as regards the worker's rights to be joined by his family and the conditions for the integration of that family into the host country."

The Regulation only covered Community workers, but as a principle, the same consideration is of course equally true for third-country national workers; in order to move freely and to establish themselves in one of the Member States, they should have a right to family reunification and once reunited, those family members should have the opportunity to integrate in the host Member State.

Indeed, all current 15 Member States of the European Union have national legislation on the right to family reunification for third-country nationals. Studies have revealed that the applicable national rules are even relatively similar on many points. There seems to be a common understanding of the right to reunite with wife and (minor) children, possibly after a few years of legal residence. The wife and children may also actively participate in the host society, in the sense that they have a right to schooling and access to the labour market. The exact conditions under which the rights may be exercised can differ from country to country, but there is consensus on the basics.

However, when it comes to harmonisation or europeanisation of the right to family reunification, many problems arise. And notwithstanding the long history of attempts to harmonise the right to family reunification for third-country nationals, no legally binding text has yet been adopted.

But before moving on to the reasons behind this, I will briefly discuss the development of the right to family reunification, from an exclusive right for Community workers at first, towards a comprehensive right for all persons legally resident within the EU. I will do this on the basis of three paradoxes. The development of the right to family reunification for migrant workers is the subject of my Ph.D. research. The two main outcomes of this research are for one that Member States are extremely reluctant to hand over any competence to the European institutions in the area of migration policy, more in particular the field of family reunification for migrant workers. Also, the level of protection in Community instruments tends to decline, but I will explain that this can, at least in part, be seen as a result of the first finding. The second outcome of my research is that the European institutions have over the years received increasingly and significantly more competence within the field of migration law, also where family reunification is concerned. This is the first paradox that will be discussed.

II. Paradox No. 1:

The reluctance of Member States to hand over any competence in the field of migration policy and the increased body of legislation on family reunion

Without dwelling into every little detail of the history of a European migration policy, I will just mention some of the most striking landmarks in order to illustrate my statement that Member States are reluctant to hand over any competence to the Community in the field of migration in general, and of family reunification rights in particular.

One of those landmarks is certainly the M*igration Policy* case of 1985. It was an action by five Member States (out of ten at the time!) against the Commission. They asked the Court of Justice for the annulment of a Decision to set up a "prior communication and consultation procedure on migration policies in relation to non-member countries." In short, it came down to a Decision that would enable the Commission to be informed about national migration policies and decisions. The Commission did *not* claim legislative competence with regard to migration policy. And even though the Commission had taken similar decisions in other fields of law, the five Member States concerned felt this quest for information came too close to their own national sovereignty and lodged an appeal for annulment. Their determination to exclude the Commission in every possible way from interference with national migration policies led, shortly afterwards and even *before* the Court rejected the Member States' application, to the signing of the Single European Act in 1986.

Although the SEA introduced the internal market, and according to the Commission's White Paper this necessitated co-operation in the field of migration policy, the Member States explicitly excluded this area from the Community-competences in an annexed General Declaration to the SEA: "Nothing in these provisions shall affect the right of Member States to take such measures as they consider necessary for the purpose of controlling immigration from third countries (...)".

In the meantime, the need for co-operation in the field of migration law could not be denied, not even by the most sceptic Member States. And thus, different forms of intergovernmental co-operation were established. However, this co-operation was based purely on practical, economic considerations, imposed by the creation of the internal market. Notwithstanding the Member States' scepticism towards Community action in the field of migration policy, important progress was made in the '90s. The right to free movement contained in Regulation 1612/68 was extended from workers, to include other economically active persons, formerly active persons and students. In 1992, the Maastricht Treaty partly formalised the current informal inter-governmental co-operation in the area of migration between Member States. The creation of the internal market was considered to be more important than the individual sovereignty of the Member States where the ingress of aliens was concerned, and apparently cultural differences between Member States could be overcome. It should be noted that until this moment all the progress made was a result of intergovernmental co-operation in the third pillar and that the Member States had not handed over any competence whatsoever to the Community.

Apart from legislation concerning European citizens, other instruments were developed in the Union to also harmonise the right to family reunification for third-country nationals. Of special importance are the agreements with several countries, especially the EEA countries, Turkey, Central and Eastern European Countries and the Maghreb countries. These agreements create the categories of so-called "privileged third-country nationals". As a last stage in the development of a Community policy on family reunification, the Commission in 1999 presented a draft Directive on family reunification that should cover in principle *all* legally resident persons, thus including European citizens and third-country nationals.

In short it can be said that notwithstanding the reluctance of Member States to hand over any competence to the Community in the field of migration policy, the legislative body on Union level concerning ingress and stay of migrants increased all the same. Thus, the group of persons covered by the Community legislation on family reunification increased significantly, but as a counterbalance to this development, the level of protection has also decreased quite drastically.

Without going into detail here, I will mention just a few examples. A novelty contained in the new proposed Directive in comparison to existing legislation, is the introduction of a waiting period before the sponsor can apply for reunification. This has even been raised from one to two years in the latest draft of the proposed Directive. Another new element in the draft Directive is the introduction of a reference to the *scope* of the stay of the sponsor. It is no longer sufficient that he or she is legally resident and complies with the material conditions. The sponsor should also have "reasonable prospects of obtaining the right of permanent residence." With regard to the definition of the family a shift can be noticed from the inclusion of all relatives in the ascending and descending line, towards the mere reference to a "rest-category", over which Member States can decide freely. It should be said, however, that the category of "spouses" is to be enlarged with the inclusion (at least for some Member States) of partners in a non-marital relationship, including same sex relationships. Furthermore, the financial threshold, in order to qualify for family reunification that is absent for European workers, has been introduced for third-country nationals, and has even been tightened up in the last version of the draft Directive. While, in the beginning, access to the labour market seemed a logical right for family members to have, it has since been watered down, especially in the Association Agreements. It has been suggested to introduce a kind of "cascade-principle", as is known in the Turkey Association Agreement, in the draft Directive because Member States do not agree on an automatic access to the labour market anymore.

In other words, the instruments studied mainly reflect two developments: one is a widening of the group of migrants covered by European legislation, the other is a downward development concerning the level of protection. These two developments are probably inter-linked: the more persons it concerns, the more interest to limit the protection, otherwise too many people would seek this protection. Another explanation of the declining development in the protection of family reunification rights should undoubtedly be sought in historical events. The oil crisis and the general decline of economic progress brought Member States to be more reluctant about a great influx of third-country nationals, who are seen as more mouths to feed. But apart from these considerations, there seems to be a reluctance from the side of the Member States to hand over any competence to the Community, to be extremely reserved about sharing their exclusive competence to rule on migration policy, which cannot always be explained by merely economic considerations. Where the economic need to allow entry of third-country nationals is apparent in certain sectors of industry, Member States still insist on restrictive migration policies to enhance internal election results. The protection of their own culture seems to play a bigger role than ever. Clearly, this argument played a lesser role when free movement rights were given to citizens of other European countries.

In brief, the first paradox is that over the years, Member States have become ever more reluctant to hand over any competence to the Community institutions. This seems to be in contrast with another development, which is the widening of the personal scope of the Community instruments concerning family reunification. The result is a watering down of the level of protection within the field of family reunification for an ever-larger group of persons.

The fact that the personal scope of Community legislation increases, means that Member States *do* hand over competence to the Community institutions, nolens volens. At the level of the European Council, there seems to be political agreement on the necessity of this shift of competence. The European Council has indeed on many occasions stressed the importance of the creation of a common approach to European migration policy, and the Commission has reacted to this with a flood of proposals to harmonise the European migration policy. However, this activism has not yet led to the introduction of such a policy. In the following, this paradox will be illustrated with regard to family reunification.

III. Paradox No. 2:

Political agreement on the outlines and failure to harmonise the right to family reunification for migrant workers

The reluctance of Member States to hand over any competence to the Community institutions seems to contrast with the actions of the same Member States in the framework of the European Council, that states repeatedly since the Amsterdam Treaty, the importance of the development of a European migration policy and harmonisation in every field where the free movement of persons is concerned. Indeed, in the European Council there seems to exist a political willingness to harmonise, which just cannot be translated into legally binding instruments in the day-to-day practice of the Council. An overview of the developments in the creation of an over-all legal instrument on family reunification, from the Amsterdam Treaty onwards will demonstrate this.

Progress in the harmonisation of European migration policy did not stop with the conclusion of bi-lateral agreements with third countries nor with the extension of free movement rights to other categories of European citizens. Without repeating all the details of the Amsterdam Treaty, its importance concerning the transfer of migration policy from the third to the first pillar of the EU construction should be remembered. One particularity of title IV of the Amsterdam Treaty was that it introduced a time limit of five years within which the Member States could come to an agreement in the Council. After these five years, the co-decision procedure would apply. Although the five-year incentive did not apply to all the Articles, for instance the one on family reunification, the European

Council seemed to be taking the *whole* area of European migration policy very seriously.

This becomes clear from the Tampere summit of October 1999. Point 18 of the conclusions reads: "the European Union must ensure fair treatment of third-country nationals who reside legally on the territory of its Member States. A more vigorous integration policy should aim at granting them rights and obligations comparable to those of EU citizens." And furthermore at point 21: "the legal status of third-country nationals should be approximated to that of Member States' nationals. A person, who has resided legally in a Member State for a period of time to be determined and who holds a long-term residence permit, should be granted in that Member State a set of uniform rights which are as near as possible to those enjoyed by EU citizens." These conclusions reveal a great political willingness to co-operate within the European Union to finally establish a common migration policy and to realise a common market where the free movement of persons will become reality. Within three months after the summit, the Commission presented its first draft Directive on the right to family reunification.

The proposal was very ambitious at the outset. Its objective was to regulate in one legal instrument all legal residents within the Community, including European citizens, privileged third-country nationals, refugees and other third-country nationals. The document was to be seen as a comprehensive instrument that aimed at full harmonisation. Therefore flexible elements should be reduced to a minimum and a standstill clause was not necessary. However, today, almost three years and two drafts later, this proposal for a Directive is still on the table, and consensus does not seem to be any closer.

In order to enhance the possibilities of reaching an agreement the Commission has made many concessions in its last draft from May 2002. Without mentioning it literally, the new draft bears many features of the open method of co-ordination. Many flexible provisions have been introduced, as well as a standstill clause and a deadline for further negotiations on the most controversial points. It is yet unclear how the Council has received this new proposal.

When discussing the difficulties of getting a draft Directive on family reunification adopted, some facts should be borne in mind. In reality, the discussion concerning the question on family reunification for all legal residents within the Community borders has been going on for over 10 years. In 1993, a Resolution on family reunification was adopted. And although it concerned minimum standards, Member States agreed. But now that a legally binding instrument needs to be adopted, which is in part on the Resolution, on the Member States legal practices and on existing Community law, the Council cannot come to an agreement. Too often the disagreements do not seem due to fundamental differences between Member States – as I mentioned before, there is consensus on the principles of the right to family reunification for third-country nationals. It rather seems that Member States are vigorously defending their national sovereignty, when it really comes to taking concrete decisions.

As a conclusion to this part of my paper, I would resume paradox no. 2 by saying that notwithstanding the apparent political willingness to co-operation in order to establish a common European policy on family reunification for third-country nationals, Member States are unable to agree on the effective form and exact wording of the legal texts. In the following, I will shed a light on the position of the European Commission in the described development of a European right to family reunification for third-country nationals.

IV. Paradox No. 3:

1. *An increased importance of human rights considerations and a lower standard of protection*

The developments described before, the reluctance of Member States to hand over any competence in the field of family reunification for migrant workers, with the consequence of a lower level of protection, and the increased competence of the Community to rule on family reunification, goes hand in hand with a third development. When studying closely the legal instruments on family reunification from Regulation 1612/68 to the latest draft of the proposed Directive on family reunification from May 2002, another factor becomes apparent. Whereas in the early documents the economic considerations for installing a free movement of persons (and as a part of that the right to family reunification) prevailed, with the lapse of time more and more importance was given to human rights considerations. Therefore, the lowering standard of protection for persons seeking reunification with their family members is accompanied by an increased interest for human rights considerations in legal instruments concerned with family reunification.

In order to respect the limited time and space of this intervention, I will confine myself here to a comparison of the two extremes of the development of the right to family reunification for migrant workers: Regulation 1612/68 on the freedom of movement of workers within the Community; and the draft Directive on the right to family reunification. To start with the first, the purely economical considerations lying at the foundations of this Regulation have been mentioned before. Not once does it refer to reasons beyond the economical interest of the establishment of the "customs union", as the internal market was called at the time.

The main considerations with regard to the right to family reunification in the preliminary statements are the following:

> "Whereas by reason in particular *the early establishment of the customs union* and in order to ensure the simultaneous completion of the principal foundations of the Community, provisions should be adopted to enable the objectives laid down in Articles 48 and 49 of the Treaty in the field of movement" and "Whereas the right of free movement, in order that it may be exercised, by objective standards, in freedom and dignity, requires that equality of treatment shall be ensured in fact and in law in respect of all matters relating to the actual pursuit of activities as employed persons and to eligibility for housing, and also that obstacles to the mobility of workers shall be eliminated, *in particular as regards the worker's right to be joined by his family and the conditions for the integration of that family into the host country"* (emphasis added).

The draft Directive on the right to family reunification shows a very different picture. It does not exclude economic considerations ("In the long term, there are demographic factors such as the ageing of the population, with all that this entails in terms of welfare protection and the funding of pension schemes"), but puts them on the same level, or even submits them to other considerations, linked to history and culture. At a certain point, the Commission even seems to want to claim a right to family reunification, *notwithstanding* the economical situation in the Member States:

> "It is true that the current employment market situation does not give the Community the grounds for operating an entry and residence policy of the very open kind that prevailed in the 1950s and 1960s. But the employment rate is not the only factor underlying immigration policy (...). More generally, a common immigration policy at European level will need to be flexible so that it can reflect the manifold dimensions of migratory flows, be they *economic, social, cultural or historical*, relating both to host countries and countries of origin."

Alongside these general political considerations, the Commission also mentions the importance for the *individual* to have the possibility to apply for family reunification: "family reunification is a necessary way of making a success of the integration of third-country nationals residing lawfully in the Member States. The presence of family members makes for greater stability and deepens the roots of these people since they are enabled to lead a normal family life." Another striking point to the draft Directive on the right to family reunification is, that it mentions various international human rights instruments that were taken into account: the Universal Declaration of Human Rights; the Covenants of 1966 on Civil and Political Rights and on Economic and Social Rights; the International Convention on the protection of the rights of all migrant workers and members of their families; the Convention on the Rights of the Child and the European Convention of Human Rights.

In short, paradox number 3 comes down to the following: the level of protection contained in the Community instruments on the right to family reunification for migrant workers has decreased over the last 35 years, while the human rights discourse in the same instruments has taken a high flight.

2. *The realm of psychology*

These three paradoxes present us with a challenge: to try to find an explanation for the situation as it exists today. Logical reasoning brings us to see just paradoxes. It is therefore unavoidable to shift away from the purely legalistic viewpoint, and to look also to sociological, political, economic and maybe even psychological considerations which may explain the behaviour of the different actors in this play; the single Member States, the European Council, the Council of the European Union, the European Parliament, the European Commission and, since I mentioned psychology, probably also the individuals that form these institutions.

I have already started to give an explanation with regard to the first paradox, the increase of the personal scope of harmonised instruments notwithstanding the Member States' reluctance to hand over any competence in the field of migration policies. I mentioned that the decrease of the level of protection is probably linked to the increase of the number of persons concerned and the decreasing economical situation in most Member States. But this is just part of the answer.

Member States, when forming the European Union, agreed on the setting up of a common market. This brings along the four freedoms. So far so good, where economic integration is concerned. But Member States seem to consider the question of national sovereignty more, when persons are concerned. As a result, Member States could not deny the need to establish the free movement of persons, but they opted to do this under an intergovernmental framework rather than on the supra-national Community level. This way, they secured themselves of the highest possible input from Member States, and avoided a shift of competence.

Then the second paradox, strictly linked with the first. Why is it so that Member States agree on the principle of the free movement of persons and as a corollary to a Community migration policy, but cannot agree on the actual wording of the legal instruments? Indeed, the creation of a common market requires the functioning of the four freedoms. The principles of free movement of persons and of a harmonised migration policy fit perfectly in the system of the common market and an agreement should be relatively easy to reach. But at the point of the actual drafting, what seem minor problems gain prevalence over the principle and block the decision-making process. I can only make a guess as to why this happens.

It is often mentioned that migration policy is closely linked with the question of sovereignty. But that does not mean anything in itself. As an example, I could mention the handing over of competence and a great deal of national sovereignty with the introduction of the Euro. Member States agreed to this far-reaching shift in competence on a political level, just like with family reunification. Maybe it is only thanks to the ECB, and independent body, that this idea actually came into being. Returning to the issue of family reunification and sovereignty, maybe the question is not so much "how come the Council does not manage to carry out the administrative part of a political assignment, which is the drafting of a European migration policy?" but "how come there was an agreement concerning the shift of sovereignty in the first place?" – I can only imagine it has something to do with a feeling linked with the protection of the national culture. But maybe I am venturing to deep into the realm of psychology.

Finally, the third paradox, which linked the decreased level of protection in family reunion instruments to an increased interest for human rights considerations. Although this paradox might seem more distinct from the other two, I see a clear link. The decreased level of protection in family reunion instruments was mentioned before, and so was the reluctance of the Member States to hand over any competence to Community institutions in the field of migration policy. Here might lie the key to the increased use of human rights considerations in the proposals from the Commission. With the power to call upon international human rights instruments and, importantly, the Union Charter of Human Rights, the Commission seems to give itself (and the other Community institutions) the necessary justification to interfere with national sovereignty, with national migration policy. It seems that the Commission invokes international, moral, human rights standards in order to bypass national scepticism and reluctance to hand over any competence in the field of migration law. The Commission implicitly seems to imply that it is better placed to protect human rights than national governments.

Although nobody would disagree that human rights are also defended in a very effective way on a national level, or that national constitutions contain many guarantees for a society in which human rights are accessible for all, the European Community has taken over this role where Community issues are involved. When Community policies are concerned, the human rights standards referred to are equally European, in order to safeguard the uniformity of Community legislation. This has once more been confirmed with the adoption of the EU Charter of Fundamental Rights. In a similar context, Coppel and O'Neill have qualified this use of the human rights discourse as the "offensive" or "instrumental" use of fundamental rights. This means that, rather than caring so much for the values they claim to defend, the European institutions (in that case the Court, in the present case the Commission) invoke fundamental rights in order to increase or safeguard their own competence. In the case of family reunification, the Commission seems to be supported in its approach by the European Parliament who insists on the inclusion of human rights components to the proposals. The position of the Council seems less clear, since it is stuck between the Community and the Member States.

One important element should be taken into consideration here. That is the importance of political responsibility or electoral accountability. Whereas the Member States' governments always have to respond to the feelings of their electorate, also in their function of the Council of the European Union, the Commission, and to a certain extent even the European Parliament, are not limited by similar considerations of political gain or loss. This is also why the Commission can use in full what was called before the offensive use of the human rights discourse. Because although Member States see migration rather as an economic and security issue, they can impossibly revolt against considerations of fundamental rights. That would undoubtedly be seen as politically incorrect.

One might wonder, though, why the human rights discourse is not also heard at a national level. Most recent national elections have evolved very much around migration issues. And rather than explaining that migrants are human beings with a right to family life, that the presence of family members can only help immigrants to integrate, national politicians present migration purely as security or economic matters. Only the – left – opposition parties, (maybe because of the same considerations as the Commission?) use the human rights argument.

When saying this, I am back at the beginning of my intervention. Why is this so? Why is migration more than any other issue seen as a threat to society? Is it just because of economic considerations? I doubt that. The most vigorous protesters against migration revolt the day their friendly Turkish neighbour is threatened with expulsion because he runs an illegal textile workshop. Is it then linked with a feeling that the cultural identity of the country is threatened? Finishing this paper with more questions rather than answers really forces a lawyer to venture into the realms of sociology, politics, economy or even psychology...*

Further reading:

Caracciolo di Torella, E./Reid, E., The Changing Shape of The "European Family" and Fundamental Rights, E.L.Rev. 2002, p. 80-90.

Cholewinski, R., Family Reunification and the Conditions Placed on Family Members: Dismantling a Fundamental Human Right, EJML 2002, p. 271-290.

Coppel, J./O'Neill, A.,The European Court of Justice: Taking Rights Seriously?, CMLRev. 1992, p. 669-692.

ILPA, The Alternative Scoreboard for EU Immigration and Asylum Law: Human Rights and Basic Principles – Response to the European Commission's Proposal for a Directive on the Right to Family Reunification, ILPA website (www.ilpa.org.uk) 2000.

McGlynn, C., Families and the European Union Charter of Fundamental Rights: progressive change or entrenching the status quo? E.L.Rev. 2001, p. 582-598.

Niessen, J., European Migration Policies: The Member States Against The Commission, Migrantenrecht 1992, p. 7-12.

* The contributions of Ms. Sandrine van der Velde and of Mr. Albrecht Weber and Ms. Anne Walter were treated in one discussion following the contribution of Mr. Albrecht Weber and Ms. Anne Walter.

Albrecht Weber / Anne Walter

THE RIGHT OF PROTECTION OF FAMILY FOR MIGRANTS IN EUROPE:

ACCESS AND INTEGRATION OF FAMILY REUNION

I. Some General Reflections on Family Reunification

The following paper mainly presents a summarized overview on the actual state of Community legislation in the area of "family repatriation" or "family reunification".[1]

Family repatriation is an eminent feature and essential element of integration policy of any European or EC Country.

EU family reunification of third-country nationals – from the pure legal point of view – has to comply with a number of international human rights obligations on the one hand and apparently with national constitutional standards. As for international standards, a general framework for this has been presented in the papers of Dr. Oellers-Frahm and also by Prof. Calliess who writes from the EU standpoint. The existence of these papers allows us to shorten this introduction.

On the international human rights level Article 17 para. 1 International Covenant on Civil and Political Rights guarantees defensive rights against arbitrary or unlawful interference with privacy and family whereas Article 23 para. 1 CCPR concerns the family as "the natural and fundamental group unit of society, which is entitled to protection by society and the state".

In the European context Article 8 ECHR plays the essential role in safeguarding the protection of family members.[2]

The relevance of Article 8 ECHR for the residence-permits of repatriation of Third State "family members" is not quite clear.

The earlier Commission has postulated "close factual ties" for family life (ECHR No. 9492/81 et al.). Article 8 is relevant however, if the refusal of repatriation leads to a separation of close family ties and the return to the home

1 Prepared by Ms. Anne Walter on the basis of her doctoral research within the Graduate College at IMIS.

2 For further consideration see *Oeter*, in: *Hailbronner/Klein* (eds.), Einwanderungskontrolle und Menschenrechte, 1999, p. 130.

country cannot be supposed. In the case of *Abdulaziz* (ECHR 19/2/1996, No. 53/1995 599) the Court assumes that the term "family" includes any relation of a true and lawful marriage even if the marital and familiar community is not entirely established. The Court acknowledges a wide range of discretion for the Member States how to comply with the respect of family life.

However, a general right of repatriation of family members cannot be deduced from Article 8 ECHR.

In the case *Gül v. Switzerland* (where a minor son wanted to join his Turkish parents) the Court stated

> "The present case concerns not only family life but also immigration, and the extent of a State's obligation to admit to its territory relatives of settled immigrants will vary according to the particular circumstances of the persons involved and the general interest. As a matter of well-established international law and subject to its treaty obligations, a State has the right to control the entry of non-nationals into its territory (see, among other authorities, the Abdulaziz, Cabales and Balkandali v. the United Kingdom judgment of 28 May 1985, Series A no. 94, pp. 33-34, § 67). Moreover, where immigration is concerned, Article 8 cannot be considered to impose on a State a general obligation to respect the choice by married couples of the country of their matrimonial residence and to authorise family reunion in its territory. In order to establish the scope of the State's obligations, the facts of the case must be considered (see, mutatis mutandis, the Abdulaziz, Cabales and Balkandali judgment previously cited, p. 34, § 68, and the Cruz Varas and Others v. Sweden judgment of 20 March 1991, Series A no. 201, p. 32, § 88)."

Although according to the *Berrehab* case (*Berrehab/Netherlands*, ECHR 21/6/1988, No. 10730/84) the visiting contacts of the divorced father to his minor son are protected by Article 8 ECHR, no individual right for a residence permit may be derived. To the contrary the Court ruled in the recent case *Sen v. The Netherlands* (21/12/2001, No 31456/96) that the refusal of a residence permit for minor children violates Article 8 ECHR.

Thus there is a relatively wide spectre of policy measures for EC regulations concerning family reunification. There are no international or regional human rights obligations requiring a wide definition of "family" exceeding the nuclear family or extending privileges to non-married couples or registered partnerships.

Therefore, human rights considerations can only hedge the EU policy considerations. These may vary from an assimilation of the status of EU citizens towards third state nationals to a model of distinct family reunification patterns for EU citizens and Third State Nationals. One of the essential questions mirrored in the past and present discussions of the draft Directives on family reunification apparently will be: How near should the family status of EU citizens (and intermediately vis-à-vis citizens of associated states like Turkey) be? Does community law require a differentiation between the status of these persons or does it leave large discretion to EU Member States solely bound by international human rights law? Even if we assume the latter position, factual pressures may arise from the simple fact that family members would only enjoy the same rights of free movement within community borders as tourists (no right to job search and labour market participation).

The following lines will describe the actual state of EU discussion without intending to give any final answer.

II. Proposal for a Council-Directive on the Right to Family Reunification

1. Historical Background of the Directive

The Community Law contains no regulation on family reunification as far as third-country nationals are concerned. The exceptions to this are third-country nationals who are family members of EU citizens exercising their right to free movement of persons. The Proposal for a Council Directive on the right to family reunification addresses this issue.

The Commission presented the first proposal in December 1999[3] and has presented the third proposal[4] in May 2002.[5] This proposal considerably amends the initial proposal. It contains changes made by the European Parliament and the results of several debates in the Council, which were incorporated by the Commission. While the European Parliament's changes consisted more of explanatory additions ("enrich the Directive"), the compromises reached in the Council diluted the original text significantly. Therefore, the Commission felt obliged – as they have stated – to opt for a slower harmonisation of this sensitive national topic.

This was mainly achieved in three ways:

- *Flexibility*: rules of exception for those points on which the Member States could not agree because of their existing national laws (especially: the right to reunification only for the nuclear family (Article 3 para. 1 of the proposal); openings to determine an age barrier for reunification of children with their parents (Article 5 para. 1 of the proposal); the possibility to check the resources after reunification (Article 7 para. 1 of the proposal); a waiting

3 COM (1999) 638 final.
4 COM (2002) 225 final.
5 Articles without reference refer to this Directive.

period between the submission of an application and the issuing of a residence permit (Article 8 para. 2 of the proposal); standardisation of the conditions and the duration of the residence permit according to the Directive on the status of third-country nationals who are long-term residents[6] (Article 13 para. 2 of the proposal);

- *Standstill clause* (Article 3 para. 6 of the proposal): the derogation *is only applicable* before the time of adoption of the Directive (probably at the end of 2004 according to the proposal);
- *Deadline clause* (Article 19 para. 1 sent. 1 of the proposal): the above-mentioned "flexible" rules are to be checked by way of priority two years after the date of adoption of the Directive.

2. *What are the Objectives and Goals of the Proposal?*

This proposal contains two principles:

a) *Immigration of Family Members*

Family members can immigrate because of their personal relationship. This right derives from the right to preserve family unity, which is connected with the right to protection of family life, a fundamental right, which is protected by Community law.[7] If a family has been separated during an escape or for economical reasons, the personal relationship is an equivalent reason to immigrate. It is questionable, however, whether the right to reside has to be considered as a reason of equivalent value.

The proposal is not intended to grant a general right to family reunification. It resembles Article 8 ECHR. The Objective of the proposal is (only) the determination "of the conditions in which the right to family reunification is exercised in Europe, this right being recognised in existing national legislation and international instruments".[8] In contrast to this, the initial proposal contained "the right to family reunification established by this proposal for a Directive".[9]

6 COM (2001) 127 final.
7 See commentary of the Commission, No. 2.4. COM (2001) 257 final.
8 See commentary of the Commission to Article 1 of the proposal.
9 See commentary to Article 1 COM (1999) 638 final.

b) Integration of Family Members

The proposal forms part of a comprehensive volume of rules of Immigration law. This touches upon another main principle of the Commission. This is the approach of the status of long-term resident third-country nationals (here: the family members) toward the status of EU citizens according to Tampere.

The Council of the European Union in Tampere demanded "a common approach to ensure the integration into our societies of those third-country nationals who are lawfully residents in the Union. (...)". It pointed out that "(...) a more vigorous integration policy should aim at granting them rights and obligations *comparable to those of EU citizens*" (our italics).

With reference to this principle the Commission concluded in their explanatory memorandum on the proposal on family reunification:

> "To ensure that they can look forward to being treated in the same way as Union citizens, the proposal for a directive is based on certain provisions of existing Community law as regards the family reunification of Union citizens who exercise their right to free movement."[10]

This orientation on Community law is done indirectly. The intermediate step is the applicant, i.e. the family member, who immigrated to the EU for other reasons (employment, flight). To the latter the rules of the proposed Directive concerning the status of third-country nationals who are long-term residents[11] are to be applied. This Directive represents another main issue in the integration programme of the Commission. It aims at evaluating and adjusting the legal rights of third-country nationals as far as possible to those of EU citizens and to create a uniform status of long-term residents of third countries. It is applied to third-country nationals, refugees and family members as well.

The two proposed documents, the Directive concerning the status of third-country nationals who are long-term residents, and the Directive on family reunification, are aiming at the same direction as far as their legal basis and their objectives are concerned.

The reference to the rights of EU citizens establish the upper limit on how family reunification can be regulated. One should bear in mind that Community law is also still in the process of development in order to assure EU citizens' freedom of movement. Last year the Commission presented a proposal on the right of citizens of the Union and their family members to move and reside freely

10 See No. 7.2. COM (1999) 638 final.

11 COM (2001) 127 final.

within the territory of the Member States.[12] I will refer to the amendments in this document when they become relevant.

The minimum limit for the planned regulation is established by international law standards, in particular Article 8 ECHR, to which the Community has committed itself.

As mentioned above, it is the aim of the Directive on family reunification to adjust the status of the family members to that of third-country nationals, i.e. the status of the applicants. Therefore no reference is made to the status of EU citizens anymore as there was in the initial proposal. Only in the considerations there is still a reference to the rights of Union Citizens from the Conclusions of the Tampere European Council.[13] The following reason is given: "This will avert the risk of differences in treatment within one and the same family".[14]

A comprehensive description of entry and residence regulations will demonstrate that this system establishes a hierarchical order between EU citizens, third-country nationals and contains a (de)grading between Union citizens and third-country nationals as well as a (de)grading between the third-country national who is the applicant and his family members. The question is this: To which extent are the rights of family members adjusted to those of third-country nationals (e.g. the applicant) in a way that would promote their integration? What are the main differences between the two? Did the objective of integration benefit from this Directive?

2. *Entry Requirements*

Family members of third-country nationals may enter the EU if they fulfil several personal and economic requirements.

a) *Personal: Who is allowed to apply?*

The Directive applies to all third-country nationals who are long-term residents. This includes neither third-country nationals with non-permanent residence nor family members of EU citizens (Article 3 para. 3 of the proposal).

Long-term residence means that the third-country national applying for family reunification has been holding a residence permit for at least one year and has

12 COM (2001) 257 final.

13 See consideration No. 6 of the proposal.

14 See commentary to Article 14 of the proposal, p. 10.

"reasonable prospects of obtaining the right of permanent residence" (Article 3 para. 1 of the proposal).[15]

According to the Commission, this rule was designed with regard to immigrants who were staying only temporarily (for example, au pairs and exchange students). Exchange students are therefore now excluded in the Directive, which was not the case in the initial proposal or in the law of the EU citizen.

b) Personal: Who is allowed to come?

The number of family members who are allowed to enter the EU was reduced widely during the negotiations.

(a) Nuclear Family

An obligation to grant entry and residence exists now only for members of the nuclear family, in other words the spouse and minor children (Article 4 para. 1 of the proposal).[16] There are, however, substantial restrictions: While the earlier proposal contained an age limit of 18 years, national exceptions are now possible as a result of Council debates, in which Germany played a major role. According to those derogations, the family reunification with children above the age of 12 years may be regulated by an additional integration criterion (Article 4 para. 1 lit. c) subpara. 3 of the proposal: "... may ... verify whether he or she [the child] meets a condition for integration"). In the Community law concerning EU citizens such a criterion does not exist; there, the age limit is 21 years.

Additionally the possibility to set an age limit for the reunification of spouses was added (Article 4 para. 5 of the proposal).[17]

(b) Unmarried Partners

In contrast to the initial proposal unmarried partners and their children may only be admitted if they have had a longstanding relationship or a registered partnership, and if the Member States' laws guarantee equal rights to unmarried and married partners (Article 4 para. 3 of the proposal). As far as this is concerned, the proposal goes further than current Community law. However, it is equally

---

15 Note: According to the Directive concerning the status of long-term resident third-country nationals (COM (2001) 127 final) it is required to have been a resident for five years without interruption, a regular sufficient resources and health insurance covering all risks of sickness.

16 Adopted children are included (Article 4 para. 1 lit. c) subpara. 1 of the proposal).

17 Background is the Danish alien law.

intended to extend the definition of family for Union citizens to unmarried couples in the above-mentioned proposal COM (2001) 257. The Commission argues that the EU cannot ignore the rapid changes from the "family group" to "de-facto" couples (often) with children.[18]

(c) Further Relatives

The Member States may limit the admittance to the spouses' 1st degree relatives in the direct ascending line (e.g. father/mother). It is required that they are dependent on the applicant or on his or her spouse and that they do not enjoy proper family support in the country of origin. In the initial proposal this provision represented an example for comparable rights for third-country nationals to that of EU Union citizens. The new proposal with its respective limitations differs considerably from the earlier proposal in this regard.

It should be noted, that with the reforms, children over 21 and parents of EU residents, even if they do not require immediate support, will be considered family members of *Union citizens* with the right to come into the EU (regardless of their nationality). This change is of special significance for third-country nationals. According to the Commission's proposal, this means that Union citizens are treated the same as the citizens of the host Member State. The Commission's reasoning states that "there is no good reason to deny"[19] children above 21 and parents who are not dependant. We will have to remember this argument.

(d) Economic Requirements

The Member State may ask the applicant to provide proof of accommodation, health insurance and sufficient financial resources. This is in line with the Community law standard.

For the first time, however, the resources may be checked after the family was reunified.[20] This was not part of the initial proposal of the Directive.

Community law does not prescribe waiting periods for the time period between the submission of an application and the issuing of a residence permit. The waiting period of one year suggested in the initial proposal was extended to two years and – as derogation – even to three years.

---

18 See commentary to Article 2 Nr. 2 COM (2001) 257 final, pp. 7 s.

19 See Commentary to Article 2 of the proposal COM (2001) 257 final, No. 2, p. 8.

20 If the family members residence documents are up for renewal (Article 7 para. 1 subpara. 2 of the proposal).

3. *Conditions of Residence of Family Members*

The rules of residence are the primary questions of integration. The three articles in the proposal, however, contain only rough outlines and they are limited to legal status. This however does not reduce their significance.

a) *The Legal Status of Family Members*

On the one hand, the legal status determines further aspects of integration and may therefore facilitate it. On the other hand, integration requires having the *same legal rights* as the host country's citizens.[21] Therefore the recitals (No. 13) of the proposal state, that in order to promote the integration of family members "they should be granted a status independent of that of the applicant after a period of residence" and "they must enjoy access to education, employment, and vocational training".

This first attempt of this kind in Community law is regulated as follows:

"The Member States shall issue to family members a renewable residence permit *of the same duration* as that held by the applicant." (Article 13 para. 2 of the proposal). "If the applicant has long-term resident status, the Member States shall issue to family members a residence permit of at least one-year's duration, until they satisfy the conditions laid down by Directive COM (2001) 127 for obtaining long-term resident status in their own right" (Article 13 para. 2 subpara. 1 of the proposal).

This limited residence permit is a derived right and consistent with the applicant's right to stay. Those regulations are consistent with current Community law. If the residence permit is granted, "the (...) family members[22] shall be entitled, *in the same way as the applicant*" to several rights. In this context only the following rights are mentioned:

- Access to education;
- Access to employment and self-employed activity;

---

21 See Commentary to Article 12 COM (1999) 638: "Family members authorised to enter and reside in a Member State are entitled to a number of rights needed to help them integrate into their new social environment on the same basis as nationals of the Member State in which they reside. This follows directly from the conclusions of the Tampere European Council of 15 and 16 October 1999 relating to immigration policy and fair treatment for third-country nationals."

22 Only those of the nuclear family. This limitation would also cease to exist for family members of Union citizens according to COM (2001) 257.

– Access to vocational guidance, initial and further training, and retraining.[23]

It is possible to terminate the residence according to Article 6 para. 2 of the proposal on grounds of public policy and domestic security, but not on the sole ground of illness or disability (para. 4), and furthermore, according to Article 16 of the proposal, when the economic requirements or the family relation are not met (para. 1), in case of false statements, information, or documents, if family relations were only mended with the purpose to come into the EU (para. 2) or if the applicant's residence comes to an end (para. 3).

b) Legal Status of the Applicant

Pursuant to Presidency conclusions of Tampere the legal status of third-country nationals should be approximated to that of Member States' nationals.[24] The proposal COM (2001) 127 has foreseen the following "set of uniform rights which are "*as near as possible*" to those enjoyed by citizens of the European Union" (Article 12 of this proposal):

– Access to employment and self-employed activity,[25]
– Education and vocational training, including study grants;
– Recognition of diplomas, certificates and other qualifications issued by a competent authority,
– Social protection, including social security and health-care;
– Social assistance;
– Social tax and benefits;
– Access to goods and services and the supply of goods and services made available to the public, including housing;
– Freedom of association and affiliation and membership of an organisation representing workers or employers or of any organisation whose members are engaged in a specific occupation, including the benefits conferred by such organisations;
– Free access to the entire territory of the Member State concerned.
– Right of residence in the other Member States. The long-term resident can be accompanied by members of his family, as already constituted in the first

23 Article 14 para. 1 lit. a)-c) of the proposal.

24 See the explanatory memorandum of the proposal of a Directive on the status of third-country nationals who are long-term residents COM (2001) 127 final, No. 1.2. and 5.1. s., and consideration No. 3 of the proposal.

25 Provided such activities do not entail even occasional involvement in the exercise of public authority.

Member State. In the second Member State long-term residents shall also enjoy these rights enumerated in Article 12, with the exception of social assistance and study grants (Chapter III).

- High protection against expulsion (Article 13): expulsion is allowed solely if the personal conduct constitutes an actual and sufficiently serious threat to public order or domestic security that affects a fundamental interest of society.

c) *The Possibility of an Autonomous Legal Status*

In summary, the extent of legal rights differs widely. The rights of family members of third-country nationals are only partly listed. They are excluded from any social protection and assistance. This is because financial security is expected to be provided by the applicant.

After entering the EU, it can be checked if the economic requirements are still met. The right to move and reside freely is also dependant on the applicant. The protection against expulsion from derived law is weaker for family members.

From this we can conclude that those extended rights may only be exercised "in the same way" as by the applicant when the same long-term status has been reached. Reaching this status is possible in two ways: according to general laws for third-country nationals (Article 13 of the proposal) laid down in the Directive COM (2001) 127, and according to the specific laws of the Directive on family reunification (Article 15 of the proposal).

According to the latter Directive there are two possibilities: "autonomous" (Article 15 para. 1) or "independent" (Article 15 para. 3 of the proposal) of the family relationship:

Pursuant to Article 15 para. 1 the nuclear family members shall obtain their own autonomous residence permit, independent of that of the applicant at the latest after five years if the family relationship still exits.

However if the family relationship ceases to exist during these five years, the emergency rule of Article 15 para. 3 of the proposal is applied. In the event of widowhood, divorce, separation or death of relatives an "independent" residence permit may be issued.

In conclusion: The autonomous residence permit (para. 1) is dependent on the condition of an "existing family relationship", whereas the independent residence permit (para. 3) is not.

This residence permit – that is autonomous of the applicant – is new and distinguishes the proposal despite all other attenuation. In addition it goes further than

Community law as it stands. Pursuant to current Community law the right of residence in the host Member State may be revoked for divorced spouses and children who are no longer minors or dependant on the Union citizen, regardless of their nationality. This problem is – as the Commission recognised – particularly acute for members of the EU citizen's family who are third-country nationals.[26] But the proposal COM (2001) 257 foresees the introduction of measures providing partly equitable solutions. In the event of death (Article 12 of this proposal), divorce or annulment of marriage (Article 13 of this proposal) the third-country national spouse may receive – based on certain conditions – an independent right of residence.

III. Conclusion

In conclusion it can be observed that the harmonisation between the status of third-country nationals' family members and that of the family members of Union citizens has only been a conditioned approximation (even without the intended reform of EU law). Rather, it is the Commission's initial proposal that would have achieved a full approximation of the two states. The initial proposal, which was criticized for being a "total harmonisation", has been toned down at the expense of third-country nationals' family members.

The narrow definition of family, the change in age limit (higher for spouses, lower for children), increased obligation to produce supporting documents, longer administrative processes, and the introduction of a two/three year waiting period until family members can enter the EU, are all mechanisms to obstruct immigration of family members who are waiting to join their relatives.

For family members who have already been granted residence status, the proposal contains significant improvements over the status quo. These include the possibility to obtain personal legal status after five years of residence, and immediate access to education and employment. Only on this issue, third-country nationals would be granted comparable rights in the sense of Tampere. The new proposal's primary focus shifts attention from the applicants themselves to their family members. While originally family reunification was intended to facilitate the applicant's integration into the respective host society, the new proposal pays increased attention to the needs of the family members. On all other issues, however, a considerable distance remains between the rights of third-country nationals and EU citizens even prior to the reform of Community law.

---

26 See explanatory memorandum of the Commission in the proposal COM (2001) 257 No. 2.5.

Furthermore, applicants and family members encounter very different conditions in their attempt to reach an equivalent status. Family members have to overcome a number of difficulties before they can obtain an autonomous legal status. Those difficulties include years of separation (long administrative processes and waiting periods) followed by a period of five years in which family members are economically and legally dependant on the applicant. As a result much is being asked of the family members. Both proposals were intended to create no more favourable conditions for the acquisition of the status by family members.[27] This intention, however, yielded a counterintuitive result. In fact, the conditions for family members have become less favourable. The family members would now have to fulfil the requirements of both documents – that is, the proposed Directive on family reunification and in addition to that, the Directive concerning the status of third-country nationals [COM (2001) 127]. For all these reasons, immigration based on family cannot be considered equivalent to immigration for economic and humanitarian reasons. What is more, the proposal falls short of the intention described as "comparable treatment with Union citizens" that was laid out in Tampere in order to initiate a policy of more vigorous integration.

27 See the Commission in her commentary to Article 13 No. 2 of the proposal.

DISCUSSION

The reports about family reunification were handled in one discussion, following the speech by Ms. Walter and Mr. Weber.

Mr. von Hoffmann started the discussion by asking for some more comments on the integration of immigrants into the society of their host country. Regarding the integration of third-country nationals he stated, that quite a considerable number of immigrants would pose certain special integration problems, for example, language problems. Ms. Langenfeld agreed, that a discussion about migration has to consider these integration problems. It should be taken into account, for example, that a young person without the ability to speak properly the host country's language and/or being badly skilled would have no chance to participate in the professional life of the host society and thus be condemned to have a minor position in society on the long term. Of course, there are a lot of exceptions, but this problem had to be seen from a very general point of view, in other words, taking into account the average immigrant. Against this background drawing the borderline at the age of 12 years for minor children for the right to entry into the host country of their parents as recently proposed by the European Commission [COM (2000) 624] is according to Ms. Langenfeld the only approach which can be expected to be accepted in the European Council. Ms. Langenfeld expressed her contentment, therefore that the first proposal of the European Commission dating from 1999 [COM (1999) 638] which failed to suggest any restriction regarding the age – apart of the basic requirement of minority – has been replaced by the above-mentioned second proposal. Ms. Oellers-Frahm, Mr. Calliess and Mr. von Hoffmann agreed with her, however Ms. Apap and Ms. van der Velde disagreed, both putting emphasis on the problem of leaving a minor aged 12 to 18 years without his parents.

With regard to the first paradox elaborated on by Ms. van der Velde in the preceding speech, Ms. Oellers-Frahm gave an answer to the question why the Member States are to a wide extent reluctant to transfer competences to the European Union, but increasing the respective national body of legislation on family reunion at the same time. Ms. Oellers-Frahm pointed out, that the admission of immigrants and their families would constitute a high economic charge for each Member State. Due to this, it would be understandable, that the Member States do not easily transfer competences in this discussed field to a supranational organization in order not to have to face charges, they cannot finance – at least not at the moment. Ms. Oellers-Frahm laid particular emphasis on the fact that the EU was not primarily concerned with questions on human rights. Therefore, a difference had to be made between competences in the economic field and those concerning human rights.

In this context Mr. von Hoffmann stated, that one had to morally differentiate according to the motives of migration – between immigrants coming for economic reasons and asylum seekers asking for shelter – in order not to mix up human rights obligations with economic interests.

Ms. Apap mentioned that EU nationals often had to face similar integration problems as third-country nationals did. She then asked whether there was any EU jurisdiction on non-married partners. Answering, Mr. Calliess mentioned the cases *Reed* (Case 59/85, Reed [1986], ECR 1283, para. 16; see the contribution by Mr. Calliess in this volume) concerning registered partnership and the case *Portugal/Council* (ECJ Case 268/94, *Portugal/Council* [1996] I-6177, no. 39; see the contribution by Mr. Calliess in this volume). From these cases, he suggested, one might conclude that the non-discrimination-principle is of relevance for this question: If a Member State recognises these partnerships for nationals, he has to do the same for third-country nationals.

Ms. Medved agreed, that especially economic reasons play a big role for the Member States when admitting immigrants. This would lead to the paradox situation that the rights provided for third-country nationals by the Member States are being raised EU-wide, but for their family members the requirements for immigration are getting stricter. The question would be whether the European Union has a primarily economic character or is changing to a more political union with its own legal personality and higher international human rights standard. Mr. Weber replied, that all Member States already grant in their national basic laws a high human rights standard including the protection of family life, which would not be topped when codified on the EU level. He also pointed out that there is not much of a difference between the case law of the German Federal Court of Justice and the European Court of Human Rights as to the protection of family life. A legal personality of the European Union would not have any impact on the standards of protection of human rights within the EU. With regard to the distinction mentioned above proposed by Mr. von Hoffmann, Mr. Weber stressed that a clear distinction between asylum seekers where human rights considerations are prevailing and migrant workers where economic considerations are prevailing, is not feasible. Indeed, both of these groups were treated nearly equally once they entered the host country and acquired a legal status. Ms. Langenfeld and Mr. Calliess agreed.

Mr. von Hoffmann insisted that a refugee, who has to leave his country e.g. for political reasons had no real alternative to leaving his home country and to freely choose his place of residence, whereas other immigrants leave their home country for reasons of prosperity. Mr. Calliess then responded that the immigration and integration policy on the whole is closely interlinked with economic matters as well as with human rights considerations. Also asylum seekers will take part in the economic field of the Member State. He also reminded everyone of the change of paradigm within the EU migration policy from a zero immigration policy to a controlled immigration policy. Ms. Fernando interjected that immigrants should not only be considered under economic reasons in the sense of a national burden. Therefore, the differentiation between migrant workers and asylum seekers would be dangerous. Given her position in the former discussion regarding age restriction in the EU Commission's proposal, Ms. van der Velde agreed with Ms. Fernando, and further asserted that a refugee should be treated as a human being rather than as an economic subject.

CHRISTINE LANGENFELD

SOCIAL RIGHTS FOR IMMIGRANTS

I. Introductory Remarks

Whenever social rights are concerned and especially in case that foreigners are supposed to benefit from these rights, emotions are going high. On the one hand, much criticism is formulated to show the lack of social benefits for foreigners, on the other hand, however, many are afraid of placing too great demands on the national social systems which are in fact – and not only in Germany- in a very bad state.

The following presentation will focus on the question which kind of effects Community Immigration Policy will have on the social status of immigrants. In doing this, one first has to define what the term "social rights" means and secondly determine which groups of foreigners will be concerned by the future European Immigration Policy.

Granting social rights and benefits to third-country nationals is no longer an exclusive domain of national law and traditional international law. The Community has brought forward several proposals for directives, which both aim at the extension of the existing European social law to third-country nationals and the elimination of unequal treatment of third-country nationals by the Member States as compared to nationals. On the other hand it is to be stated that the regulation of the social rights legal order is still principally the responsibility of the Member States: There is no common social policy as to the standards of social rights and benefits.

II. What are Social Rights and What is Their Purpose?

According to the definition given by the German Sozialgesetzbuch (code of social law) social rights serve social justice and security. They are supposed to contribute to secure a life in human dignity, to establish equal chances for everybody to freely develop his or her personality, to protect and foster families, to enable everybody to gain one's life by him or herself, i.e. to organise life with your own responsibility and finally to compensate for emergency situations in life. § 2 et seq. explicitly list the following rights: the promotion of education and employment, social security rights, social compensation for health damages, help for families, rent subsidies, children's and youth allowances, state welfare assistance and the integration of the handicapped.

Community law uses a broader concept of social rights. The EC Treaty in its Articles 136-145 (chapter on social policy) also refers to issues, which according to German understanding, would belong to the field of labour law. It is clear that these rights have an important social meaning but as they do not belong to the traditional field of social rights they will not be referred to in the following.

Traditional Community social law is connected with the realization of freedom of movement as enshrined in the EC Treaty. Migrant workers shall not suffer disadvantages when moving from one country to the other. Accordingly Community law in Article 3 of the EC Regulation No. 1408/71,[1] prohibits discrimination based on nationality within the framework of national security system and with respect to "social benefits". Thus, the non-discrimination clause also applies to those branches of social security which provide for benefits in cases of illness and motherhood, invalidity, unemployment and family benefits, even if those rights and benefits are totally financed by the state. However, the regulation does not cover general state welfare assistance.

The concept of social benefits in Article 7 of the EC Regulation No. 1612/68[2] is still wider than the concept of social *security* in regulation No. 1408/71. According to the jurisprudence to the European Court of Justice the term "social benefits" also comprises all social services which are granted to employees. The crucial point for the European Court is whether the granting of a social benefit to migrant workers would be appropriate to foster mobility within the Community.[3] It follows from this that the general state welfare assistance also falls within the scope of the regulation 1612/68.

III. Category of Persons Covered

Which category of persons will be covered by European immigration policy and consequently by the effects of the future legislation in this field? The proposals for directives put forward by the Commission deal with third-country nationals who do not have a right whatsoever of entry or of residence in a EU Member State. This is not to mention a claim to social rights and benefits. As an excep-

1 Regulation of the Council of 14 June 1971 on the application of social security schemes to employed persons and their families moving within the Community, O.J. L 149/2, consolidated version in O.J. 1997, L 28/1.

2 Regulation of the Council of 15 October 1968 on freedom of workers within the Community, O.J. L 295/2.

3 Consistent practice of the Court since ECJ Case 32/75, Christini ECR 1975, 1085.

tion to this, third-country nationals who are family members of an EU citizen may claim equal treatment in many respects including the social field. Among this group of the so-called "privileged third-country nationals" we also find the nationals of those states which have concluded association treaties with the Community like the Turkish migrant workers[4] or nationals coming from the Member States of the European Economic Area.[5] This presentation will not go further into detail concerning this group of third-country nationals.

Thus, any Community immigration legislation in the field of social rights will concern third-country nationals whose legal status is at best partially regulated by existing Community legislation. The proposal for a Directive concerning the status of third-country nationals who are long-term residents,[6] providing for a comprehensive non-discrimination clause as to social protection entitlements and all forms of social assistance provided by the state in Article 12, thus refers to the so-called "non-privileged third-country nationals" who want to immigrate into and permanently settle within the Community. The Directive also applies to refugees who are entitled to be granted asylum under the Geneva Convention and who lawfully reside in a EU Member State. Refugees, who temporarily receive shelter like civil war refugees, or refugees who may not be expelled for humanitarian reasons, within the Community, do not fall under this category. But: Refugees may also turn out to be immigrants. In Germany we have a lot of examples for this: Although the majority of the refugees from Bosnia and Kosovo have returned to their countries of origin, many of them are still staying here. The same is true for asylum seekers, whose application for asylum has

---

4 EEC-Turkey Association Agreement, O.J. 1973, C 113/2 and the respective decisions of the EEC-Turkey Association Council. The Decisions are published in: EEC-Turkey Association Agreement and Protocols and Other Basic Texts, Brussels, Council of the EC, 1992. Rights are also awarded by the Maghreb Cooperation Agreements with North African States, the Euro-Mediterranean Agreements with Tunisia, Morocco and Israel, the Europe Agreements with ten Eastern European States, the Partnership and cooperation Agreements with six former Societ republics, the Custom Union and Cooperation Agreement with San Marino and the Lomé Convention and the Treaty between the EC and Switzerland. For more details cf. *Hedemann-Robinson, M.*, An Overview of recent legal developments at Community level in relation to third-country nationals resident within the European Union, with particular reference to the case law of the European Court of Justice, CMLR 2001, 525, 531 ff.; *Raible, K.*, Vorgaben und unmittelbar anwendbare Normen des supranationalen Rechts, in: *Giegerich, T./Wolfum, R.,* Einwanderungsrecht – national und international, S. 36, 53 ff.; *Steve Peers*, Towards Equality: Actual and potential rights of third-Country nationals in the European Union, CMLR 1996, 7, 8 f.

5 O.J. 1994 L 1/1; O.J. 1995, L 86/58 (Liechtenstein).

6 COM (2001) 127 final of 13/3/2001.

been rejected, but who for years dispose of a limited residence authorization or a temporary stay of deportation ("Duldung").[7] It is quite obvious that many of these refugees will become permanent residents, i.e. "factual" immigrants.

IV. The Different Levels of Regulation With Respect to the Social Status of Immigrants From Third Countries

1. Community legislation

a) Present State of Community legislation

The legal status of third-country nationals within the European Community is not regulated in a uniform way. In contrast to citizens of the European Union, third-country nationals principally have no Community right of residence in a EU-Member State. As already mentioned above, Community law so far only regulates the status of third-country nationals who are family members of EU citizens and who make use of their right of free movement, respectively who are citizens of associated states. The Directive on the elimination of any discrimination on the grounds of race and ethnic origin from June 2000[8] has not made a difference to this. The Directive prohibits discrimination in the field of employment, education and professional training, social protection and supply with commodities and services, including living accommodation. But: The Directive does not prohibit unequal treatment on grounds of citizenship. The Council did not follow the recommendation made by the Commission to extend the non-discrimination clause on grounds of citizenship to all persons, including third-country nationals. Such an extension would have been unacceptable for the Member States, especially with respect to their social rights legislation.

Finally, for sake of completeness, the European Union Charter of Fundamental Rights[9] should be mentioned which however is not (yet) legally binding. But according to Article 6 para. 2 Union Treaty the Charter will gain legal relevance as integral part of the common legal principles, which are the basis of the human rights protection system within the European Community. It is to be expected that the European Court of Justice in the future will not only refer to the European Convention on Human Rights and the respective jurisprudence of the European Court in Strasbourg, but also to the guarantees as laid down in the

7 § 56 of the German Foreigners Act.
8 O.J. 2000, L 180/22.
9 O.J. 2000 C 354/1.

Charter. However, in case the Charter will be adopted as a legally binding document, it will only apply to the Community and the Member States as long as they are applying Community law. Besides this, the provisions of the Charter, including those concerning social protection issues, regularly refer to the Community and the respective national provisions applicable.

As a result it has to be stated that the determination of the social status of non-privileged third-country nationals so far is still up to the national legislature.

b) *Proposals for directives concerning the status of immigrants under discussion*

aa) Legal basis for a Community immigration policy

The Amsterdam Treaty of 2 October 1997 transfers important areas from Title VI EUT to the new Title IV ECT. Measures with respect to external border controls, asylum, immigration, rights of third-country nationals will now be dealt with on the basis of the ECT. The European Council, at its special meeting in Tampere on 15 and 16 October 1999 acknowledged the need to ensure fair treatment of third-country nationals who reside legally on the territory of its Member States.[10] It declared that the policy of the Community should aim at granting them rights and obligations comparable to those of EU citizens. This would also comprise non-discrimination with respect to social rights and benefits in order to realize the Tampere mandate. The Commission in the meantime put forward a proposal for a Directive concerning the status of third-country nationals who are long-term residents.[11] After a five year legal stay in one of the Member States the third-country national shall be entitled to a long-term residence permit. The status of a long-term resident will be available to all third-country nationals who reside legally in the territory of a Member State on a long-term basis. The only excluded categories are those who are not intending to actually settle, in particular persons resident within the EU in order to study or to engage in a seasonal occupation and also those enjoying temporary protection.[12] Long-term residents will enjoy full equal treatment with the nationals of

10 As to the results of the Tampere meeting cf. Communication from the Commission to the Council and the European Parliament on a Community Immigration Policy, COM (2000) 757 final of 22/11/2000, p. 5 et seq.;. for details cf. *Hedemann-Robinson* (footnote 4), 528 ff.

11 Cf. footnote 6.

12 The proposal also provides for the possibility for refugees with recognised status under the Geneva Convention and for third-country nationals who are members of the family of a Union-citizen to apply for a long-term resident permit.

the state of residence and the Union citizens in a series of respects ranging from access to employment and self-employed activity to education and vocational training and also social protection and assistance.

The proposal for long-term residents has to be read together with the Commission`s proposal for a Council Directive on the right to family reunification[13] which establishes a right to family reunification on the part of third-country nationals. The applicant's spouses and minor children of the applicant are granted the right to entry and residence. Exception may be made with respect to children older than 12 years for integration reasons. The Member States may extend the right to family reunification to other relatives in the ascending line of the applicant.

In order to set up a legislative framework for the integration of those persons already resident in the territory of the Member States, the Commission has further proposed the extension of Community co-ordination of social security schemes, as laid down in EC-Regulation No. 1408/71. to also cover employed persons and self-employed persons who are insured in a Member State and who are third-country nationals.[14] The proposal is still under consideration in the Council.

V. International Legal Context

Customary international law does not provide for equal treatment of nationals and non-nationals in the field of social rights.[15] As to international treaty law,

---

13 COM (2002) 225 final of 2/5/2002. The proposal substitutes the old proposal COM (2000) 624 final of 10/10/2000. It is far more restrictive than its predecessor and leaves to the Member States a greater margin of discretion. As to the content of the old proposal cf. *Hailbronner, K.*, Migrationspolitik und Rechte der Drittstaatsangehörigen in der Europäischen Union, ZAR 2002, 84, 86.

14 COM (2002) 59 final of 6/2/2002; see also the proposal of the Commission for a directive on the rights of citizens of the Union and their family members to move and reside freely within the territory of the Member States, COM (2001) 257 final of 23/5/2001. The purpose of the proposal is to enhance the legal status of family members of Union citizens, i.e. to award residence and working rights independently from the status of the Union citizens to whose family they belong. According to the proposal family members will be entitled to apply for a permanent residence permit which means full equal treatment with nationals respectively EU citizens.

15 *Kokott, J.*, Die Staatsangehörigkeit als Unterscheidungsmerkmal für soziale Rechte von Ausländern, in: *Hailbronner*, *K.* (ed.), Die allgemeinen Regeln des völkerrechtlichen Fremdenrechts. Bilanz und Ausblick an der Jahrtausendwende, 2000, 26.

the ILO Convention No. 97[16] introduces obligations to secure equal treatment for migrant workers in a wide range of respects and to ensure security of residence after five years, even where an employment contract is terminated. In 1990 the United Nations adopted the International Convention on the Protection of the Rights of all Migrant Workers and Members of their Families.[17] The Convention has not yet entered into force. None of the Member States have ratified it so far.

At European level the Social Charter of 1961[18] applies to all the Member States and the 1996 Charter[19] to only some of them. According to the Charter the citizens of the Member States enjoy equal treatment with nationals with respect to social welfare. However, Germany and Belgium have made reservations in order not to be obliged to equal treatment with respect to social welfare benefits. Finally, the Council of Europe's Convention on Establishment 1955[20] should be mentioned, which however solely applies on the well established principle of reciprocity.[21]

The European Convention on Human Rights in Article 14 only provides for a non-discrimination clause with respect to the rights laid down in the Convention. As the Convention does not provide for social rights in general Article 14 is not applicable. However, stricter standards apply to those social rights which are considered property in the sense of constitutional and international law (Art. 1 of the Additional Protocol to the Convention). Examples of such property rights are pensions and unemployment benefits. According to the jurisprudence of the European Court on Human Rights[22] they form part of social security systems to which the members have paid contributions. A state must thus not withhold such rights to foreigners on the grounds that the foreigners' home state does not grant such rights to nationals of the withholding state either (no application of the reservation of reciprocity).

---

16 See http://ilolex.ilo.ch:1567/public/german/docs/gc097.htm.

17 ILM 1991, 1521.

18 Of 18/10/1961, Federal Law Gazette 1964 II, 1262

19 Cf. http://conventions.coe.int/treaty/en/Treaties/html/163.htm.

20 Federal Law Gazette 1959 II, 998.

21 As to the principle of reciprocity see *Kokott* (footnote 15).

22 See the decision of the Court in the Case Gaygusuz/Austria of 16/09/1996, Reports 1996 IV, with a note of *Hailbronner, K.*, Die sozialrechtliche Gleichbehandlung von Drittstaatsangehörigen – ein menschenrechtliches Postulat?, JZ 1997, 397.

VI. The National Level – the Case of Germany

Public assistance generally entitles residents of Germany to social welfare in case of need. But the principle of residence has been modified. Numerous statutes make lawful or ordinary residence a relevant criterion; moreover, Germans are privileged as compared to foreign residents from third countries. As a matter of principle it may be stated that the less consolidated the status of residence of the third-country national is, the weaker is his position with regard to social rights. This particularly applies to asylum seekers, civil war and the so-called de-facto refugees. Since 1993 the social rights of this group form part of a special regime.[23] Accordingly, they mainly receive welfare assistance in the form of benefits in kind rather than cash benefits. However, the regime provides for a gradual approximation of the social benefits to those received by Germans and permanent residents.

The constitutional guarantee of human dignity in connection with the social state clause in Article 20 para. 1 of the German Basic Law could serve to limit a decrease in the field of social benefits for foreigners. However, it is difficult to establish the extent of social welfare benefits covered by the duty to respect and protect human dignity in Article 1 Basic Law. With regard to the general level of social protection in Germany, it seems to be obvious that the degree of social protection applying to foreigners in Germany, even if it does not correspond to the social benefits granted to nationals and EU citizens, is not in violation of the human dignity clause.

Furthermore, differentiation according to citizenship does not fall within the scope of the prohibition to discriminate laid down in Art. 3 para. 3 Basic Law. However, any unequal treatment of foreign nationals with respect to the various social welfare rights must have a constitutionally valid basis. This follows from the general equality rule in Art. 3 para. 1 Basic Law. In this respect it has been argued, that the purpose of giving less social welfare benefits to certain categories of third-country nationals than to Germans and EU nationals (and their families) was to make the Federal Republic less attractive for needy foreigners in order to protect the efficiency and financial liquidity of the authorities responsible for public assistance which in first instance feel responsible for their own citizens and aliens who permanently stay in Germany. This view corresponds to the purpose of social welfare which is to reintegrate those in need of assistance into the social and economic life of society. According to the legislature, this purpose does not apply to short term residents like refugees who are supposed to

---

23 Asylbewerberleistungsgesetz, Federal Law Gazette I 1997, 2022, amended by statute of 25/8/1998, Federal Law Gazette 1998 I, 2505.

return to their country of origin as soon as possible. Consequently, the granting of social benefits depends on the duration of stay or lawful residence of the foreigner concerned. The extent of the consolidation, respectively the duration of the stay of the foreigner, is to be considered a legitimate criterion in order to justify unequal treatment of aliens compared with own nationals or EU citizens. This perception will – on the other hand – consequently lead to the conclusion that a less favourable treatment of immigrants who *permanently* stay in Germany with respect to social rights would be unconstitutional under Article 3 para. 1 Basic Law. German legislation, by granting equal treatment in the field of social rights to those who dispose of a long-term residence permit (Aufenthaltserlaubnis respectively Aufenthaltsberechtigung),[24] is in conformity with this principle.

The principle of equal treatment must also apply to those third-country nationals who are officially accepted as immigrants. The decision of a state to allow immigration of foreigners is a fundamental policy decision. By enacting the new law on immigration[25] adopted in June 2002 and supposed to enter into force in 2003,[26] Germany has decided in favour of admitting immigration. By realizing this decision the population living in Germany will be enlarged by immigrants from third countries. This policy must consequently be non-discriminatory with respect to social rights and benefits. Thus, the new German law on immigration does provide for full equal treatment with respect to social rights for those persons who hold a of a permanent residence permit (Niederlassungserlaubnis).[27]

---

24 § 27 of the German Foreigners Act.

25 Federal Law Gazette 2002 I, 1946.

26 By decision of the Federal Constitutional Court 18/12/2002, EuGRZ 2003, 67, the statute was declared void for procedure irregularities during the voting in the Bundesrat (Federal Council). In the beginning of 2003 the bill was again (without any amendments) introduced to the Bundestag by the Federal Government. The statute was adopted by the Parliament but is still under controversial discussion in the Bundesrat. The Bundesrat who in opposite to the Bundestag is currently dominated by the Christian Democrats asks for some substantial amendments in order to restrict immigration. The outcome of the negotiations in the so-called mediation committee (Vermittlungsausschuss) is open.

27 § 9 Immigration law. The new law will grant full equal treatment in social matters both to holders of a permanent residence permit and – under certain conditions - of a limited residence permit. The relevant social laws are accordingly amended (see Articles 9 and 10 Immigration law).

Equally, the proposal forwarded by the Commission concerning the status of long-term residents, grants full equal treatment in social security matters.[28]

VII. Conclusion

Both (future) EC legislation and national law grant third-country nationals who are long-term residents equality of treatment in the field of social rights. The principle of non-discrimination forms part of a consistent integration policy aiming at the long-term settlement of third-country nationals.

However, the European Union and the Member States should be aware of the fact that immigration policy is a highly controversial issue. In many cases, the population in the immigration states are highly critical towards a policy which, according to them, leads to an excessive proportion of foreigners and to the exploitation of the social security systems.

The Treaty of Amsterdam establishes for the first time a Community competence for the field of immigration and asylum. It seems that the Commission is convinced that there is a growing recognition that the "zero" immigration policies of the past 30 years are no longer appropriate. The migratory pressures would continue with an accompanying increase in illegal immigration, smuggling and trafficking. Stating this, the Commission favours a comprehensive European immigration concept: "In this situation a choice must be made between maintaining the view that the Union can continue to resist migratory pressures and accepting that immigration will continue and should be properly regulated. (...)"[29] The Commission obviously means that immigration of third-country nationals can not be haltered any more. However, by this the Commission finds itself in contrast to the public opinion in the EU Member States. Immigration policy which will be accepted by the population of the EU Member States must on the one hand regulate and limit immigration of third-country nationals and on the other hand take into account not only the economic needs of

---

28 Although the importance of voting rights and access to nationality for the integration of third-country nationals who are long-term residents is now generally acknowledged, the EC Treaty provides no specific legal basis for it. On voting rights, Community involvement is provided for only as it regards municipal and European elections and only for citizens of the Union. Access to nationality is a matter reserved solely for national powers. This proposal for a directive on long-term residents accordingly does not address these two aspects, though it is true that the Tampere European Council endorsed the objective that long-term legally resident third-country nationals should be offered the opportunity to obtain the nationality of the Member State in which they are resident.

29 Communication of the Commission (footnote 10), 3.

the labour market but also integration requirements. A closer look at the proposals for directives presented by the Commission, however, shows quite the opposite. It is to be stated that so far, the European Commission has not answered the crucial question of how to regulate the migration flows according to the economic and integration interests of the host countries.[30] According to the Commissions concept not only will there be more immigration of qualified third-country nationals who at least in the beginning will not be a burden for the state welfare system, but in view of the proposed provisions concerning family reunification there will also be immigration into the social security system with negative effects for the latter. The only solution will therefore be to leave the Member States as much margin of discretion as possible to take their own decisions in this field. It goes without saying that the Member States are under the obligation of Art. 8 ECHR in this respect.

Unregulated or wrongly regulated immigration places a risk on the balance of the social systems and the integration process. Hence, successful immigration policy must aim at regulating, but at the same time limiting immigration. On the other hand it should be clear that a third-country national who officially has been accepted as an immigrant and long-term resident must be ensured fair treatment by the host country. Above all, this means granting him/her (after a certain period of time) rights and obligations comparable to those of EU citizens. The host country will be obliged to make any effort in order to integrate the immigrant into the host society. To offer the integration process a reasonable prospect of success, an effective and socio-politically reasonable limitation of migration flows will be indispensable. It follows from this that the European Union and the Member States must make use of all margins left by the law to regulate and limit immigration. This will be especially true for the moving in of refugees. In this field the EU and the Member States are under the obligations of the Geneva Convention. However, it seems to me that the proposal of the Commission for a Directive on minimum standards for the qualification and status of third-country nationals and stateless persons as refugees or as persons who otherwise need international protection,[31] goes very far in this respect. Finally, Article 15 of the Directive will create a general refugee clause which exceeds the international legal obligations and which above all will not fail its attractive

30 *Hailbronner* (footnote 13), 84.

31 Proposal for a Council Directive on minimum standards for the qualification and status of third-country nationals and stateless persons as refugees or as persons who otherwise need international protection (COM/2001/510 of 12/9/2001). The proposal differentiates between refugees under the Geneva Convention and those persons who otherwise need international protection.

power on the refugee flows coming from all over the world. The Commission further proposes to grant long-term residence status to all kind of refugees after a five years legal stay in the EU – too short a period in my eyes – which amongst others means granting them the right to family reunification and full equal treatment with respect to the social welfare system and the labour market. Taking this into account one has to admit that the idea of regulating immigration has indeed got lost along the way.

In order to make it perfectly clear once more: The longer third-country nationals are living in a EU Member State the more pressing will be the need to fully integrate these persons into society including the welfare system, regardless of whether they came to the EU for humanitarian or other reasons. The European Union and the Member States must also be aware of the fact that refugees, who were initially supposed to return to their country of origin but have managed to stay for a term of years, may become "factual immigrants" in case the return to their home countries turns out to be impossible. Stating this, the crucial issue for the European Union and its Member States will be to reasonably manage migration and – within the limits set by international law – refugee flows in order not to place too great demands on the national social systems.

DISCUSSION

Mr. von Hoffmann opened the discussion by asking whether the term of "de-facto-immigrant" also comprised "illegal immigrants". Ms. Langenfeld disagreed. The status of a de-facto-immigrant presupposed that at the time of entry, a legal reason for the access to Germany existed which is now no longer valid. The term comprised in particular asylum seekers whose applications for asylum had been rejected but who could not be sent back due to the hostile situation in their home country. With respect to national rules they could stay for years in a – from a juridical viewpoint – uncertain situation. It resulted, that they were not treated as immigrants by social services and had no equal social rights, e.g. benefits for children, access to labour market etc. Ms. Langenfeld pointed out, that she favoured a system integrating those de-facto-immigrants after a certain period of time, e.g. five years, if the situation in their home country causing their de-facto-immigrant-status had not changed by then. However, this group of immigrants were not in the typical immigration situation mentioned within the EC-Directive.

Ms. Medved agreed on the importance of setting up a time regulation in order to resolve the integration problem of de-facto-immigrants, but the term ought to be clarified. She asked what exactly was meant by the term of "de-facto immigrants".

Ms. Langenfeld answered, that the term "de-facto-immigrants" should only include those people, who cannot return to their home country for reasons which they are not responsible for.

Mr. von Hoffmann mentioned, that it was difficult to draw the line at illegal immigrants, as the moral difference between a fake asylum seeker and an illegal immigrant was hard to tell – the social needs of both are the same.

Ms. Langenfeld responded, that the state had to be very firm during the first period of the stay. If the immigration requirements were not fulfilled, the person had to be sent back immediately. Otherwise, the states would create a situation which allowed "de-facto-immigrants" to stay.

Ms. Apap suggested another term – appreciated by Mr. Langenfeld – used for "de-facto-immigrants" at the EU level: "non-deportable-people". Ms. Apap continued, in order to prevent factual residence of longer than five years caused by a long asylum procedure, efforts to make it more efficiently should be met.

Ms. Walter commented, that the subsidiary protection of de-facto-immigrants was implemented into the recent EU Directive proposal (Proposal for a Council Directive on minimum standards for the qualification and status of third-country nationals and stateless persons as refugees or as persons who otherwise need international protection, COM/2001/0510) containing a very broad definition considering e.g. gender specific discrimination as a reason to obtain a residence permit.

Mr. Weber added, that these reasons to obtaining a residence permit were also included into the new German immigration law (Zuwanderungsgesetz), but it provided only a temporally residential right, which implemented, that these immigrants could not be called illegal immigrants. One could speak of tolerated immigrants as illegal immigrants; in his opinion, as long as there was no eviction order one could not be held to be an illegal immigrant.

Ms. Langenfeld mentioned, that the EU Directive concerning subsidiary protection was very far reaching as it covered non-state persecution and gender-specific-persecution. In fact, according to German law, people persecuted for the mentioned reasons and being at risk of their lives or physical integrity would not be sent back to their home country. They are not, however, granted the right of asylum or any other kind of "institutionalized" legal title to stay. It is up to the competent authorities to decide each case on an individual basis. The implementation of the mentioned EU Directive by regularly granting the right not to be sent back to their country of origin would probably attract a considerably higher number of refugees from all over the world than in the past. Indeed it was sufficient, to refer to the humanitarian obligations deriving from the Geneva Convention, stating that these people must not be deported.

WOLFGANG KLOOß

HISTORICIZING/CONTEMPORIZING MULTICULTURALISM IN ENGLISH-CANADIAN LITERATURE

With *The Journals of Susanna Moodie,* Canada's internationally most acclaimed writer, Margaret Atwood, presented a poem in 1970, whose title indicates the essentially intertextual quality of this work, i.e. the distinct reference to one of Canada's outstanding pioneer women and her writings. The lyrical text is complemented by an afterword in which Atwood observes that Mrs. Moodie "claims [in her own works, namely *Roughing It in the Bush (1852)* and *Life in the Clearings (1853)*] to be an ardent Canadian patriot while at the same time she is standing back from the country and criticizing it as though she were a detached observer, a stranger". Moreover, Atwood concludes from here "[that] this is perhaps the way [Canadians] still live since [they] are all immigrants to this place even if [they] were born here."[1] What Atwood has in mind when she thus phrases her reading of Moodie's experiences in colonial Canada is closely linked with the specific way in which early immigrants to Canada adapted to their new environment. Atwood discovers an ambiguity in Moodie's approach to landscape, a fear of space, which she identifies as a central feature of the Canadian character:

> "If the national mental illness of the United States is megalomania, that of Canada is paranoid schizophrenia. Mrs. Moodie is divided down the middle: she praises the Canadian landscape but accuses it of destroying her; she dislikes the people already in Canada but finds in people her only refuge from the land itself; she preaches progress and the march of civilization while brooding elegiacally upon the destruction of the wilderness [...] the country is too big for anyone to inhabit completely, and in the parts unknown to us we move in fear, exiles and invaders."[2]

In this way Atwood prolongs a psychological reading of landscape that is not only instructive for her own approach towards identity construction, i.e. the victimization of Canadians vis à vis a hostile environment, or vis à vis the economic and cultural dominance of the USA, but which can already be discovered at the core of 19th century Canadian writing.

---

1 *Atwood, M.*, The Journals of Susanna Moodie (Toronto, 1970), 62.
2 *Atwood*, 62.

Compared to certain traditions[3] in 19th century US-American literature with their "passionate idealization of nature which [...] serve[s] as a virtual *donnee* among both poets and romancers",[4] 19th century Canadian writing offers an entirely different reading of the North American landscape, thus providing a paradigm for nearly all contemporary fiction writers north of the border, whereby ethnic diversity, i.e. an obvious feature of historical and social reality, falls prey to the authors' psychological interpretation of the Canadian frontier.

At the same time, a second paradigm is introduced which is also closely linked with the Canadian reading of the frontier experience and which can already be discovered in the first Canadian, if not even first North American work of fiction, Frances Brooke's *The History of Emily Montague* (1769). Here, the author gives a detailed account of the life of the English military post in Quebec after the fall of New France. Thus, Brooke focuses an the social order of a space which Northrop Frye in his influential mytho-poetic studies on Canadian literature conceives as the major force in the shaping of the Canadian imagination. According to Frye

> "[s]mall and isolated communities surrounded with a physical or psychological "frontier", separated from one another and from their American and British cultural sources: communities that provide all that their members have in the way of distinctively human values, and that are compelled to feel a great respect for the law and order that holds them together, yet confronted with a huge, unthinking, menacing, and formidable physical setting – such communities are bound to develop what we may provisionally call a garrison mentality."[5]

In order to extend the list of paradigms that have determined identity construction in 19th century Canadian historical romance and much of 20th century Canadian historiographic fiction, William Kirby's *The Golden Dog: A Romance of Old Quebec* (1877) needs brief mentioning, too. In this historical narrative, Canada's "Walter Scott"[6] offers a portrait of La Nouvelle France prior to the fall of Quebec. Although most of the characters are historical, Kirby follows the conventions of the romantic tale and converts authentic history into legend. Thereby, he is primarily interested in a comparative view of two antagonistic value systems. Kirby depicts a

---

3 Cf. especially the influence of Ralph Waldo Emerson and Transcendentalism.

4 *McGregor, G.*, The Wacousta Syndrome: Explorations in the Canadian Landscape (Toronto, 1985), 27.

5 *Northrop, Frye*, "Conclusion", in: *Klinck*, *C. F.* (Ed.), Literary History of Canada. Canadian Literature in English, (Toronto, 1965) 318-332, 327.

6 William Kirby was born in England, later migrated to the United States, before his loyalist sympathies led him to Canada, where he settled at Niagara-on-the Lake.

> "world of intrigue and violence in which the chivalric values of the old regime and the *honnetes gens* are being replaced by the cut-throat rivalries of the new commerce. [...] It is a world of heroes and villains, of right against wrong, of the idealized old against the cynical and corrupt new."[7]

What is of greater importance in the context of this paper though, is to realize that Kirby's interest in the history of New France is not a singular phenomenon, but rather typical of English-Canadian historical narrative emerging in the decades after Confederation (1867).[8]

Likewise, Kirby's novel, for example, "concludes with the reflection that, as New France became part of British North America, it entered into a bond with its English-Canadian counterpart."[9] In this way, many authors try to establish the myth of an all-encompassing Canadian identity, a pan-Canadian version of historical consciousness, which not only ignores the historically founded difference between La Nouvelle France and her British rival, but even the existence of two, or by the same token, rather many Canadas.

Seventy years later, however, the situation appears to have changed completely. With the publication of *Two Solitudes* in 1945, Nova Scotian writer Hugh MacLennan presents a historiographic novel whose programmatic title already indicates that Anglo- and Francophone Canada are now recognized as two distinct entities. It could even be argued that the notion of alterity is a necessary prerequisite for the development of theme and plot in *Two Solitudes* which introduces a broad set of characters, who belong to different generations of French- and English-Canadians, who are often linked through family ties and

7 *Keith, W. J.*, Canadian Literature in English, (New York, 1985) 44.

8 Cf. *Adam G. M./Wetherald A. E.*, An Agonquin Maiden: A Romance of the Early Days of Upper Canada (Montreal, 1887); *Burnham H.*, Marcelle: An Historical Novel (Toronto, 1905); *Crawley M. C.*, A Daughter of New France (Toronto, 1901); *DeMille J.*, The Lily and the Cross: A Tale of Acadia (Boston, New York, 1875); *David Hickey*, William and Mary. A Tale of the Siege of Louisburg (Toronto, 1884); *Leprohon R.*, Antoinette de Mirecourt or, Secret Marrying and Secret Sorrowing (Toronto, 1864); *Lighthall W. D.*, The False Chevalier or the Lifeguard of Marie Antoinette (Montreal, 1898); *Macdonnell B. L.*, Diane of Ville Marie. A Romance of French Canada (Toronto, 1898); *Parker G. Sir*, The Power and the Glory: A Romance of the Great La Salle (New York, 1925); *ders.*, The Seats of the Mighty, Being the Memoirs of Captain Robert Moray, Sometime an Officer in the Virginia Regiment and after of Amherst's Regiment (New York, 1897); *Roberts C. G.D. Sir*, The Prisoner of Mademoiselle (Toronto, 1904). See also *Kroel ler, E.-M.*, "Walter Scott in America, English Canada, and Quebec: A Comparison", Canadian Review of Comparative Literature/Revue Canadienne de Litterature Comparee 7:1 (1980), 32-46.

9 *Duffy*, Sounding the Iceberg, 12.

who, above all, are representatives of contrasting lifestyles and value systems. MacLennan registers, compares and explains the different economic, religious or social forces, as well as the misunderstandings, disharmonies and the deeply rooted distrust that overshadow the relationship between the two Canadas. He gives a literary version of what contemporary historian A.R.M. Lower terms the "greatest factor in Canadian life, not only because [the French-English cleavage] is a racial and linguistic cleavage, but because it coincides with an economic [...], a legal [...], a cultural [...], a religious [...], and a philosophical cleavage."[10] Thus MacLennan becomes the first Canadian writer of fiction who gives a literary portrait of a nation that has to struggle with separate identities.

In the following, the novel received such wide attention that its title quickly became a catchword among both English and French Canadians. Since MacLennan is, however, not quite at ease with the Canadian *status quo*, his narrative also emerges as the first work of fiction that suggests ways and means in which a peaceful co-existence of Canada's "two solitudes" seems possible. Under these circumstances, the notion of difference offers only a meaningful concept, if it remains restricted to social and cultural forms of expression. For MacLennan, differences cannot be accepted as an infringing political reality since this would impede his immediate concern: Canada's mandatory strife for a unity in diversity. Consequently, he has his novel end with a symbolic act of appeasement. Paul Tallard and Heather Methuen, two of the younger protagonists, bridge the gap between the two Canadas with a marriage that still allows for separate identities: "[...] she knew that in spite of loving her he had never lost the sense of himself. She was not jealous of the part she could not touch. What she did have was a hundred images of him engraved in her mind, all different."[11]

Notwithstanding the previous depiction of numerous antagonisms, *Two Solitudes* is finally turned into a story of reconciliation. And yet, MacLennan's overtly didactic vision of a bicultural Canada is not quite as well founded as it appears upon first sight. Apart from the fact that the Canadian dilemma is exclusively explained with the dichotomy between the two charter groups,[12] thereby

---

10 *Lower, A.R.M.*, "Canadian Unity and Its Conditions", in: *Anderson, V.* (ed.), Problems in Canadian Unity (Toronto, 1938), 7-19, 11-12.

11 *MacLennan, H.*, Two Solitudes (New York, 1945), 319.

12 Cf. *Goldstein, J. E./Bienvenue, R.*, Ethnicity and Ethnic Relations in Canada (Toronto, 1980). In this sociological study the problem is described as follows: For new nations developed in formerly unpopulated regions, such as the United States and Canada, ethnic differentiation has arisen through immigration, which was determined by the host or charter group, who got there first, or who conquered and determined the conditions under which other groups might enter (p. 327).

leaving any other participant in the cultural mosaic[13] aside, from an ideological point of view, it could even be argued that the novel's subtext is less concerned with compromise and co-existence than with assimilation and defeat. This becomes especially apparent in the figure of Paul Tallard who receives a bilingual education in Anglo- and Francophone schools, later serves in the merchant marine, which takes him abroad, then enrols at Oxford University where he also tries a career as a writer of short fiction and, perhaps even more significant, converts from Catholicism to Protestantism. Taking all this into account, he can hardly be perceived as a trustworthy representative of French-Canada.

In this way, the development of character(s) in *Two Solitudes* runs not only counter to MacLennan's reconciliatory intentions, but unmasks the text as a literary work that supports a hegemonial approach towards identity construction. While the Confederation novelists simply subsume La Nouvelle France under a pan-Canadian reading of (hi)story, MacLennan prolongs a literary nationalism which has Francophone Canada surrender to a version of (hi)story that begins as a narrative of a Canadian unity in diversity – apparently, a rather paradoxical notion of national identity –, but concludes as a story of (interior) colonization.

Although Hugh MacLennan's pedagogic nationalism,[14] which corresponds to Canada's awakening national consciousness during the Second World War, should not be identified with William Kirby's pan-Canadianism with its roots in the Dominion's prevailing fear of a possible annexation by the United States, it at least resembles some of the major ideological features that are also constitutive elements of the Confederation novel. In either case English Canada represents a majority culture, which attracts the country's minorities by its centripetal force.

---

13 The notion of Canada's cultural mosaic was first introduced by John Murray Gibbon. Cf. *Gibbon*, Canadian Mosaic (Toronto, 1938); see also *Klooß, W.*, "Vom Bikulturalismus zum kanadischen Multikulturalismus: Historische Grundlagen und gesellschaftliche Implikationen eines politischen Programms", in: *Hoerder, D./Knauf, D.* (eds.), Gulliver 22: Einwandererland USA. Gastarbeiterland BRD (Berlin, Hamburg, 1988), 25-35.

14 MacLennan's national orientation shows also in his other novels, all of which deal with genuine Canadian topics. Likewise, Barometer Rising (1941) gives a very detailed description of the city of Halifax during the First World War, in order to make Canadian readers aware of their own history and territory. George Woodcock has therefore classified this narrative as "the first novel about a specifically Canadian city." Cf. *Woodcock*; Hugh MacLennan (Toronto, 1969), 46. Similarly, in The Precipice (1948) MacLennan dicusses the relations between Canada and the United States, while in *Each Man's Son* (1951) he elaborates an the impact of Puritanism.

So far then, Canadian literature employs a set of paradigms, which is particularly well suited to replace a story of alterity by a tale of unity. Identity construction becomes part of an (imperial) master narrative that is based on erasure rather than on the acknowledgement of difference, although ethnic, cultural and racial plurality, i.e. multicultural experiences, are deeply inscribed into Canada's historical and social life.

It does not, therefore come as a surprise that with the rapid growth of Canadian writing during the last four decades major shifts have taken place which recognize multiculturalism as a decisive force in Canadian life. Similarly alternative notions of place, as, for instance, mirrored in recent modes of prairie writing, have become especially instructive. It is at this point, where critics like Frank Davey have intervened with an understanding of literature that fosters experiment and process, rather than structure and tradition. Authors like Robert Kroetsch, Margaret Laurence and Rudy Wiebe, or later David Arnason, Sandra Birdsell, Doug Barbour, Dennis Cooley and Smaro Kamboureli, to mention only a few representatives of the contemporary writing community, have largely contributed to what could be termed the (de-)construction of a hegemonial, or, for that matter, colonial reading of the "Canadianness" of Canadian literature.

Another important aspect that would deserve investigation, but will escape further attention here, is the general impact of the new mass media, which according to Marshall McLuhan have led to a "revulsion against imposed patterns."[15] Deriving from a different base, Eli Mandel proposed as early as 1966 that "literature is 'beyond system' and requires subjective and emotionally-engaged criticism rather than systematic analysis and explication".[16] Mandel then replied to the opening forms of literature with the request for "a response, which does not attempt to impose an individual works or an art itself a structure of reason or indeed a pattern of any kind except that of perception."[17] In much the same spirit Frank Davey pointed out that Mandel found in Canada "a new writing that wanders inconsistently and incoherently amidst the fragments of personality and history, mixing space and time [...]."[18] The following discussion will therefore try to examine some of the major forces behind this obvious shift in perception and perspective, namely the interchange between multiculturalism, regionalism, ethnicity and the postmodern in Canadian writing.

15 Quoted after *Davey, F.*, From There to Here (Erin, Ont.: Press Porcepic, 1974), 18.

16 *Davey*, 18.

17 *Davey*, 18, 19.

18 *Davey*, 19.

Even at first glance, it becomes obvious that a multicultural awareness in literature goes hand in hand with both the encouragement of ethnic[19] writing as well as the rejection of ethnic bias in literature. At the same time, a multicultural awareness in literature fosters regional forms of literary expression, since ethnic distribution in Canada is largely regional in character. It should, however, not be overlooked that political and literary multiculturalism derive originally from two antagonistic ideological concepts. Whereas political multiculturalism is largely the result of another centralist approach towards Canadian identity, multiculturalism in literature has its roots in an anti-"centralist", namely "regional" consciousness.

This advance is not least reflected in a changing infrastructure without which many of Canada's literary celebrities would have remained in obscurity. The establishment of writing which, as an institution fifteen years earlier was exceedingly marginal in the west, has been largely the result of a change in readers and publishers. Robert Kroetsch's example is instructive: he makes readers receptive to postmodernism by publishing his letters in *Boundary 2* (Spring 1975), or his journals in *The "Crow"Journals* (1980); he commits himself to many communities of writers and readers in his involvement with the periodical *Dandelion* in Calgary, in profoundly supporting the development of the NeWest Press and Turnstone Press. Poets like Frank Davey and B.P. Nichol begin to write essays of simplified explication. All in all, writers begin to gain, or take, more control over the criticism and editing of their work. The decentralization of economic power to the provinces, which follows on the OPEC oil crisis of the mid-1970s, leads not only to a demand for more decentralization of political power, but, eventually, to a recognition of the merits of regional cultural definition. The new publishing houses are at the centre of an enthusiastic interest in regional cultures, in specific place, and in local speech. The intimacy of the regional communities of poets seems essential to a clarifying of purpose: here poets listen for differences in dialect, and develop literary forms, which can claim to be rooted in the specific locale.[20] Again the importance of organisational patterns comes to bear. They provide not only the logistic framework for the promotion of a se-

---

19 "Ethnic" is understood here as a terminological marker characterizing both the racially and culturally distinctive features of a certain group. This allows for an application of the term to indigenous peoples like the Indians or Inuit as well as confessional denominations like the Mennonites, or groups who have preserved a unique cultural heritage like the Ukrainians and Italians.

20 The previous argument is partially based on *Ricou, L.*, "Poetry", in: *New, W. H.* (ed.), Literary History of Canada. Canadian Literature in English, vol. 4 (Toronto, Buffalo, London, 21990), 3-45.

lective tradition, but serve the purposes of alternating discursive strategies, i.e. forms of counter-discourse, equally well.

What appears especially noteworthy is the fact that the multicultural orientation in recent Canadian writing goes hand in hand with postmodernist conceptions of literary discourse. Those presuppositions have fostered a critical reconsideration of the relationship between fact and fiction – and consequently the (de-) construction of previous literary treatments of historical data, or as Walter Pache has argued: "[...] the invention of a collective past [marks] a central concept of postmodernism in Canada."[21] The new beliefs also have helped to initiate the revival of historical fiction, poetry and drama. This, of course, can hardly come as a surprise, since it is constitutive of meta-literature to approach its topics not only from a thematic point of view, but to include the whole process of narration as well. In this way, authors like Laurence, Kroetsch, Wiebe, Bowering et al. also comment on the problems of "reference in language."[22] In other words, the multicultural perspective in contemporary Canadian writing results not least from a critical approach towards conventional forms of (literary) perception.

Multiculturalism is further confirmed by the rediscovery of Canada's native cultures. In 1973 three works appeared, which focused on a topic that – as already indicated above – had been so widely neglected by modern Canadian writers that W.H. New could up until then speak of the "historical absence of an Indian presence in Canadian Literature."[23] W.O. Mitchell's *The Vanishing Point,* Rudy Wiebe's *The Temptations of Big Bear* and Robert Kroetsch's *Gone Indian,* all novels that promote a de-colonized vision of Canada's native peoples, helped to correct this picture. (De-)constructing a master-narrative, of course, implies the recognition and acceptance of liminal standpoints,[24] which is probably even best expressed by the awakening of the aboriginal voice in Canadian literature.

Meanwhile, native literature in Canada has reached an impressive stage. Native writers manage a degree of autonomy that makes them full masters of the English language. They are well aware of its symbolical and metaphorical levels,

---

21 *Pache, W.*, "'The Fiction Makes Us Real': Aspects of Postmodernism in Canada", in: *Kroetsch, R./Nischik, R. M.* (eds.), Gaining Ground. European Critics an Canadian Literature (Edmonton, 1985), 6478, 64.

22 *Hutcheon, L.*, "History and/as Intertext", in: *Moss, J.* (ed.), Future Indicative: Literary Theory and Canadian Literature (Ottawa, 1987), 169-184, 176.

23 New, W. H., "Fiction", in: *Klinck C. F et al.* (eds.), Literary History of Canada: Canadian Literature in English (Toronto, 21973),111, 248.

24 See in this context *Isernhagen, H.*, "Literature - Language - Country: The Preservation of Difference and the Possibility of Relation", Zeitschrift der Gesellschaft für Kanada-Studien 6 (1986), No. 1, 81-94.

fully incorporate it as a vehicle for the creative expression of their own lives and as members of a distinctly marginal or liminal culture.[25] Multicultural perspectives in Canadian society incorporate almost any Canadian ethnicity. Prairie-based Kristjana Gunnars experiences Canada's Icelandic ancestry in her writings, whereas a collection of short fiction published on behalf of Vancouver's centennial celebrations, contains two stories, which deal with the Japanese experience in Canada's Pacific metropolis.[26] Similarly, the Japanese fishing community Steveston, just south of Vancouver, has attracted the attention of Daphne Marlatt in one of her documentary long poems,[27] and the Japanese are at the centre of the poems *transcanadaletters* (1975) by Roy Kiyooka and A *Choice of Dreams* (1974) by Joy Kagowa, not to mention the latter's famous novel *Obasan* (1981) or more recent texts by Asian immigrant writers such as M.G.Vassanji, Neil Bissoondath and Rohinton Mistry, no to mention Sri Lankan born Michael Ondaatje who has easily made it into the premier league of world writers in English.

Under these premises, it seems only logical that contemporary writers and literary critics have countered the Laurentian approach towards literature[28] by acknowledging the regional and multicultural in Canadian literature. In contrast to earlier concepts, literature is no longer seen as an instructive force in the process of defining a single national identity, but it is instead conceived as a form of cultural expression that has its roots in regional and cultural diversity. Furthermore, this form of cultural multiplicity is paralleled by notions of discontinuity, which reject any belief in linear development. Quoting Frank Davey again, the new literary world appears unorganized and chaotic, while the "narrative structures take unpredictable shifts and turns, and invariably terminate in ambiguity."[29]

In this respect, Canada's interior conflict between the attempt towards an identity construction based on selective tradition and its regionally determined (de-) construction, parallels within national boundaries what in broader scale has emerged as the confrontation between colonial and post-colonial discourse in the English-speaking world. At the same time, the above-mentioned linkage between a new multicultural awareness in Canadian writing and post-structuralist forms of literary expression proves that Canadian postmodernist poetics are strongly political in their aspirations. Although many critics argue that "the

---

25 *Peyer, B.*, "Autobiographical Works Written by Native Americans", Amerikastudien/American Studies (Amst) 26 (1981), 386-402, 399.

26 Cf. *Gerson, C.* (ed.), Vancouver Short Stories (Vancouver, 1985).

27 Cf. *Marlatt, D.*, Steveston (1974).

28 Cf. *Frye N.*, "Conclusion", 318-332.

29 *Davey*, From There to Here, 155.

postmodern is disqualified from political involvement because of its narcissistic and ironic appropriation of existing images and stories",[30] it only seems legitimate in view of contemporary Canadian aesthetics, when Linda Hutcheon emphatically asserts that "postmodernism is a phenomenon whose mode is resolutely contradictory as well as unavoidably political."[31]

The West as well as Pacific and perhaps to a lesser extend maritime Canada are no longer objects, but have become powerful subjects in the literary process. The fringes have not only learned how to write back, but also helped to restructure the former placement of "centre" and "periphery". Subsequently, a (re-) definition of the "Canadianness" of Canadian writing has become necessary. Just as the traditional cultural hegemony of the east has been challenged by regional forms of cultural expression and distribution, there is no longer one clearly defined notion of Canadian literature. Instead the "Canadianness" of Canadian writing is conceived as a paradigm, which is open to linguistic and topical shifts and changes, thus serving a Canadian identity, which is defined by its disparity.

In order to substantiate this argument a few basic facts may be briefly recalled. The 1991 census mentions a total population of 27.3 million people then living in Canada as opposed to approximately 3.7. million which are listed in the first Canadian census taken in 1871, i.e. within the last 120 years Canada's population has been increased by almost 24 million people. This can only be explained by the fact that Canada has strongly fostered immigration – before the arrival of the first Europeans the Native peoples without counting the Inuit amounted to some 1 million people. Without going into too much detail it may suffice to point out that immigration has always been subject to political and economic decisions in Canada as well as to the social and political circumstances in the countries of departure. Likewise, immigration was very high between 1911 and 1913 when more than one million people arrived in Canada, whereas the lowest rate of immigration is linked with the period between 1941 and 1943 (25.000 immigrants). Subsequently, immigration has also shaped Canada's social and economic appearance after World War II. It is particularly noteworthy that the ethnic distribution has drastically changed. For example: only a quarter of the total of 192.000 immigrants in 1989 came from Europe, the largest group of whom had not left the British isles, but were of Polish descent. 50% of these new Canadians had an Asian background, namely Hong Kong, the Philippines, Vietnam and India. There was also a substantial number of South Americans

30 *Hutcheon L.*, The Politics of Postmoderism (London, New York, 1989), 3.

31 *Hutcheon*, 1.

among the immigrants of 1989. One could, of course, go on with this list and show how Canadians of non-European ancestry are increasingly turning Canada not only into a multicultural, but also a multi-coloured society. This is particularly visible in metropolitan centres like Vancouver or Toronto which suggests that ethnic difference is as much a general feature of Canada's historical and social reality as it is a matter of regional distribution.

From an historical point of view it is interesting to note that cultural diversity as a distinct feature of Canada's public discourse has found as much expression in the notion of a "mosaic of peoples", an idea which can be traced back to Murray Gibbon's famous study *Canadian Mosaic* (1938), as it has been suppressed by the highly limited and imperial view of Canada's division into an English- and a French-speaking population. With respect to Canada's social practice, both chartered groups have exercised their political and economic influence on non-British and non-French immigrants by simply subsuming them under either of the two power structures. Social reality thus challenges the concept of a cultural mosaic, which implies

> "that Canada is composed of a multiplicity of collectives or sub-groups, each with its own cultural, racial or historical identity, who co-exist in an atmosphere of mutual toleration within a liberal democratic form of political economy."32

While Gibbon's analysis therefore originally resulted in hardly more than a neat catchword used by politicians and public administrators alike, it gained new momentum when Canada's rapidly changing population after World War II, the urge for the nationalization of cultural expression as for instance reflected in the foundation of the Canada Council, the rejection of US-American influence and the subsequent demand for adequate new forms of identity construction revitalized the notion of Canada's cultural mosaic – and here I return to my primary point. Almost exactly one year after Atwood's acknowledgement of the immigrant status of the Canadian society with its ethnic differences and multiplicity of cultural heritages Canada's liberal government under the leadership of Prime Minister Jean Pierre Trudeau from Quebec announced a new policy which since then has figured under the magic label "multiculturalism".33

Seen in merely semantic terms and detached from any historical contextualization, Trudeau's political programme implies an attempt towards identity construction in Canada, which, regardless of any ethnic boundaries, considers all

32 *Goldstein, J. E./Bienvenue, R. M.*, Ethnicity and Ethnic Relations in Canada (Toronto, 1980), 313.

33 "Multiculturalism" was introduced as an official government policy on 8 October, 1971.

participants in the cultural process as equal partners. This is, for instance, reflected in the following statements:

> "First, resources permitting, the government will seek to assist all Canadian cultural groups that have demonstrated a desire and effort to continue to develop a capacity to grow and contribute to Canada, and a clear need for assistance, the small and weak groups no less than the strong and highly organised. Second, the government will assist members of all cultural groups to overcome cultural barriers to full participation in Canadian society. Third, the government will promote creative encounters and interchange among all Canadian cultural groups in the interests of national unity. Fourth, the government will continue to assist immigrants to acquire at least one of Canada's official languages in order to become full participants in Canadian society."[34]

Unity via difference, homogeneity via heterogeneity, sameness via otherness, national identity based on the principle of alterity these are prime issues on the political agenda of a country which, just like elsewhere, fifty years ago had not even heard of the term multiculturalism. Instead, Canadians, as I have just pointed out, then began to subscribe to the notion of a cultural mosaic in order to distinguish their own sameness, or by the same token, their national otherness from countries like Britain or, perhaps even more so from the mighty neighbour south of the 49th parallel. With respect to literary expression, Canadian writing, regardless of the enormous influence of authors such as German-born Frederick Philip Grove, Scandinavian Martha Ostenso or previously the English gentle woman Susanna Moodie "did not reflect this mosaic until the late 1940s, when, beginning with Jewish writers such as A.M. Klein, a new generation of writers looked to their cultural roots for inspiration."[35] Nowadays, "multiculturalism" belongs to the most inflated terms in public discourse. What is of even greater importance though, "multiculturalism", if viewed in historical perspective, emerges as yet another version of a pan-Canadian, i.e. centralist form of identity formation. The paradox inherent in the nationalist concept of a unity in diversity is easily dissolved since the acknowledgement of difference as a political and economic practice is reduced to an ideology that pretends to explain otherness while it actually erases it. This becomes most obvious, if one looks at the economic implications of multiculturalism. And here the Canadian experience serves as an example that can easily be transferred to other territories.

---

34 House of Commons, Debates, 1971.

35 *Hutcheon, L./Richmond, M.* (eds.), Other Solitudes. Canadian Multicultural Fictions (Toronto, 1990), preface.

In an essay published in *Harper's* a few years ago, David Rieff argued that multiculturalism is a phenomenon with a silent partner: the broad and radical change now taking place within world capitalism. It is the most salient phenomenon of an increasingly globalized system. Multiculturalism helps to legitimize whole new areas of consumerism. One of its central tenets is to undermine the idea of the masterpiece as the aesthetic expression of an antidemocratic, absolutist concept of quality. In general, western culture has excluded many things; art in the traditional sense is anti-egalitarian, in that it demands that people judge a given work to be not only subjectively, but objectively superior to another, an idea which is also strongly supported by canon-formation in traditional English Studies. In as much as multiculturalists challenge the notion of hierarchy, they, at the same time, support some of the fundamental interests of capitalism. In the cynical words of David Rieff:

> "If all art is deemed as good as all other art, and, for that matter, if the point of art is not greatness but the production of works of art that reflect the culture and aspirations of various ethnic, sexual, or racial subgroups within a society, then one is in a position to increase supply almost at will in order to meet increases in demand. [...] The result is that the consumption of culture can increasingly come to resemble the consumption of goods."

One may not have to go all the way with this argument although terminological markers and claims such as "cultural diversity", "difference", the need to abandon "boundaries" etc. are by no means restricted to academic discourse, but resemble the stock phrases of the modern corporation – "product diversification", "the global marketplace", the "boundary-less company", where conventional "vertical hierarchies" are being replaced by "horizontal networks". Capital and labour have become mobile and as it seems, with time passing, national borders, not to mention national identities, become less relevant either to consciousness or to commerce. This is substantiated by the fact that with the communications revolution, with fibre cables, it is hard to say just where the centre is anymore, or if one even needs one. Multiculturalism has transgressed its social and artistic boundaries. It has become a multi-facetted reality, not only in Canada.

DISCUSSION

The discussion was started by Ms. Medved, who expressed her excitement about the discussed topic, since she considered the development of "multiculturalism" as mirrored in literature to be very interesting. She referred to the book *Option Québec* by Réne Lévesque (1968) who, in his view on the status of the Canadian province of Quebec, was obviously inspired by the then development of the European Community. She also mentioned Elijah Harper who had a decisive "no" word on behalf of the "First Nations" to "eleven white men" concerning the so-called Meech Lake Constitutional Accord, which, inter alia, provided for a "distinct society" of Quebec. Ms. Medved stressed that the Canadian policy of multiculturalism and citizenship and the writings on multiculturalism, for example by Charles Taylor, had exercised a strong influence on Europe, inter alia, on the adoption of the Swedish integration policy in 1975. According to her, the glue of the Canadian cultural mosaic and multiculturalism was citizenship. She wondered if the EU citizenship would be able to provide such "glue" for a new common European identity.

In addition, Ms. Medved remarked that Quebec had succeeded both within Canada and in the NAFTA agreement to sustain its own immigration policy. She believed that Canada's example could – in some respects – be regarded as suitable for negotiations within the European Union for the framework of common immigration policy as well.

Ms. Apap, a Belgian herself, made a comparison between Canada and Belgium concluding that Belgians – unlike Canadians – tended to look for differences rather than for features they have in common. Moreover, she added, that Canada as an immigration country showed better acceptance towards new emigrants. In her viewpoint, Belgium seems to be insecure about its own national identity.

Mr. Klooß reminded the participants of the discussion of Canadian literature as coming from a part of the so-called postcolonial world. He pointed out that historically Canada had been representing the extension of British imperial policy. Thus, the development of Canada had been characterised by seeking to avoid its heritage and to detach itself from colonial policy. He marked that until 1931 Canadians had not been allowed to pursue their own foreign policy. As a result, Canada could be described as being multicultural on the one hand and strongly impacted by the colonial regime on the other.

Mr. von Hoffmann noted that the recent discussion of multiculturalism in Europe had shown that this term could hold various meanings in different contexts and could sometimes also prove to be misleading.

Mr. Klooß stated that Canadian policy still remained largely centralist rather than marginal. Hence, though in reality there was a diversity represented by a lot of small communities, the policy of multiculturalism was installed as a political program on a federal level and therefore represented an "impact from above."

At the request of Mr. von Hoffmann, Mr. Klooß described the situation of these small communities and admitted that there was in fact some ethnic or even racial cleavage now to be observed. Referring to the example of Vancouver, he stated that racism had not been thoroughly avoidable even in a multicultural society.

Ms. Fernando commented that whether a person tended to restrict his or her social contacts to people of his or her nation and develop a certain "ghetto habit" or not was more a question of individual character than a national feature. She nevertheless stressed the importance of maintaining checks and balances to make sure that not too many people congregate for the wrong reasons. As to multiculturalism, she suggested that it should not be defined as a totality of very strictly separated cultures, since people were often infused by other cultures either through communication or in some other way. In this context she referred to Michael Ondaatje, a writer from Sri Lanka, who lived in different countries and had been influenced by each of them, thus uniting diverse cultures in his personality and his writing.

Mr. Weber marked that, although the notion of a cultural mosaic had even been implemented in the Canadian constitution, he personally considered this notion to be a myth and an artificial construction. He therefore raised the question of whether the different notions relevant to the construction of national identity in Canada and the US-cultural mosaic/multiculturalism or melting pot had in fact resulted in any significant differences between the two nations regarding the factual situation relating to immigration and integration.

Mr. Klooß admitted that to a large extent differences could not be found. He also marked that in the US the notion of the melting pot no longer prevailed but had been replaced by that of "new ethnicity", which reflected an approach already more similar to the Canadian one. He also agreed with Mr. Weber that the notion of the cultural mosaic was indeed a myth and a construction like several other forms of identity construction – the frontier, the 49th parallel etc. which did not match reality: these notions and myths had each been created for a certain purpose through a process of selective tradition.

FINAL DISCUSSION

After all individual lecturers had given their speeches, Mr. von Hoffmann opened the final discussion, which concentrated on the main aspects touched upon in the workshop and envisaged to formulate final conclusions.

Mr. von Hoffmann started the discussion by inviting the participants to name, according to their own views, the main issues involved in the subject of the workshop. This brainstorming process resulted in the following list of aspects and questions, which were then dealt with more specifically during the course of the final discussion.

- Selection of foreigners/immigrants and the needs of the labour market
- What degree of communitarization and harmonization of immigration policy in the EU would be desirable?
- What model of a European immigration policy should be adopted and to what extent can the models introduced by Mr. Münz and Mr. Calliess serve as guideline?
- Non-discrimination of immigrants, in particular with regard to cultural and social rights
- Integration concepts

Ms. Medved made the first contribution, illustrating the interrelation of these aspects by putting them into chronological order according to the three door admission model, which had been introduced by Mr. Münz in the course of the discussion of her own speech. In her opinion, the selection of immigrants before the entry to the territory of a Member State would be represented by the first door pertaining to the outer circle. Once having entered the EU Member State, she pointed out, the immigrant would accumulate certain rights, which touched upon the question of non-discrimination of immigrants regarding also social rights. The issue of naturalization of immigrants would finally arise at the third door.

Subsequently she turned to the model introduced by Mr. Calliess, asking him, whether his concept did not only cover the issue of entry, i.e. the first of the three doors.

Mr. Calliess explained that the "freedom of goods model" not only related to the entry of immigrants but also to their status after entry: like a product that has once entered the EU after entry controls, they should participate in the four freedoms of the internal market. Hereby, his model implemented the principle of non-discrimination, which was in fact located on the second level. He admitted, however, that the issue of naturalization was indeed not covered by the "freedom of goods model". Due to its simplicity it could nevertheless serve as a guideline, he suggested.

It would, however, as Mr. Weber argued, presuppose a sort of international labour convention in this area, a non-discrimination principle regarding free movement of persons, which at present does not exist. Ms. Langenfeld stressed that the proposal for the Directive only grants freedom of movement within the first state, even after the lapse of the five-year period, which leads to a permanent residence permit in that first state. To illustrate this, she pointed out that in the case that the immigrant did not find a job in the second Member State, he could be expelled from that second Member State. The model by Mr. Calliess, she concluded, was therefore not fully implemented in the proposal.

In this context several questions regarding the "free movement of goods model" were brought up by the participants. Would the free movement of immigrants within the EU – lacking a control mechanism comparable to that of supply and demand of goods – not pose a threat to the Member States' social systems? Would the implementation of this model not transfer the discretion of each Member State to decide what kind of and how many immigrant workers should be allowed to enter its territory from the Member State in question to every single other EU Member State? Would the model not presuppose a common policy and equal conditions for entry in all Member States to prevent the accumulation of superfluous labour force in some of the Member States?

In his response to these questions, Mr. Calliess stressed that, according to his model, immigrants should only participate in the four freedoms of the ECT, and nothing more, which would therefore not result in unrestricted free movement. As any citizen of a European Member State before the introduction of the EC Citizenship, immigrants would only be allowed to enter other Member States for the purpose of finding a job and would have to return to the first state after a certain time, if they failed in finding one.

Mr. von Hoffmann then turned the discussion towards the question of who should select immigrants. Ms. Medved suggested to follow the method of open coordination, which could effectuate the exchange of information between the states. According to this method, she explained, each state should report to the other Member States how many immigrants it had admitted to its territory within the past year and what the country's future plans regarding immigration policy were. Ms. Oellers-Frahm (Max Planck Institute, Heidelberg) remarked, that coordination and an assessment of the need of labour force on a community wide level could prevent an overflow of immigrants, which might result from the approach by individual Member States, not taking into account the need of other members.

Mr. Werner, however, favouring the concept of consultation, was reluctant to follow a centralistic approach. Mr. von Hoffmann agreed, that given the weak democratic legitimacy of community organs at the present time it was open to doubt whether citizens would accept community decisions concerning an issue as serious as immigration.

Ms. Fernando proposed to implement a selection process, based on a points system, comparable to those systems used in Australia and Canada, with the selection being carried out in the country of origin and not in the host nation. This way certain professional groups could be directed to European regions in need of their skills. Additionally, registration procedures should be simplified and to some extent connected to each other in order to prevent needless expenditure. This way migration could be managed more efficiently, as it could provide helpful feedback to immigrants, motivating them to take the necessary steps to qualify for entry. Furthermore, she suggested that the Member States should introduce an exchange of experience concerning their national integration programs. She also stressed the importance of selecting the potential migrants in their home countries already (comparable to the Australian Oversees Immigration Offices), in order to prevent illegal immigration. Mr. von Hoffmann added that it was vital to prevent illegal immigration and illegal employment by enforcing laws more strictly, e.g. sending employers to jail in cases where they employ someone who does not have a valid permit.

Focusing on the next step following the implementation of a selection procedure and certain entry preconditions, Ms. Langenfeld raised the question of whether there would be an automatic right to entry if all conditions are fulfilled or whether the final decision would still lye with the Member State. In her view, the proposal for a Directive was not yet clear on this point. Ms. Fernando suggested that even with a points system the final decision should stay with the receiving country.

Then the issue of integration was examined more closely. According to Mr. von Hoffmann, it required knowledge of the language and of the (political and social) system of the country of residence. Ms. Oellers-Frahm confirmed that as a minimum a knowledge of the every day language was comprised in most of the national integration systems. Additionally, she proposed to have integration tests after a 5-year stay, in order to avoid ghettoization. As Ms. Langenfeld reported, this was included in the new German immigration law already, which, in her view may be in conflict with the European legislation in this respect: She was doubtful as to whether it allowed Member States to impose new and additional requirements on immigrants. However, the willingness of the immigrant to integrate. A visible effort by the immigrant to learn the language of the host country should be one of the prerequisites for an extension of the resident permit, which in turn would increase the legal status of the foreigner.

Mr. von Hoffmann then began the last stage of the discussion by asking whether any of the participants could specify a "vision" of a common European immigration policy. According to his opinion, it would probably not consist in full communitarization but at least it would encompass information exchange and voluntary harmonization of standards with the final decision still remaining with the Member States.

Ms. Apap submitted that the future immigration policy would depend on the future of the European integration process. Still, she added, that the future might allow further steps than seem feasible today, in the frame of the present "three door model".

Ms. Langenfeld agreed with her on the first point but stressed, that the development of a common European immigration policy would also depend on the development of the labour market. The development of the latter she found hard to predict

Mr. Calliess and Ms. Medved, on the other hand, were confident, that a process had been put into motion that might finally lead to a common policy. Nevertheless, both speakers emphasized the need to steer this difficult process using legislation. Mr. von Hoffmann pointed out that the Treaty of Amsterdam with its unanimous decision created an obstacle for major changes within the area of immigration.

However, a consensus as to whether a common European immigration policy was desirable could not be found.

Finally, Mr. Calliess stressed that, as illegal immigration was perceived to be the cause of many social problems, effective measures in this respect would possibly produce a more positive attitude towards immigrants legally entering "Fortress Europe". Referring to his paper, he suggested, that a European Coast Guards might be helpful in assisting the Member States in this task.

LIST OF CONTRIBUTORS

Dr. *Joanna Apap**, D.Phil, MA, BA (Hons), Head of Unit and Research Fellow on Justice and Home Affairs at the Centre for European Policy Studies (CEPS), Brussels, Belgium

Dr. *Anastasios Bisopoulos,* Ph.D. (Economics), MPA, Principal Administrator, European Commission, Brussels, Belgium

Prof. Dr. *Christian Calliess*, M.A.E.S. (Brügge), LL.M.Eur., Director of the Institute for European Law at Karl-Franzens-University Graz, Austria.

Prof. Dr. *Bernd von Hoffmann*, Director of the Institute for Legal Policy at the University of Trier, Germany

Prof. Dr. *Wolfgang Klooß*, University of Trier, Germany

Prof. Dr. *Christine Langenfeld*, University of Göttingen, Law faculty, Germany

Felicita Medved, Centre for Research in International Migration and Ethnic Relations (CEIFO), Stockholm University, Sweden

Prof. Dr. *Rainer Münz*, Humboldt-University Berlin, Germany

Dr. *Karin Oellers-Frahm*, Max-Planck-Institute for Comparative Public Law and International Law Heidelberg, Germany

Sandrine van der Velde, LL.M., European University Institute of Florence, Italy

Anne Walter, Graduate at Graduiertenkolleg IMIS Osnabrück, Germany

Prof. Dr. *Albrecht Weber*, University of Osnabrück, Germany

Dr. *Heinz Werner*, Studies in Economics, Institute for Employment Research (IAB) Nuremberg, Germany

* Ms. Joanna Apap was accompanied by her assistant, Ms. Gayathri Fernando.

Rechtspolitisches Symposium
Legal Policy Symposium

Herausgegeben im Institut für Rechtspolitik an der Universität Trier
von Bernd von Hoffmann und Gerhard Robbers

Band 1 Bernd von Hoffmann (ed.): Towards a Common European Immigration Policy. Reports and Discussions of a Symposium held in Trier on October 24th and 25th, 2002. 2003.

FSC
www.fsc.org
MIX
Papier | Fördert
gute Waldnutzung
FSC® C083411

Kolibri 360 GmbH
Ferdinand-Jühlke-Straße 7
99095 Erfurt, Deutschland
produktsicherheit@kolibri360.de

Druck:
CPI Druckdienstleistungen GmbH
im Auftrag der
Kolibri 360 GmbH
Ferdinand-Jühlke-Str. 7
99095 Erfurt